THE Bureaucratic Experience

THE Bureaucratic Experience

FIFTH EDITION

The Post-Modern Challenge

Ralph P. Hummel

M.E.Sharpe
Armonk, New York
London, England

Library of Congress Cataloging-in-Publication Data

Hummel, Ralph P.
The bureaucratic experience : the post-modern challenge / by Ralph P. Hummel.—5th ed.
  p. cm.
Includes bibliographical references and index.
ISBN 978-0-7656-1010-2 (cloth : alk. paper)—ISBN 978-0-7656-1011-9 (pbk. : alk. paper)
  1. Bureaucracy. I. Title.

HD38.4.H85 2007
302.3´5--dc22   2007002133

Printed in the United States of America

The paper used in this publication meets the minimum requirements of
American National Standard for Information Sciences
Permanence of Paper for Printed Library Materials,
ANSI Z 39.48-1984.

∞

BM (c)   10   9   8   7   6   5   4   3   2   1
BM (p)   10   9   8   7   6   5   4   3   2   1

In Memory of

Larry D. Terry

Contents

Foreword

I will here confess my purpose: it is to find hope that my mother tongue and my freedom to say what I want to say in my own terms will not be lost.

Ralph Hummel, 2003

The fifth edition of *The Bureaucratic Experience* transcends the traditional discourse between the critical school of bureaucratic analysis and those who find a measure of virtue in the operations of bureaucratic institutions. That is long overdue.

Traditional bureaucracy remains in place and continues to assault the social, cultural, and psychological commitments of contemporary life. It influences the way we think and speak and has profound consequences for political life.

Theorists of the critical school agree that the bureaucratic mind—the hard residue of the institution itself—is a threat to freedom. They counter the "don't blame bureaucracy" school of thinking that places the alleged sins of bureaucracy at the feet of its political masters.

Those considerate of bureaucratic institutions applaud their contributions to the maturation of societies. Bureaucratic apologists extol the accomplishments of a misunderstood institution operating under duress.

The fifth edition of *The Bureaucratic Experience* recognizes that the choices posed in the traditional quarrel between critics and sympathizers of bureaucracy are limiting. This edition uses another perspective to shed light on the essentially two-sided debate to see if there is a fresh antithetical understanding that helps appreciate the bureaucratic experience.

The reach for a new way of thinking about bureaucracy may end the artificial duality created between critical theorists and traditionalists, who, for instance, put Hummel's previous editions in the hands of students along with Charles Goodsell's work, which defends bureaucracy. This is done ostensibly to create a fair debate about bureaucracy. It's a setup. Goodsell's books are more readable than Hummel's and are mainline public administration, reasonable, and hopeful. Hummel's manuscripts are more intricate, argumentative, and even contentious, taking on subjects not normally reviewed by PA students.

The books do not address the same subjects. Hummel is not writing just about bureaucracy as a kind of administrative instrument. He does not particularly care how efficient bureaucracy might be—in fact, the more smoothly it operates the more horrified he becomes. In the end, those who are comfortable with reasonableness probably prefer Goodsell and those with a predilection for the edge likely go for Hummel and probably careers away from the public service. At bottom, the issue is about comfort with high doses of rationalism or humanism.

Hummel's new edition moves away from traditional forms of debating bureaucracy. It entertains the post-modern point of view and then rejects much of it as long on deconstruction and short on faith in any future worth living. Hummel finds that post-modernism reveals much of what is happening, but offers little on what to do about it. The author acknowledges, often with a fair measure of enthusiasm, the work of several post-modernists. In the end, he finds no humanly tolerable attitude in their avowed strategy of tearing one foundation down and announcing it cannot be replaced by any other.

Deconstruction of this variety is like a union organizer who helps people see exploitation and the façade of power that dominates their lives. The workers then boil for a fight against their oppressors. They begin to rebel. The workers roar out a question about what to do, and the organizer's response is "nothing"—as if knowing alone is sufficient.

The fifth edition remains true to the idea that humans are not a form of intelligence easily replicated by machines and takes on the computer as the representation of bureaucracy itself. Chapter 6 is the gem of the text. It takes on Herbert Simon, an icon in public administration. Hummel argues that it is machines that are bounded, if not in rationality, then in sensibility and felt sense for what to do where feelings of people count in the equation, where feelings, for instance, may be a variable.

It is the proverbs of administration that dominate nearly every popular text on how to lead organizations. These days the ability to understand and choose between contingencies, not comprehensive analysis and overwhelming data, gets us through most things. "Trust your stomach" might be worth teaching in a management course in public administration. Data are immediate and often reliable, however irrational they might seem. Inconsistent proverbs can be true in any situation. It is judgment about what to do with them that matters. It is the underlying values, the know-how born of experience, that drive judgment that is consequential. These things defy programming.

After the journey through philosophical thinking still new to public administration, the latest edition makes its way to an independent point, a tradition with this author. The soul of the book remains true to the author's lasting concern that bureaucracy continues to serve as conversion machinery, flanked by what is human and what is mechanistic, between conformism and individuality, things rules say to do and what judgment and felt sense tender. The chapter on what living in a bureaucratic world does to the psychology of people is exceptional. What happens to the *self*, assuming people are in touch with one, after the massive assault on it by institutions, allegedly benign ones, over the course of *one's existence?* How much order can one ingest, even in the spirit of good organizational citizenship, without it having some corrosive effect on one's *being in the world*—even a world that admittedly runs more efficiently and economically? Hummel goes after these questions starting with the engaging "identity is not personality."

Each edition of *The Bureaucratic Experience* is hard at the core. Its essential concepts are unfailingly about freedom. The book is not a simple argument about the evils of bureaucracy as a mechanism for accomplishing the instrumental goals of modern society. It is too often miscast that way. The text reveals the face of the mechanical system and its implications for the human. It is not about how to get the trains running on time.

The volume is political theory in the sense demanded by John Gaus and Dwight Waldo as the precondition for administrative theory.

Everyone should be able to identify with the meaning of the title of the book—*The Bureaucratic Experience.* Who among us has not had a bureaucratic experience? You stand before the machine—the inquisitor. Even if you behave, that is, follow the rules, your humanity is compromised. The machine decides. The program chooses. The tools of the machine decide. The functionaries rule. One is fitted to the system. Woe to the person who is the deviant case.

The experience of fitting in correctly is not a simple annoyance, although we learn over time in the name of "maturity" not to lose our equilibrium in the face of the offense. We cooperate. Still, our bureaucratic experiences are signals of something alien to our being in the world. We sense something foreign in front of us, not created for our use. It does not really matter to us, in those disquieting moments, if the machine is efficient or economical.

Perversely, the antidotes to the problems of organizational bureaucracy become TQM, "in search of excellence programs," quality circles, reinvention, re-engineering, civil service reform, budget process reform, and other programs that sharpen the tool that stands against us. We are working on the wrong problem. We are helping the machine, not the human. It is extension of the assumption that what helps the machines aids humans in all their aspects. It is a thoroughly discredited idea, at least for people down the line in most societies.

This is a compelling text. Reading it will not reinvent anything, except perhaps ourselves. It is a classical treatment of a classic book.

David G. Carnevale
Norman, Oklahoma

Acknowledgments

Over the course of five editions, I have incurred debts for intellectual and physical survival to Guy Adams, Howell Baum, Peter L. Berger, Renee Berger, Morton Berkowitz, Paul Bernstein, David Carnevale, Bayard Catron, Glen Cowley, Raymond Cox, Fred Dallmayr, Robert Denhardt, Michael Diamond, Stephen Dracopoulos, John Everett, Karl Everett, Frank Fischer, Sandra Fish, Claudette Ford, John Forester, James M. Glass, Charles Goodsell, Mary Hale, Michael Harmon, Charles Hayes, Hans Held, Larry Hill, Marc Holzer, Patricia Ingraham, Robert Isaak, Jong S. Jun, Hwa Yol Jung, Louis Koenig, Douglas LaBier, Donna Lavins, Charles Levine, Bert Lummus, Max Mark, Bruce Marquand, Edward Mazze, Roger Mazze, Cynthia and Orion McSwite, Brinton Milward, Tommie Sue Montgomery, Kirsten Moy, Carl Nelson, Dail Neugarten, J. Steven Ott, H. Mark Roelofs, David Rosenbloom, Barry Rossinoff (who first published the book), Conrad P. Rutkowski, Mary Schmidt, David Schuman, Howard Schwartz, Jay Shafritz, Eli Silverman, Kalman Silvert, Michael P. Smith, Patricia Snow, Kathryn Speicher, Harry Steinberg, Camilla Stivers, Clarence Stone, Peter Vaill, Richard VrMeer, Dwight Waldo, Stephen Wasby, Richard Wells, and constantly Jay White.

The current edition has benefited from the dedicated and thoughtful labors of four students: Brenda Westbrook, Ishmael al-Amin, George Edward Richards II, and Seth Darkwa.

The publisher and the author wish to thank the following for their support: Charles Goodsell, for writing and maintaining a book directly opposing this book; Mel Dubnick, for upholding against all evidence that management can be a science; and Cynthia McSwain and Orion White, for taking me seriously while taking a quite different tack.

The credit for any success of this fifth edition belongs to Camilla Stivers.

Ralph P. Hummel
Akron, Ohio, and Spruce Head Island, Maine

Prologue

Imagine an age of terror. The icons of American economic, political, and military power are attacked. Thousands die among horrific scenes of courage and sacrifice. Government attempts a defense. Civil rights are curtailed. A war on terrorism is declared. Government itself becomes terror's medium. The populace wishes nothing more than a return to normalcy. Others may disappear into secret jails supervised by secret courts, but—What's it to me? Academe promptly falls in line echoing a theme struck in an earlier crisis: "No sacrifice is too great for our democracy, least of all the temporary sacrifice of democracy itself" (Rossiter, 1963 [1948]: 314).

What would be the responsibility of scholars in such imaginary dark days? What if we can shed light on what would come next?

The fact is any twenty-first-century political leadership imagined in this scenario needs to expand the role of government. This means expanding modern organization design—bureaucracy in the strictly technical sense of rationalist administration driven by a single will. An independent civil service is a counterweight to politics and is treated as an obstacle. And this for good reason. Public administrators take an oath to defend the Constitution. Bureaucracy promises control—constitutional or not. The honor of the bureaucrat lies in obeying orders; the honor of the civil servant rests on obeying the Constitution. Leadership in hard times requires an application of government will that is coherent, direct, and certain. Civil service—with its diffuse structures and clienteles united only by a general social contract—gets in the way of executing the unified will of the moment.

A new kind of government evolves. This kind of government is no accident. It can stand only on historically prepared ground.

What would be that ground? Ironically, it is bureaucracy itself that has done the preparing. This fact emerges only when we examine what bureaucracy has already done to erode modern civilization itself. A willful government can stand more easily on grounds of society reduced to organization, culture reduced to economics, psychology reduced to identity, language reduced to information, thinking reduced to logic, and politics to administration.

It is time to apply previous analysis of bureaucracy to the question of our times. This is the question that, under the current will to power, cannot be asked with impunity. Failure to ask it, however, condemns us forever to the contempt of posterity—that dismal universal hiss of which the poet spoke to mark the sound of public scorn.

What is the future of free men and women thought capable of reasoning out their own fate and order?

This fifth edition continues that examination of bureaucracy but turns to emphasize its impact on freedom, reason, and the self-made order of a free people.

Bureaucracy—modern self-critique has shown—has been the perfectly logical structuring of the delivery vehicle for public policy. Its threat to democracy was recognized by the beginning of the twentieth century (Max Weber). The threat was enacted in Germany in the 1930s and 1940s. It has been criticized most recently by a critical school in public administration, planning, and policy analysis in the last thirty years, and also again by post-modernists.

So far I am not saying anything new. But the results resonate with all of us who have been subjected to authoritarian government. Civil society and democratic rule require independent citizens; their power base rests in the economy. Today we are without our own roots in power. We spend most of our working day in bureaucracies: modern organizations whether public or private, governmental or corporate or non-profit. There we are unmade and transformed.

The transformations by bureaucracy have been identified for nearly thirty years by a critical school that continues applying the insights of modern self-criticism rooted in modern philosophy. This school recognizes that bureaucracy transforms citizens into clients. A new kind of human beings evolves: Their psyche is made dependent and fragmented. Their social relations are reduced to masks and roles. Their values are converted from personal to procedural. Their thinking mirrors internally what the political leadership seeks externally: single-premise logic corresponds to single-minded government. Their speech is caught up in a pre-set matrix. And their politics is a mass politics. It matters not what political party, class, status group, or gender you belong to; the sense of isolation and impotence in the political sphere and loneliness in the social sphere pervades.

The observations of single-premise logic, isolation, impotence, and loneliness, and the search for a unified and unifying will to hold the world together—these are Hannah Arendt's. The fact that they come from a book entitled *The Origins of Totalitarianism* should not disturb anyone, though they have a resonance to those who have gone through something like this before. I am not (repeat: NOT) saying we have or will have a totalitarian government. No one can predict such an outcome from the data at hand. But I am saying that we no longer are what we say we are and that the bureaucratization of the world has made us so.

If we claim to know this much, if there is a chance that this is so, then to speak of this is our responsibility.

The Chapters

The fifth edition of *The Bureaucratic Experience* pursues the idea that bureaucracy serves as the conversion machinery for turning a project for a humanistic way of life into a mechanistic one. To deepen the argument, I lay the pattern of earlier studies alongside newer ones: modern self-criticism alongside the criticism by post-modernists. The result is a picture of bureaucracy preparing an authoritarian human condition. (See Chapters 2–7.)

It is never too soon give an early warning of totalizing trends.

Chapter 1 now updates earlier contrasts between a bureaucratized world and the Enlightenment project of the early modern world. Contrasting charts summarize the early effects in organizations against later ones in society at large.

Chapter 2 uncovers the decline of society. The early hopes for human enlightenment are contrasted with the constrictions observed by Weberians and are arrayed against the critique by post-modernists. A warning is issued against the all-too-facile transposition of the French post-modern experience onto the American playing field.

Chapter 3 is the core chapter. It takes the Enlightenment as the baseline against which bureaucratic conversion creates a new concept of human nature. It traces the collapse of modern culture to its origins: contradictory assumptions of the Enlightenment and the subversive role played by bureaucracy in its implementation. Here we find a first counter-challenge to post-modernists' charge of inadequacy in modernist self-reflection. Modern critics can take credit for identifying the source of the Enlightenment project's failure. They saw this in an inversion of means and ends. The post-modern claim to be the linear successors to modernism can be questioned. In other words, modern self-criticism answered post-modernism's challenge before it was issued.

Chapter 4 exposes a scandal in psychology. Sigmund Freud posited an autonomous psyche. Modern analysis shows an autonomous psyche has no place in the workplace. Freud might have found the soul of the bourgeois, but failed to observe the condition of the worker. The worker's individual psyche is now merged with that of a manager, substituting submission and dependency for mastery and conscience. For the first time, a part of post-modernism becomes suspect of serving the system's ideological interests. The analysis finds in Jacques Lacan's new trans-personal psychology, though it denies serving bourgeois interests, a surprising echo and possible endorsement of the psyche-destroying state of affairs.

Chapter 5 shows bureaucracy's destruction of human language, the stifling of its sources in everyday life and work, and the attempt to constrain thinking within the limits of a matrix imposed by a bureaucratic grammar and vocabulary. Here the seed work of modern critics, specifically Wittgenstein and Searle, is compared with the more recent work of Derrida, Lyotard, and (not usually considered a post-modernist) Bourdieu. Both schools record an all-out attack on language, but to different effect. The modern side hopes to correct the situation by exposing control to ever greater demands for clarity and sense-making; the other side sees spaces for escape opening up precisely where control tightens.

Chapter 6 indicts bureaucracy for undermining reason. Its procedures force us to reduce thinking to an inferior form of logic that leaves us only with deadly choices. Both modern and post-modern analysis see that bureaucracy teaches us to accept thought control. But here the post-modernist criticism is forced to confess to a paradox. It attacks modern thought for misreading modernity's true position, and yet it owes its own thought to modern origins: rereading Kant, Husserl, and Heidegger. Here, Derrida provides the bridge between warnings about misuse of reason given by the first among modern philosophers (i.e., Kant) and practical problems of today—for example, the launch of a missile defense.

Chapter 7 outlines the political implications of the bureaucratic transformation of modern life. Weber, Lasswell, and Habermas already observed—and in Lasswell's case unintentionally celebrated—the tendency of politics to devolve into administration. Among post-modernists it is perhaps Foucault who finds, in attempts to hold the political world together, the most room for escape.

In the Epilogue, I sum up the effects of the bureaucratic experience and ask how bureaucracy's preparations can possibly lead to politics, democracy, and government as we, in a brief shining moment, used to know them.

THE Bureaucratic Experience

1

Understanding Bureaucracy

One city planner, shown a plan of a road cutting through a medieval city's houses: Won't people object?
Second city planner: One must force them to be free!
> —From a documentary on the medieval
> city of Rothenburg on the river Tauber

It was a series of random events that killed thousands and saved hundreds. Not many people did anything right that day, but not many people did anything wrong either.
> —A firefighter who escaped the North Tower

What are we calling postmodernity? I'm not up to date.
> —Michel Foucault

This is a practical guide to bureaucracy. Or, it will be if you can make it so. Not an easy job, when you consider: "As soon as you step into bureaucracy, the handcuffs go on your mind as well as your hand" (Ishmael al-Amin, Personal communication).

If you can't at some point in reading this say, "Yeah, that's how it is on my job, in my life," you have not made the practical connection. This is not a message from me to you; if you understand, you understand only because in some way you already knew *what* I was going to say.

Doing something practical means letting go of some illusions and delusions. One illusion is that bureaucracy is compatible with democracy (see Goodsell, 2003). A delusion is that, whatever the faults of modern organizations, these are just anomalies that can be fixed. We all subscribe to this delusion. Without it there is no hope. Yet behind this delusion stands a grim reality. It is captured in defense computers run amuck, international aid that starves populations, but most directly in the desperate phone call of a friend who announces, without introduction or saying who is calling:

"Ralph, it's worse than you say it is."

Imagine having adopted a baby. A year later, you get a phone call: "Return the baby!" "What!?" you say. "The father didn't sign the papers," they say.

Bureaucratic Experiences

In some way, we have all had our experiences with bureaucracy. Everyone has trouble with bureaucracy. Citizens and politicians have trouble controlling the runaway bureaucratic machine. Managers have trouble running it. Employees dislike working in it. Clients can't get the goods from it. Teachers have trouble getting a grip on it. Students are mystified by the complexity of it.

Let's take a closer look at what is so troubling.

Firefighters

New York firefighters are civil servants. Are they bureaucrats, too? Kicked off the fully manned rigs, some of those off-duty took the bus to the World Trade Center. Some came without clear direction. Some came without working radios. Some came against orders. All came because they heard behind the sirens and the alarms a silent call. Sixty of the total of 343 firefighters who died on 9/11 were off-duty. Would better support from the administration of the fire department have helped?

Consultants called for stricter training, routine obedience to orders, tauter command and control, better coordination with the police. These can enhance the ability to take care of our fellow human beings. Can they create or command sacrifice? (Contrast this with the Fire Department of the City of New York, 2002.)

And this is the practical case against bureaucracy. It is at the same time the moral case. Bureaucracy beats what we do freely into order, and it does so blindly. It multiplies the potential of organizations to get things done, but it does not do the doing. Bureaucracies set up the invasion of Normandy; human beings won the battle. Bureaucracy, whether too much of it or not enough, set up the organization of firefighters—it did not create the will to self-sacrifice. No matter how tough the rules, how rational the plans, how tight the tolerances and controls, some human being somewhere has to judge whether, when, and how there is an opening for applying those rules.

This is not only a judgment of technical fit. It is to judge whether what you do next upholds or damages the potential of human beings to whom you do it. We not only judge whether rational plans are objectively reasonable, but whether they fit the human being. Freedom, not order, opens the room for sacrifice. Know-how and freedom are inescapably partners.

One thing we know about you who choose public service, whether you become immersed in bureaucratic demands or not. You, in contrast to those choosing business, are not in it for the money. You do not blanch or pull a wry smile at the word "service." Service, not profit, is your aim. But service is freely given. No one has warned you that you would be entering not a world of service but a world of control. When you first enter a bureaucracy—and most organizations today are—you are entering an entire new world.

Welfare Managers

In this brave new world, a baby entrusted to a welfare agency may die of neglect while sleeping on the floor of the welfare office while welfare workers for days step gingerly around it—and yet the welfare administrator will be able to say sincerely that "everyone concerned did his or her job conscientiously" (Basler, 1985: B1).

Corporate Executives

In this new world, parallels are enacted (but more easily defended) in the business bureaucracy. When the accounting firm of Arthur Andersen missed a \$3.5-billion discrepancy because the communications firm of WorldCom had disguised operating expenses as profits, the *New York Times* reporters thought "it was conceivable that Andersen's auditors at WorldCom could have done their job properly and nonetheless failed to detect the problems with the company's financial reports" (Glater and Eichenwald, 2002: C1).

FBI Agents

In this new world, nearly 3,000 people are killed in an attack on the United States and a tip by lower-ranking officials does not get to the top because, in the words of one whistle-blower, "We have a culture in the F.B.I. that there's a certain pecking order, and it's pretty strong. And it's very rare that someone picks up the phone and calls a rank or two above themselves" (Federal News Service, 2002).

The IMF—International Bureaucrats

In this world of global reach, nations are asked to change their cultures to meet the demands of the macro-bureaucracies—the International Monetary Fund or the World Bank—in other words, that they modernize or be killed in economic competition. In the words of a former global bureaucrat: "To heap paradox upon paradox, because I worked with investment bankers I was surrounded by free-market fundamentalists who roamed the globe preaching a triumphant gospel of deregulation from which all freedoms would flow, yet returned to a bureaucratic roost perfectly Soviet in its rigidity" (Jennings, 2002: 15).

Computerized Citizens

In this world's most intimate touch, we ourselves become prisoners of a micro-bureaucracy of the mind. We willingly carry it with us even as it distorts our reasoning. Each use of the laptop, palm pilot, pager, and so on trains us daily in a kind of thinking that is so logical that we forget we have to make it sensible. Inner logic becomes the standard rather than the question: Does this serve the ultimate human capacity to set our own purposes? Instruments that technically connect us practically keep us apart. No need for a central power to force us to obey a central law. We happily subscribe to the electronic network. This provides not orders but only a matrix for all thinking, sensing, and acting. Within it we are free to think we are free.

Nitwits begin to say that when air controllers and a computer disagree, the solution is "removing the human from the loop." In a flurry of sneers at science fiction horribles, conveniently forgotten are examples from the Cold War. Then humans repeatedly saved computers from launching a war based on reading a flock of geese or a rising moon as a missile attack. (Quotation on airliner safety from Johnson, 2002; on missile attack, see Hummel, 2002.)

There is a danger in this wired world. It is not only that the baby died, that the economy was endangered, that peace collapsed, or even that we are hardwired to be part of the techno-bureaucracy. The danger lies not in technology or bureaucracy themselves, but in the ease with which we fall into lockstep with their programs and reproduce their excuses: Everybody did their jobs, but the baby died. Somebody didn't do their job: same result: Return the baby!

Bureaucratic Patterns

There is a pattern in all this, a consistent pattern of misunderstandings covering up the understanding of what bureaucracy is and does.

Consider its word origins. Bureaucracy: from the Greek for power (*kratos*) and from the French for office (*bureau*). In conceiving the thought that an office could rule, the designers had made a discovery: people could orient their actions toward an idea instead of a human leader. This idea could become law for them. And this law would be legitimate, a product of their own making, by becoming embedded and available to all in published rules. To assure compliance, there would be regulation and enforcement by the impersonal office. In this office, the present tenant is held accountable. But he or she will claim to be not personally responsible as long as he or she follows the rules, the law, the impersonal idea.

All these—idea, law, legitimacy, even force—could be made thoroughly intelligible to human reason, technical and moral. Promised was a power of social control never before seen on this earth. The price simply was that the particular human being would be subjected to the general rules.

Now consider the implications: The office rules, not the man or woman in it. It rules by policies, programs, and standards. These are the most inhuman of standards that can be imagined: the general laws of pure reason untainted by the particular individual or situation determine the fate of each of us. Without fear or favor does this office uniformly apply its assigned tasks; but also without compassion or sensibility. A mis-fit is unavoidable.

Reason rationalizes. It modernizes. It creates the modern world. Modernity replaces tradition: the sentiments and sensibilities of the family, the clan and tribe, the kingdoms of faith or fear.

The cradle of modernity lay in Europe. There bureaucracy was expected to carry into human affairs reason's light—the light that would enlighten the world. Europeans called it the Enlightenment, and named bureaucracy to be its administrator. Just so do we still rely on schools, armies, prisons and world bureaucracies to modernize the globe.

What happened?

For centuries we have lived that failed promise. The system developed its own inner logic. Its logic runs contrary to what humans who have desires, feelings, and emotions might consider reasonable. Bureaucracy—as distinct from civil service in general—structures that service under dehumanizing conditions. These favor top-down control but guarantee insensibility to outsiders and a pathological lack of care for the health of its inmates. The claim that it is the most perfect control instrument for its masters in business or government has long been disproved; yet its myth persists.

Consider our conventional expectations (I call them misunderstandings) in contrast to cues from reality (I call them understandings) (see Exhibit 1.1).

Today these misunderstandings and understandings work themselves out in three distinct arenas of human struggle for the human spirit.

Conventional bureaucracy. Exhibit 1.1 covers this familiar arena of bureaucratic struggles that we are used to. The institutions are in local, state, and national arenas of power. But today there are two more: computer bureaucracy, the bureaucracy without bureaucrats; and global bureaucracy, the bureaucracies of globalization.

Computer bureaucracy. With the coming of the computer, bureaucracy has become a state of mind. With every stroke of the laptop keyboard, we key in to the demands of the perfectly rational machine, the machine totally without human sensibility.

Global bureaucracy. Here the Enlightenment project continues unabated. It claims to bring the light to "dark" continents. It spreads the economics of modernity along with the gospel of democracy.

Bureaucracy is spreading, rather than contracting. It spreads across the globe. It invades our minds. Where is the light?

Modern Self-Critique

In the Enlightenment project something seems to have gone wrong. Who will tell us what it is?

The project had expected free men (and eventually women) to use their own imaginative reason to construct their own political order.

Exhibit 1.1

Misunderstandings and Understandings
of Bureaucracy

Misunderstandings	Understandings
Socially Bureaucrats deal with people.	Bureaucrats deal with cases.
Culturally Bureaucrats care about the same things we do: justice, freedom, violence, oppression, illness, death, victory, defeat, love, hate, salvation, and damnation.	Bureaucrats aim at control and efficiency.
Psychologically Bureaucrats are people like us.	Bureaucrats are a new personality type, headless and soulless.*
Linguistically Communication with bureaucrats is possible: We all speak the same language, we think the same way.	Bureaucrats shape and inform rather than communicate.
Cognitively Bureaucrats think the way we do: logically *and* sensibly.	Bureaucrats use logic only: They are trained to think the way computers think.
Politically Bureaucracies are service institutions accountable to society and ruled by politics and government.	Bureaucracies are control institutions increasingly ruling society, politics, and government.

*The terms "headless" and "soulless" here evoked strong protests from some employees of modern organizations. It may be worthwhile to point out that these terms reflect a tendency that bureaucratic life forces on bureaucrats, rather than the actual characteristics of specific individuals.

In the transition, an administrative mechanism would keep a delicate balance of order.

By 1900, this temporary order had, in the words of the sociologist Max Weber, become "a cage of steel." Bureaucracy places order before freedom. Its inmates distrust imagination. Reason, the source of light, becomes half-reason. Without imagination of how things might be otherwise, it becomes the mere logic of turning other traditions into carbon copies of the modern Western original.

By 2000+, in personal life, in computer use, in globalization, we still face the same familiar bureaucratic problem: How can human imagination be free to construct an order fit for human beings when the tools are in the hands of a force heading in another direction?

Modern social science critical of this contrary development asks typically modern questions. As the father of modern bureaucracy study, Max Weber, put it in regard to the increasing bureaucratization of life:

1. How can we save *any* remnants of "individualist" freedom in any sense?
2. How will democracy even in a limited sense be *at all possible*?
3. How will politics remain possible? (Weber 1968a [1918]: 1403–4; Weber's emphases)

These are profound questions. But they seek to protect the essential concepts of modernity from itself. Post-modernism questions today's validity of the use of concepts like freedom, democracy, even politics. Such terms are considered out of date. They no longer cover experiences and entities in reality (a concept also threatened). On top of that, post-modernists ask about the choices presented. The individual, freedom, democracy are defined by the Enlightenment itself. How can its laughing heir, modern social science, protect their integrity when its tools are tainted?

Yet Max Weber's questions have profound consequences. They orient us to the vast indifferent expanses of the modern world. Most recently similar questions were extended to apply to other aspects of modern life (e.g., Hummel, 1977; Denhardt, 1981; Baum, 1987; Diamond, 1993; Forester, 1989; Schwartz, 1990; Adams and Balfour, 1998; J. White, 1999). In the study of public administration, private management, policy, and planning, a whole critical school appeared.

This critical school, believers in full reason and hopeful of modernity, now stands confronted by a school we may call post-modern, unbelievers or at least challengers of reason.

If bureaucracy is a state of mind, this school asks, how did we get into that state of mind? And how do we get out of that state without losing our mind? Perhaps traditional institutions—individualism, freedom, politics itself—are not the issue. Perhaps the problem is precisely in thinking of human beings as individuals, of freedom as license, of politics as power, of reason as just logic. In which case, modern self-critique is not enough.

Modern self-critique of modern institutions begins with Max Weber. Still the first and foremost student of bureaucracy, Weber even today presents us with his definitive outline of what it takes to construct this control instrument without compare (see Chapter 3).

Post-modern critics do not fundamentally disagree with the tally of the costs:

- *Socially*, bureaucracy cancels *who* you are and tells you *what* you are—your assigned role in the program or the job.
- *Culturally*, the substance of what is worthwhile to you is translated into a formal shadow of your values: for example, justice into law.
- *Psychologically*, you are asked to surrender your full personality to fit into program or job identity.
- *In speaking*, you learn a strange new language that enables you to speak without meaning what you say.
- *In thinking*, you learn to be strictly logical—even if the result makes no sense.
- *Politically*, you accept being managed and are taught to despise politics because it falls far short of rational administration.

But post-modernists go beyond this list. They ask: Is there any other way of thinking about how this became so? And: What are the further-most implications of where we are headed? A version of Exhibit 1.1 was first published in 1977 as a modern anti-bureaucratic manifesto. Today even we moderns realize that, as the adoptive father of the baby said, it's really worse than that.

Post-Modern Critique

Post-modern critics try to show just how much worse. They cast suspicion on even the tools of modern self-critique. Their attack on institutions becomes a critique and criticism of modern social science itself. They question our very ways of knowing what is going on around us.

At the very least, post-modern critique confirms what modern self-critique had already exposed. At it best, post-modern critique shows new routes of escape. At its worst, the attack of the post-modern critics—often obscured by baroque flourishes of style and impressive though unnecessary detours—merely repeats the modern social scientists' own self-critique.

Yet the post-modern critique is a challenge. We must come to terms with it. It is not only the latest attack on modernity and its organizations, but it is an attack on how we think about these. How to evaluate its contribution? Perhaps it is time to draw up a new chart (see Exhibit 1.2).

A Brief Survey of Post-Modernism

What do the post-modernists hold? What new concepts replace the modern ones? What new propositions and theories? A quick survey of Exhibit 1.2 answers. The transitions observed in Exhibit 1.1 begin to show themselves in clearer outlines.

Socially, some post-modernists fear our transition from social person to organizational tenant of job or case may have resulted in the loss of the social altogether (e.g., Baudrillard).

Culturally, modern organizations' recent culture games (Japanese management, quality management, TQM, and so forth) stand out as desperate attempts to repair control in the face of disintegration. Culture, we now see, is in transition from being a center of homegrown and cultivated values toward hothouse corporate and governmental redesign. Corporate and government attempts to seize hold of culture are exposed as efforts to mask what is really going on in capitalist enterprises: loss of quality and effectiveness. In a countercurrent, there emerge lots of little stories people tell and practices they create to orient themselves to the actuality behind the curtain. Global victims of cultural hegemony are seen as having rediscovered that "culture" is a specific European invention. Attempts to "cultivate" so-called emerging nations are seen as cultural colonialism of powers burdened with the heritage of a particular religion and submissive to a particular European vision of economics: that of reinvestment capitalism.

Psychologically, in bureaucracy, I submerge my own mastery and conscience in the mastery and conscience of the manager. I lose my sense of being the author of my work. "It was done," the worker says of something he did, revealing a hidden injury of class (see Sennett). The worker is alienated, as Karl Marx would say, from himself. Post-modernists now recognize what tradition-to-modern analysis already saw: the splitting of psychological functions between manager and worker resulting in a unit for analysis that is centered in neither of them.

In language use, once we left the home of a mother tongue and started consciously making language and using it as a tool, post-modernists point out, the obverse side also began to flourish. This is the impossibility of controlling human action perfectly through controlling the language (Derrida, Jameson, Baudrillard).

Cognitively: "The once-existing centered subject, in the period of classical capitalism and the nuclear family, has today in the world of organizational bureaucracy dissolved" (Jameson, 1991: 15). Effects had already been observed by the early 1900s: the descent of science scouring reality to find general laws—Truth writ large—and the capture of science by technology. Now one post-modernist in particular has traced a vicious circle in which the knower is shaped by official "truth" already established, resulting in his or her capture in disciplines that, in turn, reinforce official reality (Foucault). In the extreme, what we see are signs pointing to a reality that does not exist: for instance, stock market numbers.

Finally, post-modernists have been disappointed by political ideologies and mass movements. They turn instead to small-scale politics. This is to be based on anything but the knowledge assumptions of the power politics inherited from the Enlightenment. Specifically, the faults of political representation as the ruin of reason are pointed out, and hopeful participants are warned not to fall in love with power (Foucault; Deleuze and Guattari.)

To the further exploration of this chart, the rest of this book is dedicated. For now an illustration of the use of post-modern analysis. What does it see that modern self-analysis does not see?

A Case in Point: Post-Modernism Meets Sewage

Changing the charts enables us to navigate differently. We can better see where we are coming from and where we are headed. The post-modern chart opens up new channels by going to the depths. It asks how free modern social science is from the assumptions of modernity thinking. Can there be self-criticism of modernity by modernity?

Exhibit 1.2

Bureaucracy and the Post-Modern Challenge

Modern society—as seen by itself	Bureaucracy—as seen in modern critique	Post-Modernity—as seen through post-modernism
Socially Who we are is defined by a set of relationships. Social identity: status, class, gender, etc. Work is one aspect. (*Weber*)	Work defines who you are: The job, the case are both defined by the organization. They-relations. (*Berger, Schütz*)	In the extreme: loss of social bond. Selves as atoms in random motion (*Baudrillard*), as nodal points in flexible networks (*Lyotard*).
Culturally Culture as self-development. Humans create the worthwhile. Meaning is shared by reference to core values. Spirit of capitalism is religious.	Culture by design. Formal universal values and procedure replace substance (*Weber, Mannheim*). Functions. Capitalism without spirit.	Culture as economics. Loss of universal values: little narratives, not grand narratives (*Lyotard*). Relativism (*G.B. Madison*). Reduced to power (*Foucault*); as capitalism. Hermeneutics.
Understanding.	Explanation.	
Psychologically A centered psyche. Individual personality. (*Freud*)	An alienated psyche. Organizational identity. Truncated individual identifies with manager: Work bond (*Hummel*); Narcissism (*Diamond, Schwartz*).	A decentered psyche. We are all decentered selves dependent on others, diffused over structures, and in the grip of insatiable desire. (*Lacan*).

Linguistically We are embedded in language, the "mother tongue." Meaning is created in our talking back and forth (*Searle*). Communication.	Language as tool of hierarchy; machine "language"; retreat from meaning and committed speech (*Wittgenstein, Searle*). Information.	Language not controllable (*Derrida*); rule of the differend, the phrase (*Lyotard*, 1988: 9); Language games (*Jameson*); Tests (*Baudrillard*).
Cognitively Knowing subject (ego). We are subjects seeking knowledge of objects: Big Truth through Science about Reality. (*Kant*)	Knower and known overlap, but: descent into technique (*Husserl*); enframing (*Heidegger*).	Death of the subject. Knower is function of knowledge and power (*Foucault*). Little truths. Simulacra (*Baudrillard*).
Politically We engage in power politics. "Responsible" politicians: citizenship (*Weber, Lasswell*).	Politics replaced by administration; politicians by managers; citizens by functionaries (*Habermas, Heidegger*).	Micropolitics (*Foucault, Jameson, Lyotard*). We are functions in collectivities. The individual becomes an effect of power (*Foucault*).

I am reminded of the consultant who was asked by the city manager of a southwestern city to look into the recurrent failure of its sewage clearance plant. Stressed beyond its limits, it regularly floods in heavy rains. When the consultant arrived at the plant, he was greeted with silence. Finally, clearly anticipating being blamed for the plant's incapacity, a worker said: "Why should we tell you anything?" Said the consultant: "Because I won't give you up" (Anonymous, personal communication).

You don't give up the baby. You don't surrender substance for procedure. Post-modern analysis does not stop with tracing the human causes of an event; it asks how humans were put in the situation to begin with.

To the consultant using this approach, getting to the bottom of things means looking at the setup. You don't stop at immediate causes or go on running down one-way-path analyses. You suspect your client and the people who do the work have been set up: Is the silence imposed by isolation? Is it torture to be put to work in an impossible situation and then be forced to talk about it as if it were possible? (See Lyotard, 1988: 11)

Perhaps the citizens and taxpayers had something to do with the setup? Assumptions that there is only one single truth about this should be questioned. And so should the assumption that what exists is all there is: a single reality, a futureless now.

Perhaps the issue should not be seen in terms of power, but in terms of opportunity?

And if the words spoken here do not point directly to an opening, what prevents them from doing what comes naturally—that the phrase I speak resonates in you and that you pick up before I leave off? This encounter is a potential opening to rethink the sources of the need for clearing sewage to begin with. The consultant must get to the bottom of things, but the bottom may not lie at the base of the clearance pool.

So far, the pitch and tone of a post-modern analysis. Modern analysis deals with what is; post-modern analysis goes to what prevents us from imagining how things might be otherwise.

To be effective in the *modern* way, the consultant must be an honest broker to all sides yet get to the heart of the matter as it stands. To be effective in the *post-modern* way, the consultant needs to see where the modern tools—the modern concepts, the modern science, the modern theory—no longer work.

Truth is an issue for both kinds of analysis. But where modern analysis seeks the Truth in general, *post-modern analysis* looks for lots of little truths as they emerge in particular situations. The consultant must know how these little truths emerge. This is the move from Grand Narratives to little narratives.

As he himself moves from department to department, the consultant's stock of stories told in one place opens up the situation in another. The truth he seeks is not adherence to a standard; it is what can be discovered from out of what is otherwise covered over. Conversely he will know that what he knows in general about men at work must yield to local interpretation (see Derrida).

The city manager, in post-modern analysis, is well advised to restrain the tendency to use power to force compliance to his wishes. Not only would the little truth of the plant not emerge, but there would be unspoken costs.

And why should the workers speak up in the face of power? There is a baby they must not give up. But it is not one of the Truth about the plant, not even a small truth. What they must preserve is their own ability to speak in a situation that offers a dilemma. The dilemma is this: to speak is to accept responsibility for what one knows, and not to speak may be perceived by management as equally incriminating. Both moves may reinforce the manager's suspicion that the workers are up to something.

It takes courage to speak. But it is speech that makes us fully human. And this is the baby not to be given up at work. The test, of course, will come when even a little truth confronts political power. But even power is a two-edged sword for post-modernism: it depends on resistances (see Foucault). Where it suppresses speech, workers can fail to resist by simply not telling management what is going on, a worse outcome than workers who resist but are engaged.

Post-modern analysis questions the conventional way of looking at how things stand; the consultant—and the rest of us—must try to think and speak in unconventional ways. We live—we come to life—in what we now say. In my telling you what to do, I am not sending you a message; I am opening up a world in which you and I have existence only because we are able to say what needs to be said: Don't give up the baby!

Similarly, where one party to a dispute must speak in terms of the other, not only can there be no satisfaction of its needs (see Lacan) but it becomes a victim not a partner (see Lyotard).

In short, post-modern analysis asks whether the conditions are present that leave the future open to possibilities even where the choices seem mutually exclusive: Don't return *this* baby.

The Danger

The bureaucratic society exalts reason that measures, calculates, and aggregates what is countable. Don't we all believe that what is real is what is measurable? Wielding this tool, bureaucracy—wielding in the one hand reason and in the other science—rides roughshod over experience, emotion, belief, faith, purpose, meaning, feeling, judgment, deliberation, resistance. But without these—and a sense for how all these fit together in human life—it is not possible to see what is there, trust how we know, judge what we must do (Socrates).

These human tasks are not helped by reason as analysis that merely takes the problem apart. The analyst who merely takes problems apart ends up dissecting *you*.

The Politics of Good and Evil

Reason alone is a false companion. Where it is allowed to determine the way we live, it imprisons and distorts our human possibilities. Those who know this courageously point out the consequences: reason declines into administrative evil (Adams and Balfour, 1998). They may stand accused of going too far. They have not gone far enough.

Auschwitz is not an anomaly.

The question is whether we can stop this descent before all choices become choices between evils: between a prisoner being denied a head of cabbage, in which case, he starves—and that prisoner being given the cabbage, in which case he dies of dysentery (see Borowski, 1976).

Every day, in every small and seemingly trivial way, we commit this kind of evil. Any one of us, given even the smallest portion of power, is in the position of committing little unspeakable acts against our fellow citizens. This may take the form of dilemmas: To proceed, you need form X; but we give you form X only after you proceed. To work in the automotive industry, you need a union card; but to get a union card, you need to work in the industry. When such an act is backed up by an entire institution, by the logic of all modernity, its force becomes irresistible.

And yet, there may still be a place where we know what is good and what is evil. There we know what is right, we just don't do it once we calculate the personal consequences. There what is right is what keeps and increases the potential of human beings; what is evil is whatever forecloses that potential.

The daily injuries of bureaucratic reason are not trivial. In a bureaucratic society, each of us holds the fate of many others in his or her hands. The price is not cheap.

On the national scale, a senator calling for "the best security we can have" fingers the tradeoff between order and freedom: "We never had, ever in this country, a police state, and I don't know, gosh, I hope we never have one" (Shelby, 2002: A14).

Who or what is making him choose? A police state reaction to terrorism is not a mere misstep. It is an outrage against humanity. It is being forced to die by eating the cabbage or not eating it. We have been down that road before. Its origins in our own heart of darkness are captured in the words of the presidential scholar who, in dark times like ours, uttered these fatal words: "No sacrifice is too great for our democracy, least of all the temporary sacrifice of democracy itself" (Rossiter, 1963 [1948]: 314).

On September 13, 2002, another U.S. senator, speaking to an empty chamber (except for the majority whip), uttered these words about the Founders: "They were writing a Constitution that would protect the common people against tyranny." Speaking on behalf of requiring Senate confirmation of a presidential aide seconded to control homeland security, he evoked the spirit of senators who had served before him, saying they would not have "stood aside" for "that kind of noose placed around their necks" (Sen. Harry Bird, D-West Virginia, C-Span 2).

Bureaucracies, including departments of justice, are not a trustworthy guardian of democracy. A "temporary" sacrifice of freedom to the forces of order is never temporary. If, as Max Weber said, "In a modern state the real ruler is necessarily and unavoidably the bureaucracy," was he just blowing smoke? Or have we missed something? (See Weber, 1968a [1918]: 1393.)

A critique of bureaucracy is an act on behalf of political freedom and future human possibility. It is in political terms that this book renews its claim to become a practical guide to—and warning against—rule that reduces human beings to pieces of paper, computer bytes, or pawns of financial strategy. Though, of course, the claim to practicality will be fulfilled only to the extent that you take it so and make it so.

Remember the baby!

2

Bureaucracy as Society: Loss of the Social

Bureaucracy is the means of transforming social action into rationally organized action . . . a power instrument of the first order for one who controls the bureaucratic apparatus.

—Max Weber

Perfect control over a system, which is supposed to improve its performance, is inconsistent with respect to the law of contradiction; it in fact lowers the performance level it claims to raise.

—Jean-François Lyotard

Information devours its own content. It devours communication and the social.

—Jean Baudrillard

Bureaucracy replaces society. In bureaucracy all our relationships become impersonal. In society all relationships are personal. When my daughter Kate was born, we observed a rite of passage. My professor in graduate school did the honors. "Hi!" he said to her in a booming voice. She promptly started to cry. "We say, 'Hi!' to you," he continued above the wail, "because today we welcome you." And so on.

What we make of others and what others make of us defines us. Such acts define not only who we are (a baby, a father, a professor) but *that* we are.

Society—our social relations—answers the human question, Who am I? But this contains the all-too-human question, Am I? Our parents, friends, and neighbors answer, Yes. A stranger may answer, You are nothing to me. But even this confirms *that* you are: namely he (or she) who is "nothing to me." Only when we are totally ignored by others—as in the statement, We don't know him—do I feel at a total loss. People have been known to commit suicide over this denial that they are.

Society provides recognition *that* we are by establishing *who we are to others.* People above us, people below us, people next to us—these confirm that we have a place in the world. You are a child to your parents. They are your parents to you. The boy is a male to the girl. The middle-class shopkeeper has a social position only if there is someone who can be called upper-class or working class. But we also get a chance to respond: You're no child of mine, I'll have a sex change operation, My father was upper-class and so I am, and so on.

In contrast, our relationships in the modern factory or bureaucracy are assigned to us. The issue is no longer who we are (to others) but what we are (to the work). Not until modern times has work totally dominated human beings. Is it really any wonder that work organizations replace social organizations?

The modern work organization shapes all aspects of being human, beginning with freedom to choose whose company we keep. Society—the word comes from the Latin for associate (*socius*)—*is* the company we keep. Organization—the word traces back to the Greek *ergon* and energy—chooses and controls whom we meet, know, and depend on at work. Work relations in the factory or the office displace friends and all kinship on our social map. Bureaucracy—as the key type of modern organization—replaces society.

Who we are and whom we encounter at work is determined by an anonymous someone sitting behind a desk (bureau) and exercising the power (Greek: *kratos*) of the office: bureau-cracy. We naturally resent this bureaucratic experience. As human beings we are capable of making and maintaining our own social relationships. These are now left in a backwater. Society itself becomes a backwater to the factory or office.

Modern critics say organizational domination has gone too far: devaluation of the social in favor of being functional to our work actually reduces modern organization's promise of performance.

Post-modern critics argue that even the concepts of the social and society no longer apply. The social itself is lost in organizational structuring of what we are to the work.

What is lost to humanity? What picture can we make ourselves of the brave new world gained in the bureaucratized society? What is the new social/organizational reality?

Bureaucracy replaces society. What does this do to us as human beings relating to and working with other human beings? We turn first to what people actually do.

How People Act

Society is defined by how we relate to each other. How do we act differently toward others in bureaucracy than in society? How does bureaucracy change social relations? Modernists ask these questions. What do post-modernists ask?

The next section's two subsections address this difference. Both modern critics of modernity (those committed to the modern experiment) and post-modernists (those who question the assumptions of that experiment) question the direction of human society. The first see an aberration from modernity; the second group sees the end of modernity and the rise of post-modernity.

The Worker in the Bureaucracy

Imagine you are in a box. Operating instructions tell you how to use various levers to operate tools attached to the box to work on objects outside the box. You can see the objects through a glass bottom and you can also see there are tools protruding from other boxes; these work on the same objects you work on. In these other boxes, you assume, there are people like yourself. Occasionally, you would like to speak to them to get one of their tools out of your way or to work with you in jointly grasping an object. However, this is prevented by the fact that each of you is in a box.

The good news is that you can relate to people in other boxes if you first ask permission from a person in a box above you. You can see this person because there is a glass ceiling in your box. You are linked to him or her through a speaking tube. The bad news is that the up-valve is open only when he or she decides to open a down-valve, through which come orders. In short, the system of boxes is set up so you can do the job assigned to you—but without much questioning of the orders or the job description and without contact with your coworkers.

Congratulations! You are working in a bureaucracy. You will recognize the division of labor so characteristic of bureaucracy: your box and the working boxes next to you. And you will recognize hierarchy: the box just a little higher up that has a one-way channel of ordering you around. It controls whether and how you relate to the working of others.

This is what the founding sociologist of the study of bureaucracy meant when he said: "Bureaucracy is *the* means of transforming social action into rationally organized action" (Weber, 1968a: 987). Its guiding image is the organization chart. It places people into the boxes of jobs, all of which are so designed as to be perfectly logical means to the goal of the totality of boxes: the organization. The organization looks like this:

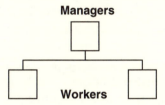

Its advantages and frustrations are cut from the same blueprint. Workers in their assigned jobs soon work out more sensible ways of relating to their work than can be contained in the instructions.* Since workers in related jobs focus on the same work, they soon respond to the possibility of using their tools in a coordinated way that makes sense from their own observation of how the object responds. In short, their natural contact with the work inspires them to turn the shape of hierarchy upside down:

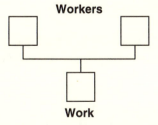

This conflict represents the core tension in the social relations of bureaucracy. The conflict is that between bureaucracy and society. To the extent this rebellion succeeds, the organization falls apart or is destroyed. But to the extent that the organization can keep people from relating to

---

*The special problems this creates for modern organizations are discussed in the chapters on language and thought.

work and others in their own way, it becomes, in Weber's words, *the control instrument without compare.*

All the pathologies of social relationships associated with bureaucracy —between clients and bureaucracy, between citizens and bureaucracy, between managers and functionaries of bureaucracy, and most important between workers and their work—result from this original seizure of the society-building impulse of human beings.

The Citizen versus Bureaucracy

The man and woman in the street experience the upside-down nature of bureaucratic society every day.* They feel the coldness and impersonality with which they are typically treated by the street-level functionaries of a bureaucracy. They, of course, mistake these for fellow citizens, not realizing that these are functionaries imprisoned in the box of their jobs. Citizens expect to be treated as citizens, but the job instructs functionaries to treat them as objects on which to perform work. Before he walked into the doors of, say, the New York Motor Vehicles Department, our man in the street was a proud car owner, a man of substance because he could own a car, a man with some degree of self-esteem because he just steered that car through difficult traffic—in other words, a human being with class, status, and unique personality. Once inside the door, he is told to stand in line, fill out forms just so, accept the rejection of the way he filled out his forms, told to stand in the same line again to wait another hour or so, required to answer the questions of the man or woman behind the desk, directed to another line, and so on.

> They made me feel like a kid, like I didn't have a brain in my head. The whole thing didn't make sense. First one line, then another. Then they sent me back to my insurance agent for my F-1 form I didn't know I was supposed to have. I told them I just took off the day to get my license plates and couldn't take off another. Couldn't they just give me my plates and I would mail in my form? No! The rules say . . . blah, blah . . . another day shot.
> —*Man interviewed by author outside a Motor Vehicles Department*

---

*As throughout the book, each difference between society and bureaucracy is here first treated experientially. A theory of the bureaucratic society is offered at the end after insights of experts, whose work serves as a foundation for the theory.

"They made me feel like a kid. . . ." The client here commits his first and almost universal error in misunderstanding bureaucracy. Actually, he is turned into less than a child in the eyes of the bureaucrat. He is turned into a "case." The bureaucrat has no time and no permission to become involved in the personal problems of clients. From the bureaucrats' point of view, the more they can depersonalize the client into a thing devoid of unique features, the more easily and smoothly they will be able to handle cases before them.

Here is where the client commits a second mistake of misunderstanding. In the world from which the client has just come, the world outside the bureaucracy's door, there are many areas of life in which it is absolutely necessary to take into account the unique personality of the person with whom you are dealing. Friendship and salesmanship are two of these areas. When you go to a friend for help, he or she helps you in a personal and intimate way precisely because you are unique—because you are you, a friend. If you are trying to sell door-to-door, whether it is cosmetics or life insurance, you had better take into account the unique state of mind of the individual you are selling to. It may make a difference to know that a woman's spouse has just put her on a strict budget or that the person you are trying to sell life insurance to has just that day lost a relative.

The Bureaucrat and the Work

There are many ways of giving public service. The Salvation Army gives public service. Parishioners in your local church collect money to give to the poor at Christmas. Society women hold a charity ball. You give to a poorly dressed man holding out his hand on a street corner. Whether any of these ways of giving are bureaucratic remains to be examined. The last two examples are likely to be unbureaucratic.

Bureaucracy is a particular strategy, chosen from among others, through which public service can be given. Weber indicated the chief characteristic of bureaucracy as a specific organizational strategy for giving service: It is characterized by "rationally organized action," not by "social action." In fact, it transforms social action into rationally organized action.

The newcomer to a bureaucracy, intending to keep the job, and the client approaching a bureaucracy, wanting to get service and still remain sane, had better understand the difference in the codes of behavior built into society and bureaucracy; that is, the conflict of "social action" versus "rationally organized action."

The alternative, even for the experienced bureaucrat, can be eternal puzzlement. A social worker for Catholic Charities talks about her attempts to get humane, personal attention for her clients from social services caseworkers:

> In dealing with clients we would eventually have to take certain clients down to welfare, Social Security, the board of education and they would see a caseworker.
>
> Still, no one is interested in what your problem is. The caseworker screens you like you have applied for a Banker's Trust loan.
>
> Eventually you get pretty tired of all the bullshit questions and ask, Are you so inhuman that you can't deal with the client as a person? Then, being the dedicated caseworkers that they are, they'll give you some crap about the manual not allowing for that.
>
> If you still continue along this line of questioning the caseworker—or, as they call it, harassment of the caseworker—they will read you the rules and regulations of the welfare department.
>
> All of this keeps you in line and keeps them uninvolved. . . .
>
> Bureaucracy, as you say, is *the* means of transforming social action into rationally organized action. Which is what any well-organized agency will do, in that they cut through the bull and get to *their* main objectives, not *yours.*
>
> *—Anonymous Respondent, Catholic Charities*

Ultimately, functionaries who cannot accept the restrictions of bureaucratic service leave, or are forced to leave, the bureaucracy. A former social worker tells of the frustrations that led to her being fired:

> For two and a half years, I was a social worker for a private child caring agency which cared for dependent and neglected children. Since these children were all from New York City, our agency was funded by the City of New York and thus we were bound by the rules of the Bureau of Child Welfare of the city's Social Service Department.
>
> My job was to provide casework services to the children and their families. The goal was to come up with some long-range plans for the child—hopefully to reunite him with his family or to place him in a long-range foster home. I had a regular caseload and visited the families every two weeks.
>
> I had a difficult time adjusting to some of the rules set up by both New York City and the agency that employed me. We always had to become somewhat detached from our clients. It was not my job to get involved

in determining how much welfare money my clients received. Almost all of them were receiving public assistance and it was easy to see that it wasn't enough.

I recall using my own money to buy Christmas gifts so that the parents would give them to the children when they spent the holidays with them. I occasionally brought food with me to my clients because it was easy to see that their public assistance allotment wasn't enough.

I never told this to my employer.

Our agency had a rule that the parents could come and visit the children every other Sunday. I remember feeling frustrated over this, as I felt that it was hardly enough contact. I remember asking how this decision was arrived at and being told by my supervisor that he didn't know: It had always been that way.

I always felt that the bureaucratic process placed a great gap between the social worker and the client. This created much frustration because I guess I felt some human feelings toward these people and couldn't give them what I wanted to. There were too many regulations and forms that got in the way of what I considered to be a good relationship based on needs and feelings.

Thus, I didn't last too long.

—*Elaine G., currently personnel director for a detention shelter for juveniles* (Written report to the author, May 1974)

Despite puzzlement, resentment, and an overpowering sense of frustration, both the Catholic Charities social worker and the child care social worker put their finger on essential characteristics of bureaucracy. Their only problem is that they perceive these essentials as pathology. In their own words, these essentials are:

1. Bureaucracies "get to *their* main objectives, not *yours*."
2. "Regulations and forms" get in the way of "a good [social] relationship based on needs and feelings."

Why is this so? Why should this be so?

The Client as "Case" and the Policy Maker

Bureaucracy is an efficient means for handling large numbers of people —"efficient" in its own terms. It would be impossible to handle large numbers of people in their full depth and complexity. As a result, only those facts in the complex lives of individuals that are relevant to the task at hand are taken up by the organization.

To achieve this simplification, the modern bureaucrat has invented the "case." At the intake level, individual personalities are converted into cases. Only if a person can qualify as a case is he or she allowed treatment. More accurately, a bureaucracy is never set up to treat or deal with persons: It "processes" only "cases."

What is a case? A case is never a real person. A case is a series of characteristics abstracted from persons; it is a model of those characteristics that a potential client must display in order to qualify for the attention of a bureaucracy, whether for service or control. Definitions of what constitutes a case have far-flung impact not only directly on clients but on policy formation.

For example, case definition was crucial when one of the watchdog organizations appointed to keep an eye on New York City's shaky finances noted a strange phenomenon in 1984: The city's public assistance "caseload" was continuing to rise at a time of high economic growth at both the national and local level. In its attempts to explain such public assistance growth and to forecast future trends, the state's Office of the Special Deputy Comptroller for the City of New York needed to model case definitions.

The Deputy Comptroller's Office defined public assistance as including benefits to indigent people under two major programs: Aid to Families with Dependent Children (AFDC) and Home Relief (HR). AFDC was defined as providing "assistance to families with dependent children that are deprived of support due to the death, prolonged absence, incapacity or unemployment of a parent." HR was defined as providing "financial assistance to indigent persons who do not meet Federal eligibility requirements for the AFDC program, including persons with substantial physical or mental impairments, unemployed young adults with limited training or work experience, and families with very low incomes." It was further defined as providing "temporary assistance to persons who are awaiting eligibility determination for the Supplemental Security Income (SSI) program, a Federally administered program which provided assistance to certain aged, blind or disabled individuals."

The Policy Analyst and the Case

Without definitions of who is likely to come onto the city's "case rolls," it would be impossible to explain or predict the financial load on the city's coffers. Using such definitions, the State Deputy Comptroller's Office was able to construct an econometric model to explain the relationship between caseload and fluctuations in the city's economy as measured by gross city product,* an indicator of the city's economic strength.

Technical staff concluded that any trickle-down effect of prosperity on the poor was delayed. Based on the past pattern of such delay, staff was able to predict that the growth in the city's AFDC caseload would level off or possibly decline over the near term, a trend already evident in a recipient decline of ten thousand between May and October of 1984—a drop of about 1 percent.

Even for those less than interested in whether the City of New York can survive carrying its public assistance caseload, there is a lesson here. The "case" is not only the basic definition of whether a person in need officially can come to exist to the eyes and ears of bureaucracy; it is also the basis for all calculation of future needs of a bureaucracy and of the entire political system as it engages in providing government services and controls. By the time a human being is allowed to enter a bureaucracy as a case, that human being already no longer exists as a human being.

Herein lies a fundamental difference between people's self-perception when they stand in society and the client's official status as perceived by bureaucrats as the clients enter bureaucracy. Can a policy and an administrative system based on calculations of *sameness* be designed to satisfy the needs of a population defining itself on the basis of *differentness*? To the extent that this is not possible, the calculations may be exact and even aesthetically pleasing, but they will have little or nothing to do with reality as the calculations find it—though, of course, the calculations do encompass reality as they make it.

The Worker and Management: Control and Visibility

The dehumanization of the functionary–client relationship is paralleled in the relationship between employees and management.

Bureaucracy's purpose is "rational" action. Action is rational on two grounds: first, if an action is a logical means to a clearly defined end; second, if and only if action is performed in such a manner that its

---

*Gross city product is defined as the total output of city goods and services adjusted for inflation. It is analogous to gross national product.

means–ends logic is visible. Action within bureaucracy must not only be action; it must also be subject to control. If it is not subject to control, it is not action. Or, rather, it may be action, but bureaucracy itself cannot take official notice of it.

The sociologist Talcott Parsons includes the double demand for both logic and visibility in a definition: "Action is rational in so far as it pursues ends possible within the conditions of the situation, and by the means which, among those available to the actor, are intrinsically best adapted to the end for reasons understandable and verifiable by positive empirical science" (Parsons, 1937: 58).

Functionaries have a hard time accepting the double aspect. "Why," they typically ask, "do I have to spend hours filling out reports when anybody can see that I've got my work done?" The demand for visibility is especially irritating to civil service managers whose work is already highly visible to them. A battalion chief in the Fire Department of the City of New York complains:

> When the fire's out, the fire's out. Anybody can see that. We've done our job. There's a lot of satisfaction in that.
>
> I don't even mind going over what happened at a big fire with the captains involved. I think it's necessary to debrief. You learn from that. Other people can see things that happened that you missed.
>
> But then there are the reports. And the second guessing from upstairs. And the insisting on regs [regulations]: Does your watch guy have his shirt buttoned, are shoes shined, are buttons on?
>
> If I've got a good team that turns out a topnotch performance at a fire, I'm going to hassle them about a missing button?
>
> —*Battalion Chief, 1977*

Yet bureaucracy is a control instrument and a control instrument without compare. Control is the source of power for this type of organization, and it is natural that those charged with control will emphasize the visible portions of what their subordinates do. As a result, instituting standard operating procedures and basing assessment of performance on observed compliance with these is a natural and normal demand. The results of such emphasis on the visible are also inevitable. Eventually control comes to mean largely checking that procedures are followed—instead of looking at impact.

What can be controlled are jobs; these are merely the boxes that contain the work. Jobs are defined top down according to goals as understood rationalistically by management; work is what functionaries actually do. These actions then must be made to resemble job descriptions in official reports. A weakness of bureaucracy is that, when jobs and work diverge, managers tend to mistake official reports for work actually done. In other words, for the sake of visible procedures that can be easily supervised by control personnel (management), the first condition of modern rational action—that action be logically connected to some substantive end or purpose—is finally abandoned. Formality conquers substance.

Logic, however, is neither human motivation nor spirit. In seeking control over the people who carry out assigned jobs, management still must deal with human beings who have both. Yet the single-minded logic of control persists, especially when workers seem "out of control." That logic creates a picture of simple robots who only wait for the proper stimulus to do exactly what they are ordered to do.

In the wake of the sacrifice of 343 firefighters at the World Trade Center, a consultant's report critically cited a supposed need for stricter training, routine obedience to orders, tauter command and control, better coordination with the police—all control issues.

As so-called tough-minded consultants will tell us the world over, control is more important than care. This ignores not only the willingness for self-sacrifice so typical of firefighters but reflects a typical bureaucratic attitude toward the devotion of many civil servants. What was the effect that the mortal sacrifice of the firefighters had on the remaining living? Are we seriously asked to believe it was merely motivated by pension money or family pressure? Between January and July 26, 2002, a total of 661 firefighters of all ranks filed for retirement, as against 274 retiring in the same period of 2001 (Baker, 2002). What will be the human effect of implementing the consultants' advice?

On all these issues, what do the experts say?

What the Experts Say

Modern Critique: Weber, Schütz, Berger

People who enter bureaucracy complain that their social relations now are dictated by the organization. Modern social theorists agree that this change is systemic. Max Weber writes in his *Economy and Society* that "Bureaucracy is *the* means of transforming social action into rationally organized action" (Weber, 1968a: 987). Whom we work with is not determined by our preferences but by whether we and our coworkers are logically evaluated as the fitting tool to reach a working goal.

The breach in sociality is real. Social acts are real. They are real to the people involved. They are made real because each social act is directed with the purpose of being understood by at least one other person. Organizational dictatorship over the social insults and injures not only social process but purpose.

What purpose? The purpose of making a life together. And this making of a life, a joint life-world, includes other concerns beyond work. Each member in the relation engages in a social process: he or she attributes meaning both to what the other does and to the action he or she directs toward the other. When any of these elements is lacking—as on the job—people complain of the rationalistic transformation of basic human relationships: those ranging from love to kinship to friendship. A stranger is more likely to be your intimate coworker than anyone in your family or your extended kin. His or her commitment, not to say any loyalty, is not to you but to the personnel department. "Under the spreading chestnut tree, I sold you and you sold me," writes the author of *Brave New World*.

Post-modernists see more than a transformation. They see a loss of the social altogether. "Language games" replace commitment and relationships. Social relations are now treated as mere talk. Their seriousness is undermined by "play" of language games. But post-modernists find hope here, too. The bureaucratic game breaks down into little sub-games. Each game is seen to arise from what people are able to say about their particular experiences in different environments opposed to the official word that comes from the bureaucratic center.

The concept of language games originally was grounded in actual experience—in what its originator, the philosopher Ludwig Wittgenstein, called "life forms." There is a tendency among post-modernists to let this foundation in reality slip by looking at what people say as a text, rather than what they do—the context.

Whether this adds anything to our depth of analysis, or whether this belongs in a movie entitled *Attack of the English Teachers*, is left for further discussion under the heading of post-modern critics. First to the modern critics of modernity.

Modern critics as early as Max Weber have pointed to taking the human element out as the strength of bureaucracy. Looking at how this move is experienced by real people (a form of inquiry called phenomenol-ogy), the sociologist Alfred Schütz clarifies the cost: the succession of "we-relations" typical of society by "they relations." His student Peter L. Berger in turn grounds these developments in the way we know our world. His sociology of knowledge shows how the bureaucratized society gets stuck in the middle stage of what used to be a natural cycle of the creation, maintenance, and reproduction of society.

It may be useful to see how far their critique takes Weber, Schütz, and Berger before taking up the post-modern challenge that it does not take them far enough.

Weber

The classic, and still leading, expert on bureaucracy is Max Weber, who also gives us a definition of social action outside bureaucracy that un-derlies much of current sociology.

Social Action. In *Economy and Society*, the theoretical groundwork for his sociology, Weber offers this definition of action and social action: "We shall speak of 'action' insofar as the acting individual attaches a subjective meaning to his behavior—be it overt or covert, omission or acquiescence. Action is 'social' insofar as its subjective meaning takes account of the behavior of others and is thereby oriented in its course" (Weber, 1968a: 4). What does he mean, and how is what he means rel-evant for any attempt to distinguish between social action in bureaucracy and in society?

If we take Weber personally, his meaning becomes clear: I am engaged in action when I do something and attach some sort of meaning to what I do. For example, I may be swinging an ax and hacking away at a piece of wood. This behavior, in itself just a physical exercise, becomes action when I attach to my swinging and hacking the intention of ending up with some kindling for the fire.

So far Weber's point about action is merely definitional. He is simply saying to us: This is how I shall define "action" in a purely arbitrary way. But, of course, he has a hidden purpose, and this becomes apparent when we look at the definition of social action.

Social action is action not simply of the sort to which I, as the actor, attach my personal meaning. It is action in which I take into account the meaning that others may attach to it. For example, if I am in the woods by myself and want some kindling, I may swing and hack at anything that comes along. If Joe is with me, however, I do not want him to misunderstand my wild swinging and hacking as an attack on him. I therefore chop in a very organized way at one piece of wood at a time, hoping Joe will recognize in my care and direction the meaning I attach to my action: "Hey, Joe, I'm chopping at this piece of wood, you see? Not at you!" When I so design my actions that I take into account how others might react, I have begun to transform action, with its purely personal meaning, into social action, which is intended to have meaning for myself and at least one other person.

From this, Weber progresses to the form "social relationship." "The term 'social relationship' will be used to denote the behavior of a plurality of actors insofar as, in its meaningful content, the action of each takes account of that of others and is oriented in these terms" (Weber, 1968a: 26). Now we have at least two actors, you and I, for example; and each of us acts in such a way that the other can understand the meaning of the action. I, for example, am now writing these words with the intention of having you understand them. And, you, to the degree that you want to engage in a reader-author (social) relationship with me, read with the intention of understanding me. To the extent that we each direct our actions toward the other, we are engaged in a social relationship.

Now let us ask ourselves to what extent bureaucrats are allowed to engage in either social action or social relationships with their clients. To answer the question, we can simply ask ourselves:

1. To what extent do bureaucrats intend to have their actions understood by clients?
2. To what extent do bureaucrats intend to engage in relationships with clients in which all action rests on mutual understanding?

In our ordinary human life, we treat people as people. We try to understand them and give them a chance to understand us. But what of the bureaucrats' position? Do they wait—can they wait—until they are engaged in a relationship of mutual understanding with their clients? The fact is that the machinery of bureaucracy must grind on long before that. What Weber meant to tell all of us working in and living with bureaucracy is that the pressures we feel from being unable to deal with clients as human beings are not occasional. They are not symptomatic of something gone wrong in bureaucracy. They are built into bureaucracy. They are essential to bureaucracy if the great claims of modern organization to greater efficiency and their ability to manipulate large masses of people are to be achieved. Bureaucracy is the rational organization of action.

That leaves us with one more of Weber's terms to understand. What is rationally organized action?

Rationally Organized Action. Weber clarifies the character of rationally organized action in another essay, "On Some Categories of a Sociology of Understanding." He distinguishes three stages of development. Of these the last is dominated by a logic that subordinates human relations as totally as possible to service of a larger purpose. In the earliest stage, in community, "the normal form of entry" is "to be born into" participating and "to be reared [*hineinerzogen*] into it." This is communal action in which the individual yields to community practices (Weber, 1913: 471).

In the second step, social arrangements are arrived at by increasingly conscious and mostly voluntary agreement. This is the beginning of modern society and social action with its growing demand that individuals serve a larger social purpose; the very fact that this becomes an issue reflects increasing individuation, which social arrangements must coordinate. Increasingly rationalistic, social action tends to be dominated by voluntary contract, which, however, can ultimately be enforced by "a coercive apparatus" such as the State and the Church (468).

Finally, even society yields to the onward march of a rationalism that says meaning comes from having a purpose and that it is our human duty to design logical means to achieve these purposes. Society's successor becomes the modern organization: the factory and the bureaucracy. The way we act in these institutions puts us in the vanguard of modernization, but also reflects a loss of personal loyalty and personal duty, which are now superseded by calculating prudence in role performance. "The transition to the 'institution'," says Weber, "is fluid." Rationally organized action becomes "institutionally mandated action" (468).

Rationally organized action thus dominates the step that follows community and society in the history of human existence in the West. These stages and their dominant types of action can be portrayed as follows:

community = communal action based on mutual understanding.
society = social action: general rules mixed with discretion for exercise of understanding within the rules.
bureaucracy = rationally organized action: design of all action from above; shrinkage of discretion.

The insight that bureaucracy is a new type of social relationship, first outlined by Weber, is subsequently developed in three directions. Talcott Parsons and the functionalists accept rationally organized action as a necessary condition of the large-scale organizations into which human beings had fitted themselves for survival in the twentieth century (Parsons, 1951). Jürgen Habermas, a successor of both Weber and Karl Marx, criticizes the decline of true social relationships of a personal kind and penetrates the farthest of any sociologist into the consequences of the new form of human relationships in spheres such as education, technology, and politics (Habermas, 1970). But the third direction in which Weber's insight is developed contributes most intimately to the understanding of our personal experience with bureaucracy. This direction is pursued in the phenomenological sociology of Alfred Schütz.

Schütz

Phenomenology in this context refers to nothing more than a way for reducing our experience of life in bureaucracy to its basics. This type of phenomenology begins with ordinary everyday experience, brackets out the accidental and unessential, and ends up by exposing the fundamentals of any experience.

Where Weber distinguished between social action as constituting ordinary social life and rationally organized action as constituting bureaucratic life, Alfred Schütz asks how such differences are experienced by ordinary human beings. He observed that such ordinary experience divides relationships I have with you into two types: In one I perceive you and myself as part of the same group, as part of a "we"; in the other I perceive you as alien to me, as part of a "they." Phenomenology thus points to two essential and different types of human relationships: the "pure we-relationship" and the "they-relationship."

We-Relationships. In the pure we-relationship I create my social life with others who have intentions similar to mine. In the they-relationship the social world has been preconstructed for me and my contemporaries, and the problem becomes to get to know them in terms of the significance and role already assigned them by the system. It is easy to see that the we-relationship describes the situation between close friends, whereas the they-relationship describes that between bureaucrat and client, with the bureaucrat being forced to think of the client in terms predefined by the bureaucracy.

The same distinction can be observed between creative or revolutionary political action and institutionalized political action. In creative politics at least two individuals must go through the effort of determining what each of them wants or intends. If their goals or intentions are similar, they then can work out a shared social act that will bring them together, laboring toward those goals. Once this act has worked for them in achieving their shared goals, they may want to repeat it under the assumption: We have done it once, we can do it again. But at that point, institutionalization begins. The second time around, the problem of achieving a want or intention does not have to be apprehended anew. All the participants have to do is identify the want or intention. If it fits into the category of a want or intention previously accomplished by a political action, all they need to say is: "It fits under Political Routine No. 1001B; let's do Political Routine No. 1001B." Typical routines of action replace original and creative action. Bureaucracies and specifically their organizational structures are such routines frozen into permanently repeated patterns; that is, they are institutions.

They-Relationships. They-relationships tend toward just the opposite pole. Routines, stereotyping, recipes for action coded in work rules—and the evenhanded application of these to all comers—dominate they-relationships. The relationship between bureaucrat and client is easily recognized as the extreme example. Not that human relationships of a personal sort are never used, but they represent a deviation. The bureaucrat who becomes deeply involved in the life of a client is regarded as either undependable or corrupt.

Schütz's concept of the they-relationship corresponds to Weber's concept of action that is not social. If we recall the example of the clerk in the license plate office, pressed by office rules and the number of clients, Schütz's concept helps us understand more closely the situation the clerk is in:

> I cannot assume, for instance, that my partner in a They-relationship will necessarily grasp the particular significance I am attaching to my words, or the broader context of what I am saying, unless I explicitly clue him in (Schütz, 1967: 204). For me, as a hard-pressed clerk, there just isn't enough time to penetrate through the cloak of anonymity that having to treat people as cases has thrown over them. "As a result, I do not know, during the process of choosing my words, whether I am being understood or not." (204)

Two Separate Worlds. According to Schütz, the worlds of we-relations and they-relations remain distinct. As a client dealing with a bureaucrat, our ideal type of they-relationship, I am not allowed to know him intimately "unless, of course, I decide to go to see him or to call him up; but in this case I have left the They-relationship behind and have initiated a face-to-face situation" (204). Schütz continues that

> in the We-relationship I assume that your environment is identical with my own in all its variations. If I have any doubt about it, I can check on my assumption simply by pointing and asking you if that is what you mean. Such an identification is out of the question in the They-relationship. (204)

The results of the functionary–client relationship can be disastrous. A mother and her children applying for welfare may even suffer and die because the mother is one child short of becoming a "case." A patient is denied treatment at a hospital, not on medical grounds, but on grounds of being an insurance card short of qualifying financially for admission.

Berger

The complaint that bureaucrats are robots, not human beings, is commonly voiced by disappointed clients. It is just as commonly dismissed as a kind of folk wisdom. Yet, Max Weber and Alfred Schütz, as leading sociologists and founders of important schools of thought, confirm that there is a central element of truth in this popular perception. Similar supporting evidence comes from sociologist Peter L. Berger, who founded an entire sociology of knowledge.

Acutely aware of the transformation of social action into bureaucratic action, Berger and his coworkers argue that "technological production brings with it *anonymous social relations*" in industry as well as in bureaucracy:

> Actually, it is not concrete individuals but abstract categories that interact in the bureaucratic process. The bureaucrat is not concerned with the individual in the flesh before him but with his "file." Thus bureaucracy is an autonomous world of "papers in motion," or at least it is so in principle. (Berger, Berger, and Kellner, 1974)

Constructing Society. This understanding of the difference between society and bureaucracy has its roots in earlier work Berger did with Thomas

Luckmann, like Berger a student of Schütz's. This work was a description of how society is created to begin with. It runs as follows:

Human beings create society. They begin this process by each expressing his or her needs or wants or designs for society, interacting face-to-face with others, and engaging with others in the construction of the social world. This first step of expressing one's intentions is called *externalization*. The process of constructing the social world, beginning with simple social relationships and ending with institutions, is called *objectification*, and the products—the formations of social reality that I encounter outside myself—are called *objectivations*. These objectivations, when they are encountered as parts of a reality "out there," are then in turn taken by individuals as guidelines for future conduct. That is, human beings internalize the patterns of their social reality and behave according to the standards explicit or implicit in them. This last part of the dialectic of constructing and living within the social world is called *internalization*.* In the words of the authors, *"Society is a human product. Society is an objective reality. Man is a social product"* (Berger and Luckmann, 1967: 465–66).

All three phases of society construction are here considered as perfectly normal and legitimate. Human beings have a natural need to externalize, to express their designs *for* the world and impress these designs *onto* the world. Human beings also need external objects, whether human or inanimate, connected into patterns: it will not do to have to re-create the New York City subway system all over again every time I get up in the morning and want to go to work. And human beings have a natural tendency to learn the patterns in the objective world, that is, to internalize them.

The problem relevant to the understanding of bureaucracy is that there is an immense gap between the creative activities of social life involved in externalization and the passive activities that are forced on individuals by their need to accept existing social structures as guidelines and background for everyday behavior.

Berger argues that the initial face-to-face situation is the matrix of all forms of social relations. The face-to-face relationship is for him the foundation of social life. It is in this situation that "the most important experience of others takes place." According to Habermas:

---

*In this triad of externalization, objectivation, and internalization, Berger and Luckmann combine the sociological insights of Weber, Marx, and Durkheim into an attempted synthesis.

> In the face-to-face situation the other is appresented to me in a vivid present shared by us both. I know him in the same vivid present I am appresented to him. . . . I see him smile, then react to my frown by stopping the smile, then smile again as I smile, and so on. Every expression of mine is oriented toward him, and vice versa, and this continuous reciprocity of expressive acts is simultaneously available to both of us. . . .
>
> In the face-to-face situation, the other is fully real. . . . [He] becomes real to me in the fullest sense of the word only when I meet him face to face. (Berger and Luckmann, 1967: 29).

Here Berger, in describing the essential interaction in society in much the same words that Weber and Schütz used, already presents us with a situation that we hardly ever find in bureaucracy. It is exactly the fullness of the face-to-face relationship that is absent there—and it is commanded to be absent!

Bureaucratizing Society. But Berger does more than describe the creative phase of society in contrast to its objectivated phase, which we may begin to associate with bureaucracy as an objectivation. He shows how and why bureaucracy is a natural product of society. This in turn helps us understand why the inhuman characteristics of bureaucracy exist, not as mere accident and mistakes, but as logical extensions of a perfectly natural human tendency.

Here bureaucracy is a kind of objectivation. In the extreme case it is an example of *reification.* In this process it is human beings who lose consciousness of their potential and their past as creators. They treat their social institutions as if they had a life of their own above and beyond human control.

Objectification in this context is a process in which human subjective consciousness produces certain products. These then embody it and are available in the world we share with others. Reification is a step beyond objectification. While objectification is absolutely necessary for society and for human survival, reification is a process in which the link between the producer and the product is broken. The world humans have produced now appears to them as an *alien* reality. Reification is a phenomenon of unconsciousness. The experience of reification is a dwindling of consciousness to the point where humans forget they have made their world. Eventually, consciousness fades to such a point that "the real relationship between man and his world is reversed in consciousness. Man, the producer of a world, is apprehended as its product, and human activity as an epiphenomenon of non-human processes" (Schütz, 1967: 205). Thus students become the "products" of universities, workers become the "tools" of management, and individuals holding roles within an institution become subsystems performing functions within a system—functionaries.

Such instances point out not only that society and bureaucracy, as examples of externalization and reification, are polar opposites, but also that the claim of bureaucracies to be something other than social relationships is intrinsic to them. In other words, as long as bureaucracies can lower consciousness, leading clients to perceive them as reifications without which life would be unthinkable, if not "unnatural," that is as long as they will survive.

Bergerian analysis shows that the supercession of fundamental human relationships by dehumanized relationships is a condition for bureaucracy's very existence. All attempts to "humanize" relationships between a bureaucracy and society must therefore be considered as suicidal or window dressing when they come from within bureaucracy itself, and as declarations of war when they originate in society.

Post-Modern Critique: Baudrillard, Lyotard

Where modernist critics of bureaucratic life share a concern for the creation and maintenance of society, all the post-modern critics aim to expose opportunities for rebirth even in decay. Most focus on how new knowledge—and therefore new social structure—is stillborn in modern times. They blame the ingrained influence of the modern Western way of looking at things. This way of looking, they say, prevents new ideas of creating and running a society from coming to power. Post-modern criticism's own focus is to anticipate newly emerging social arrangements on the evidence of social decay and social fragmentation.

Society's core values, to which all can refer to give meaning or detect meaning, are seen to fall apart. Attempts to create new consensus fail. As Jean-François Lyotard puts it, such consensus is not possible in the proliferation of "language games." Consensus covers up the real goal of knowing, which is discovery not agreement.

What happens to the social is conceived in three ways by post-modernists: Society continues but is transformed by the bureaucracy (Lyotard: system), it dissolves into the randomness of Brownian motion (Baudrillard), or it is converted into relations of mere power—that is, it becomes mere power relations.

Americans may question whether the last two possibilities represent a change: Aren't all social relations seen as exchange relations? Given Thomas Hobbes's political Man, are we not always fearful of others who can make our life solitary, nasty, brutish, and short? From that perspective, the descent of the social into politics is not something we would call post-modern. Nor would it seem absurd to see ourselves as a mass of individuals in some kind of random motion, a charge Lyotard levels at Baudrillard.

A warning about this American context. Social critics from other countries tend to project wishful thinking on America: "But in America . . ." This takes them out of their own realities, but it does not necessarily give them insight into the American reality.

Society in the American Context

There are only two positions on the question of society in America: that of the political theorist H. Mark Roelofs and everyone else. Roelofs argues that America lacks a concept of the social, society, or social movements. This accusation might be painful to Americans. It is not. Americans treasure their individualism.

But there is a problem for post-modernists, especially if they are French. The French, like all Europeans including the English, have a strong sense for the social. To lose it is for them inconceivable. What would happen to *esprit de corps*? To Rousseau's *contrat social*? *Fraternité?* Or for that matter, what would happen to the English solid footing in social status prejudice, Burkean political tradition, and the class system? In Germany, what would happen to the life-long commitment to *Freundschaft*, formed in grade school (at least among boys). The binding nature of the legally established and rationally explainable rules of *Gesellschaft*? The still romanticized and natural community of *Gemeinschaft*?

Neglect of this difference between Europe and America can lead to quite erroneous assumptions. Say a French post-modernist sees America lacking the concept of the social. Will he not reason as follows? "America is the most advanced modern country. As we enter post-modernity, we observe it lacks the social. Therefore America must be already quite advanced along post-modern lines." He would be wrong. (See for example the reference to the development of hypermarkets "especially in the United States" by Baudrillard, 1994: 77.)

As Mark Roelofs has said in his lectures at New York University, not only does America not have the concept of the social, but "America is the only 19th century [*sic*] country left in the world that has not dealt with Marx." This makes us hardly a candidate for post-modernity.

American individualism is rampant. Class, status, gender, ethnicity? What others think of me? I am a self-made man (or woman). Others be damned! The result is a political climate of barely pacified war of all against all—nature's state of war pursued by other means. And deliberations of the sovereign—the people—are marked by a social thoughtlessness. This lies in the inability to either retrieve a social past or experience the absence—and opportunities—of the social in the future: "These missing concepts have essentially to do with social structure and social movement. . . . Because we lack concepts of social structure and social change, we cannot create in our political imaginations any revolutionary vision, even one to be achieved peacefully" (Roelofs, 1976: 240, 241).

If we consider these cautions, we will need to proceed carefully in any analysis of the social. We will keep in mind the question: What effect might American radical individualism have on the thesis that, in social disintegration, the late modern bureaucratic chickens are coming home to roost? Can Americans in their social isolation imagine such an insinuation for the present or such a warning of a future fate? Here we need to turn to the individual post-modernists.

Post-modernists deal with modern problems not by offering new answers but by raising new questions. So, for example, Jean Baudrillard and Jean-François Lyotard paint a new picture of post-modern social life. Within that picture, the questions change just as late modernity now is seen as post-modernity. For bureaucracy, always at the cutting edge of modernity, the question becomes: What is the function of modern organization (bureaucracy) in post-modern times?

Baudrillard

Consider who you are. Is it not true that you are increasingly defined not by your role in work, but by what you eat, drink, wear, view, listen to, take as a medicine, travel to—in short, by what you consume?

A leading post-modernist, Jean Baudrillard, observes that modernity's obsession with the production of goods of late is overshadowed by the production of needs (or wants). The *producer* society, running low on markets for its goods (or overproducing its own capacity) has turned us into a *consumer* society. Our needs become something of value, something marketable. We ourselves are converted into objects—commodities as Karl Marx called us—to be traded in the marketplace. The more needs we have, and the more these can be changed, the higher our market value.

Not only is the production of consumer needs a simulation of what once would be called real needs, the system's answer to them is to produce "simulacra." What is a "simulacrum"?

Recall the last time you met a beggar in the street. You could say that you don't have any money with you. That is dissimulation. Or you could give him the copy of a dollar bill you just ran off on the xerox machine and say, "Here is a dollar bill. Bless you, my man." Which is the greater offense? To say one has nothing when one has something is to dissimulate: to lie. But to say you have something when there is nothing. . . . That is the production of a "simulacrum." What if the whole world were simulated? A lie, as Martin Heidegger says, still refers to a truth. Simulacra refer to nothing, and yet are valued. And yet they are the more valued the less they refer to anything. (This should remind you of the dot.com bubble in the 2002 stock market or Enron.)

The production of simulacra opens new markets. Say someone invents a new disease—by the simple process of rearranging some old ones into a "new" syndrome, preferably one with vague symptoms. This in turn produces a new and ill-defined need for the products of drug companies. The inventor is a hero of producing consumption.

What is the role of state bureaucracy in such conversion? It was no accident that Max Weber described the state as the legally created institution that exercises a monopoly of force over a given territory. But to what purpose? Will the state—government and administration—exercise the same role of enforcer in the consumer society? Does it make sense that—just as in modern society Man was forced to be free—we will be forced to produce and display ever new needs?* Again, Baudrillard suggests we look afresh at our situation.

We go to "hypermarkets." There who and what we are in the new hyper-society is defined.

---

*Throughout this book, in the tradition of philosophical discussion, "Man" is used wherever the reference is to homo sapiens; this is all the more necessary in dealing with German philosophers in whose language "Man" is the generic *Mensch*, referring to both genders.

The object commodities are no longer commodities: they are no longer even signs whose meaning and message one could decipher and appropriate for oneself, they are *tests*, they are the ones that interrogate us, and we are summoned to answer them, and the answer is included in the question. (Baudrillard, 1994: 75)

Baudrillard sees all this as a late effect of capitalism. From its beginnings, capitalism turned everything and everybody into a commodity. Labor as much as things could be bought and sold as essentially equivalent—and, eventually, be consumed. "The whole world still produces, and increasingly, but subtly, work has become something else: a need (as Marx ideally envisioned it but not in the same sense), the object of a social 'demand,' like leisure, to which it is equivalent in everyday life" (26).

An iron law has now been broken. Or, better, exceeded with a vengeance. We observe the logical extension of commodity fetishism to all things. We now treat the fetish as more real than the reality. This results in a number of ironies:

- Capitalism once dealt in things and matters considered real. It lost that connection where it played at *deterrence* (of not seeing things in their human use due to commodification), their *abstraction* (from human life), their *disconnection* (from other things), their *deterritorialization* (or loss of their grounds).
- Even capitalism now has run into its limits: treating all things as potential commodities has produced so many signs standing for its reality that reality has been lost. It is surrendered to *hyperreality* populated not by things with use value but by *simulacra*—not mere simulations of things but symbols standing for nothing.
- We begin to recognize that even under capitalism, the map we had of it was not the real, but a simulacrum, and that today the simulacrum has become more real than capitalism: we buy and sell objects of the hyperreal.

With the loss of the real, capitalism seeks to regain its power. It tries to produce not values or commodities but tries to produce a copy or imitate the now nonexistent real: the hyperreal. Here we can think of stock market bubbles, creative accounting practices, virtual stocks like dot.coms bought with virtual money and crashing in virtual terrorism.

Already the consumer adapts. Is the pension down the drain? "It was only paper money anyway." Is the boss at Enron accountable but not responsible? "He does have a nice image on TV." Are the so-called federal regulators watchdogs without teeth? "They do the best they can." Will you reinvest in the market? "Sure. Where else can you put your money?" Is there any reality behind stock recommendations? "Who knows?"

In the words of Baudrillard: "What every society looks for in consuming to produce, and to overproduce, is to restore the real that escapes it. That is why today *this material production is that of the hyperreal itself*" (Baudrillard, 1994: 23).

Media Terrorism. The market and the state are not the only institutions being converted in the post-modern era. Baudrillard specifically picks out the media for reanalysis. Media—newspapers, radio, early television—used to "mediate." Media bridged the gap between modern society's estranged individuals.

Baudrillard contends that this connecting function is lost. Instead of enhancing communication to bridge social differences and restore social relations, media are producers "of the implosion of the social in the masses."

In short, media institutions were designed to connect. Now they disconnect us from others in cutting our social relationships. But, most important, they convert us from individuals-in-relationships into faceless and mindless undifferentiated masses. These are formed and fed by a joint fascination such as that produced by terror. Baudrillard says:

> The media make themselves into the vehicle of the moral condemnation of terrorism and the exploitation of fear for political ends, but simultaneously, in the most complex ambiguity, they propagate the brutal charm of the terrorist act, they are themselves terrorists, insofar as they themselves march to the tune of seduction. (Baudrillard, 1994: 84)

The Need to Rename. Why these new concepts? Why not say that when we see the commercial on television, and we go out to buy the product, we are not buying the product but actually are buying the satisfactions offered by the commercial? Why not simply say we ourselves are seduced from our own dull lives by the excitement of terrorism? We could also say that "simulacra," the stuff of dreams in hyperreality, are advertisements in a world of advertising.

And what about the ideological implications of the new concepts?

The old ones—money, capital, surplus value, labor—served to obscure exploitive relationships. What do the new ones hide, and whose interests do they serve? But perhaps, the hype of the hyper gets to be a bit much at times; soon we'll be called back to reality.

Baudrillard would object, saying that advertisements represent something that exists. The "simulacrum" is a concept that calls our attention to the unreal in the world. Simulacra, which can be created only when all reference to something real is lost, refer to something that does not exist but for which there are signs marking its absence.

Still, why not stick with known words? A dissimulation is a lie. A simulacrum is . . . ? Something that has no reality? The unreal. The hyperreal is the entire universe of simulacra. Why not say hyperreality is an unreality? We begin to see the difficulty: The new concepts must express an entire new world. And it is post-modernists' position that we are caught up in the dynamics of that world without having a say over it.

A New World? But is Baudrillard's world really new?

I concluded the first edition of this book by observing that "each of the changes first noticed in the 1960s has been exploited by entrepreneurs, who have responded to 'new needs' with new products and service." I added: "In the end, it is bureaucracy itself that has produced the kind of dehumanized fragment—socially crippled, culturally normless, psychologically dependent, linguistically mute, and politically powerless—that has become the economy's favorite object of manipulation" (Hummel, 1977: 221). Does that make me a post-modernist—as the organizational theorist David Boje has suggested?

Similarly, the Marxist Georg Lukacs writes about Marx's observation that "a new thinghood (*Dinghaftigkeit*)" is produced by viewing things only as commodities to be exchanged on the basis of their use value. Lukacs adds the thought: "So, if the singular thing, which the human being encounters in immediacy as producer or consumer, is distorted in its thinghood through its characteristic as commodity, then this process must by all lights intensify itself all the more, the more mediated are the relations that the human being grants these things as objects of the life process in his societal activity" (Lukacs, 1967: 104; my translation).

Does the reference to "consumers" make Lukacs a prescient postmodernist? Does he anticipate the intensity of abstraction? Is his view of history one of history of "*forms* of encounters with things"? It is only a small step from there to proclaiming a world dominated by abstractions.

However, there are several crucial points in favor of Baudrillard. Like all post-modernists he gives us new grounds for asking afresh longstanding questions. One such question is whether bureaucracy as an instrument of power will be unchanged by the changing of the objects of administration: from objects that are real in the sense of meaningful to people to objects that are become unreal but yet valued, such as the changing status of their own needs.

Then there is the ability to capture the dual and often self-contradictory meaning of events as exemplified by media treatment of terrorism. Terrorism is both abhorred by media executives—and marketed. But the position of these executives is itself paradoxical: they themselves are caught up in a quandary. If they condemn terrorism and withhold the worst pictures, they at the same time elevate it to a hidden mystery. "The media carry meaning and counter-meaning, they manipulate in all directions at once," Baudrillard writes, adding that nothing can control this process (Baudrillard, 1994: 84).

Then there is his challenge to psychoanalysis, which ironically wins an answer that satisfies in post-modernity's leading psychoanalyst, Jacques Lacan. Lacan writes of human life as one long chase to satisfy desires. These cannot be fulfilled. They involve the attempt in adulthood to resolve the helpless baby's need to get its satisfactions through the desire and satisfactions of an Other, usually the mother. Baudrillard similarly writes of simulacra as signs that attract and command our desires. But the reality assumed to be behind the objects of desire is unattainable because of our knowledge "that truth, reference, objective cause have ceased to exist" (3).

In short, Baudrillard gives us a new start by getting us to look at the underside of old truisms such as that the effectiveness of an administration increases with greater control or that making social relations at work visible (personnel administration) makes them more controllable. Reading his exploration of the economic substructure's virtualism suggests the advent of an equally subtle and virtual stealth administration, whose unplanned effects remain hidden even from itself simply because you can't see what you aren't, in some sense, looking for. An example may be the voluntary self-indoctrination into phrasing our problems in computer terms.

In addition, Baudrillard's map of post-modernity gains in credibility by integrating well with other post-modernists' maps—just the sort of thing post-modernists hate. And as to the American problem, someone else will have to see to the exploration of what Baudrillard missed: Are Americans as individuals perhaps especially vulnerable to post-modernization *precisely because of the absence of a society to protect them?*

Lyotard

Another perennial question concerns bureaucracy's dependence on rules and their effect on freedom. Can any sort of freedom survive? This question was asked by Max Weber, who gave a modernist's negative answer. The question is reopened by the post-modernist Jean-François Lyotard, who finds a new source for freedom precisely among the rules. We may think of his answer as a new thesis on an old theme well put by the historian R.G. Collingwood: "action according to rules always involves a certain misfit between yourself and the situation" (Collingwood, 1939: 104).

Lyotard's work suggests this: The more an organization tries to constrain the work of its workers, the more workers notice the difference between how work is organized to be done (the job) and how it actually turns out (the work). This frees up a space for countermoves. The official "Grand Narratives" are being replaced by lots of little narratives, *petits récits*, that arise from the working experience itself.

Challenging Jean Baudrillard and Michel Foucault, Lyotard rejects the suggestion of disintegration of the social. But he also objects to the concept of the social as being useful today. Such a claim to usefulness could be sustained only as long as there is a central and absolute idea—Weber's core of values—to which social actions can be referred for shared meaning. Lyotard questions that there is such a core that remains steady and steadfast. He asks: if there is no such object for orienting our human interactions and finding shared meaning in them, how can orders issued by a central command be expected to be obeyed without other sources of interpretation?

Modernists used to say that a concept "covers" a reality. That is exactly Lyotard's objection. In covering the social reality, the concept "social" hides more than it reveals.

What does Lyotard want to reveal? He wants us to get past our surrender that lets late modern organizations capture us in rules, and so establish our identity (Lyotard, 1984: 74). He urges us to move ahead to what we can do about it, in other words: to get a life.

Beyond Concepts. Here Lyotard uses a Kantian insight. The modern mind has developed a special way of grasping how things stand in the world: the concept. In a concept we bring independent sense data as seen by us ("intuitions") into the context of reason and logic. As Immanuel Kant already showed, we thus capture what is the same in what is different in many things. In so doing we gain immense power of efficiency. We can now treat in the same way, with the same desired effect, many things—and even people—without being overwhelmed by their differences. So, for example, the modern legal system considers all equal before the law—and formally treats them that way. Equality of procedure is raised up and over the obvious inequality of people and substantive outcomes.

In an example of his own, Lyotard points to how technology has changed our making ourselves pictures of things. He observes that the multiplication of "the fantasies of realism" through the use of photographs instead of portraits is, in modern times, considered "faster, better" (Lyotard, 1984: 74). So is, we may add, bureaucracy's treatment of the case rather than the individual. Lyotard challenges the lack of attention to individual differences in all these situations. This parallels the objection of a well-known physicist to the tendency to measure everything in human affairs: "A lot of good things are left out, a lot of good guys are missed" (Feynman, 1998: 90).

We can sit back and feel comfortably stuck in the way things are, including established society. But society's center no longer holds, which is the bad news. There is, according to Lyotard, also good news.

A move in all games calls up countermoves. Play develops in the interaction of these moves and countermoves. It is in the countermoves that I *find* myself in the game. The unexpected (and unexpectable!) play makes the game. In industry or bureaucracy, only in these countermoves, the feared discretion of the worker, does the game come to life.

The game is not the rules. An order spoken is not the execution of it. The post-modern approach to human lives, as these play into each other, must always try to present the unpresentable: that which we can conceive but have trouble thinking of ways of presenting (Lyotard, 1984: 81). In this case, to make room for the new play that gives life to social development, Lyotard wants to replace the concept "social."

Language Games. To replace "the social," Lyotard borrows from Ludwig Wittgenstein the concept of "language games." His intent is to uncover aspects of the social not uncovered before. However, a concept is supposed to "cover" reality the way a map matches the ground it "covers." Language games would cover what the social concept used to cover, while at the same time uncovering a difference. Conceiving of society as the whole of social actions in Max Weber's sense is seen as no longer useful in a time in which people rapidly shift in and out of different jobs, locations, affiliations, situations. The one tool for orienting ourselves is that in all these changed relationships there are local language games. These we learn to play. The new language approach would take account of the varying ways we relate to each other, with emphasis on their differences. The focus is on things social that are a-changing.

Some, Lyotard says, have extended his idea that the social center is fading to the great stories civilizations tell, the Grand Narratives. The captains and the kings depart; Far-called, our navies melt away—as Rudyard Kipling would say. But does this mean the loss of the social? Those who say so he holds in error. There is no dissolution of the social bond—no "disintegration," proposed by some authors (the reference is to Baudrillard), "of social aggregates into a mass of individual atoms thrown into the absurdity of Brownian motion" (Lyotard, 1984: 15).

Understanding the social in terms of "language games" enables us to recognize what systems theory already saw. Even weak relations between selves located at nodal points of communications circuits have an effect. This is an image to which Foucault on occasion subscribes, but here it must be read in the context of systems theory. Here "performativity" is king. Systems theory reveals that those exercising even minor functions retain powers of self-adjustment and these are useful for the system to fight entropy.

Lyotard does not claim all social relations are systems functions: "—that will remain an open question." He simply uses the insights of systems theory to unpack the power of freedom in society. In asserting that "language games are the minimum relation required for society to exist," he draws on systems insights only to end up arguing against systems theory as a whole: "It would be superficial to reduce its [the language game's] significance to the traditional alternative between manipulated speech and the unilateral transmission of messages on the one hand and free expression and dialogue on the other." To reduce messages and their sending and receiving to a systems-maintaining function "unduly privileges the system's own interests and point of view" (16).

In these words, Lyotard does not as yet reject people's bureaucratic experience of being dominated. But he begins to see a new chance for freedom. True, we are being manipulated by systems rules, but our sense of this actually causes us to go beyond mere reactive responses to make really "good" countermoves. A normative prescription for the bureaucratic age: " . . . increase displacement in the games . . . disorient it[,] in such a way as to make an unexpected 'move' (a new statement)" (17). In short go in the system's door and come out yours.

It might be argued, Lyotard admits, that bureaucracy tries to confine the resulting innovations in the war of words, that it tries to impose a set of rules. But, he claims, "bureaucratization is the outer limits of this tendency." In any game, play moves on. So language "moves" are "never defined once and for all (even if they have been formally defined)" (17). Here, lest we think of his solution to the problem of freedom as that of a systems or communications theorist, he introduces the lesson taught by both R.G. Collingwood and Ludwig Wittgenstein: rules never completely cover what we can and do say. (See Chapter 5.)

In summary, Lyotard calls our attention to the sources of a possible alternative to bureaucracy's capture of freedom: the more you try to constrain freedom, the more you cause those constrained to observe opportunities for escape. We may be reminded of the Polish workers under Soviet communism who had a saying, "They pretend to pay us, and we pretend to work."

* * *

What if anything have the post-modernists added to our previous modern analysis?

Bureaucracy as Society

In bureaucratic society—the modern organization—my social identity is organizational identity. The person becomes a case. Social identity was reciprocally developed between myself and others. While social identity defined the range of my social *being* (my rights), what I am as organizational identity defines the range of my permissible activity: the size of my *cage*. As a case I am defined not by my two-way relations with other people, but by one-way definition by the organization's architects and designers.

For example, official relations between offices are not defined by the people in them. They are defined by those who organize relations from

Figure 2.1 **Three Stages of Society**

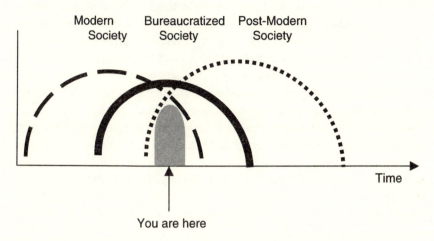

Time

You are here

the top down. The totality of such relations between offices or bureaus makes up the bureaucracy—the power of the office (*bureau* + *kratos*).

Society yields to an artificial structure populated by cases, types, cutouts. These make up the work organization centrally conceived and centrally run. Who we are socially is replaced by what we are to the organization. The power of bureaucracy derives from this surrender. It depends on the exclusion of people from the designing and running of the organization. The organization becomes a power instrument without compare for those who run it.

Post-modern analysis discovers not only further deterioration of the social (beyond modern critique) but entirely new aspects and developments. A new product is discovered by production organizations: consumption (Baudrillard). Yet the increasing manipulation of our social roles, restricting social freedom and spontaneity, also is seen to open up opportunities for freedom. Such findings envision a further stage to the developments we have observed in progressive bureaucratization from a self-critical modern perspective. (See Figure 2.1.) We could say that post-modern critique discovers yet a further stage in the decline of social structure that opens up new opportunities at the same time. Paradoxically, the post-modernists see both the failure of the Enlightenment and a recovery of freedom. The bet of the Enlightenment, that free men will creatively use the imaginative part of reason to structure their own order, is vitiated. Reason's logic is celebrated in the bureaucratic preoccupation with structuring everything monocratically, that is in terms of channeling power to the top and command from the top down. Reason's creative part—the ability to imagine an order that strikes more than the single note of modern organization's preoccupation with power—is, however, neglected and fades away. The expected sequence freedom → reason → order is now seen as too simplistic. When we say the human being has the power of reason, we must differentiate between the potential to be wise, having a sense of what is good for human beings, and being logical, which without wisdom produces a certain fatal stupidity and senselessness.

In summary, we can visualize where we are in the historical rise and fall of society → bureaucracy → post-bureaucracy as follows:

Social structures, especially of the size of societies at large, do not suddenly spring into existence. The structure of modern society does not suddenly surrender itself to the bureaucratized society based on work. In the normal curve that indicates the rise and fall of modern society, bureaucratized elements are already present, but elements of independent modern society are also still present in the bureaucratic age. In the same way, the sources of post-modern "society"—and here we should put society into ironic quotes—are already present both in modern society and its bureaucratic successor: there is some work organization even in a social organization. Following the suggestion of R.G. Collingwood: the reason we can understand both the social structure of the past and the post-social structure of the future is because both are with us in our own time. (See the "You are here" marker in Figure 2.1.)

3

Bureaucracy as the New Culture: "Economics"

Bringing to the fore the fitness of a rational being for . . . whatever . . . purposes at all . . . is culture.
—Immanuel Kant

There lurks decisively the struggle of the "specialist" type of man against the older type of the "cultivated man." . . . This struggle affects the most intimate aspects of personal culture.
—Max Weber

Riches—"A gift from heaven signifying, 'This is my beloved son, in whom I am well pleased.'"
—John D. Rockefeller

Bureaucracy replaces culture.

This tendency can be traced to the very beginnings of modern times. A first example may be a famous encounter between a philosopher and a king. "Think for yourself," said the philosopher to the subjects of the king. He meant: reason out loud and argue. Anticipating public disputes over his policies, the king responded, "Reason as much as you want and about what you want, but obey!" (For details see pp. 83–85).

The philosopher was forced to see a paradox. Making free citizens out of subjects evoked the specter of rebellion. The king was likely to object to any sudden moves, and people themselves wanted to have a peaceful progression. After all, it was said, progress toward freedom must be orderly. Freedom to think would have to come through order, though freedom is opposed to order.

Considering that this paradox emerged from the country that gave us bureaucracy of the purest type, we may be excused for thinking it a particular instance of a general law: order conquers freedom. Bureaucracy's order is from the beginning the enemy of a culture of freedom. Where bureaucracy is employed to foster culture, bureaucracy replaces culture. What does this mean? And what is culture, anyway?

What Is Culture?

Culture is the set of values we live by. Originally society is the way people organize to pursue those values. Bureaucracy takes over this function as we pay more attention to the means to fulfill our values than the values themselves.

But this is all superficial. From this vantage point, we cannot explain racism, poverty, wars, and empire building. These are not direct goals, or at least not espoused ones, of our society, yet they are consequences of what we hold worthwhile. What makes us, in the American tradition, so sure of our culture's goals? What allows us, as the richest nation on earth, to write off the poor at home and force our way abroad? Our true colors are obscured behind myth: what we say we are as distinct from what we do.

Surely other countries, other populations, other nations also have their equivalent of cultures. We feign respect for them. Of course, we respect you! Just as we are pursuing equality and social justice at home so do we pursue it for all the world. So, why the force? Veiled behind the myth stands an operational reality on the international scale similar to the division H. Mark Roelofs (1976), a political scientist, observed in the American political mind:

Our Mythical Values	Our Operational Values
We are a national **community** which, under **great leaders**, **progresses** ever onward and upward toward **equality** and **social justice**.	Each one of us is an **individual** who wins human **dignity** by earning **property** through **hard work** in **competition** with others.

One side states who we would like to be; the other what we do. But note that the values on the operational side are economic. They are universally applicable; as Americans we apply them to politics also: he or she who does not adhere to working hard in competition with others to acquire property has no standing with us—whether in acquiring property in a political position or in working. Economic values are not only the basis of day-to-day politics in America but are for us the measure of people's worth.

It is a small step from here to the arsenal of bureaucratic values. Efficiency, foremost among these, at first is simply reason put in the service of our operational goals. Who could object to making work more efficient? And, by extension, why not make politics more efficient?

But along with efficiency, which may free people, come discipline, precision, accountability, calculability, impersonality, instrumental rationality, and formal equality, which constrain us. All these are helps to the citizen at work. But what happens when the cultivated citizen becomes the specialist charged with carrying out political goals? Then these values become a culture of their own. The ends that they once served fade into the background. The transformation has been observed by the philosopher Jürgen Habermas and the sociologist Max Weber:

Values of the Society	Values of Bureaucracy
Justice	Stability
Freedom	Discipline
Violence	Reliability
Oppression	Calculability of results
Gratification	Formal rationality
Poverty	Formalistic impersonality
Illness	Formal equality of treatment
Love and hate	
Salvation and damnation	
Victory and defeat	
—Habermas 1971:76	—Weber 1968a: 956–58; 224–41

But let us go one layer deeper to how culture works. Culture is more than a list of values. The word itself connotes cultivation—a term also found in agriculture and horticulture. Culture in this sense is a strictly European invention. The concept contains the eighteenth-century thought that Man can cultivate himself. Just as the gardener prunes the rose and binds it to a trellis to show its full beauty, so human beings were thought to be capable of development.

Probing deeper yet into history, we find three further components of culture. The culturing of the human being was driven by three forces. *Free individuals* would use *reason* for setting their own goals; success would be taken as a *sign of religious salvation*. This is the culture of the self-made man.

In the words of the foremost exponent of the cultivated man, the educator Wilhelm von Humboldt: "Among men who are really free, every form of industry becomes more rapidly improved—all the arts flourish more gracefully—all the sciences extend their range" (von Humboldt, 1993 [1854]: 50–51).

Culture was further defined in the words of the philosopher Immanuel Kant. These demand to be read more slowly. Here is what culture is and does: "Bringing to the fore the fitness of a rational being for [setting] whatever preferred purposes at all (and, it follows, in its freedom) is *culture*" (Kant, 1790/1793: B 392, 393; A 388; retranslated).

And, finally, Max Weber exposes the religious component: economic activity as the ultimate meaning-giving activity. In Europe, economic success became a divine sign. God had favored you. You were predestined to heaven. An other-worldly faith was turned into the motivator for this-worldly asceticism: the Protestant ethic as the spirit of capitalism.

It is a secular version of this culture, exercised by individual will and armed with reason and secure in the promise of salvation, that has asserted itself around the world. Even in retreat, the poet of empire still has this surety: "Far-flung our navies melt away . . . the Captains and the Kings depart . . . still stands Thine ancient sacrifice, an humble and a contrite heart" (Kipling, 1941 [1897]).

The Origins of Economic Culture

Modern culture is the culture of economics.

The culture of modern economics has been a Humpty Dumpty poised on a wall. It began, about 400 years ago, as the forces of science and technology made mass production and mass marketing possible, and as the rising industrial and merchant classes were looking to justify themselves in ultimate values.

They were responding to supply the needs of a national "household," wider than a family's or a clan's. The tools of this national economics were technical and political and the ultimate meaningfulness of religion.

Technically: The tool was a new idea on how to manage the national household: expand wealth by reinvesting profits back into the enterprise.

Politically: The groundwork was *power-political:* government needed to remove the forces of traditional "household" economics (robber barons, local law) from the playing field (see Friedrich, 1937: 84, 88ff.).

In terms of ultimate meaning: Justification was religious. The rising classes adapted a sense for God's way in the world to their own purposes. Their argument: Our destiny in the next world is predetermined. However, God is not inconsistent. If He rewards your labors in this life, He is giving you a sign you are destined for heaven.

Unlike the values systems of other parts of the globe, modern Western culture linked economic success to ultimate meaning of life guaranteed by the divine.

The activity to which the early Greeks gave its name—the ordering (*nomos*) of the household (*oikos*) continues to have, in the West, divine connotations of which we are less and less sure.

Bureaucratic Intervention

It should hardly be a surprise, then, to see bureaucracy openly step in to prop up and control externally what wobbles internally. Modern economics produces a global crisis today. Sure only of the need to expand, it aims to replace traditional societies with a worldwide culture. On that scale, an international bureaucracy begins to overwhelm the individual "cultures" of nations.

How can we understand the resulting conflict? We can clearly observe the replacement when we look at the bureaucracies of the World Bank or the International Monetary Fund or the World Trade Organization. These dispense aid to countries needing economic development. Or they give help in financial crisis. Or they advance free trade. But all such moves aim at establishing a universal culture of Western-style economics.

The problem goes back to the meaning of culture. Just what do the rich Western powers mean by culture, a concept they invented, and by economics, which has become a word that covers reinvestment capitalism? Getting to the root of both may give us the foundations on which Western international bureaucracies deal with the economic life of nations.

We can already anticipate the origins of the problem: To cultivate Man, you need will and discipline. This requires not freedom but order. People would have to submit to order to free their human potential. The contra-

diction was to haunt the experiment. What was first called the culture of
the Enlightenment became a struggle between freedom and order. Order
can be a source of freedom only if they both obey the same spirit.

What if a successful culture lost its motivating spirit?

The Spirit of Culture

In its heyday, modern Western culture was as unique in spirit as it was in
form. Taking it as a secular idea, human beings could take *any* purpose
in remaking themselves, as long as the design was based on reason aiming at freedom (Kant, 1790/1793: B392, 393; A 388). But the practice
of human self-cultivation in Europe was defined by the prevailing religious spirit. This gave divine justification to the production of wealth.
It persists among the least religious among us today: if you work, you
have human dignity.

To secular minds, the motivating spirit of the populations who invented
culture might be an undefined human spirit. But in fact the acquisitive
society understood its economics as linked to divine providence. As late
as 1900, when asked about his wealth, the greatest of capitalists, John D.
Rockefeller, called it in all piety: "A gift from heaven signifying, 'This
is my beloved son, in whom I am well pleased.'" Economic success had
become the highest value. Economics had become culture.

Say an International Monetary Fund today swings into action. It sets conditions under which to rescue a nation in fiscal straits. But it imports—along
with any life preserver—this faith in being able to cultivate human beings,
complete with unconscious remnants of a specific religious/economic
ethic. The Protestant ethic had in the West become the divine, though
finally nonsectarian, background that gave ultimate meaning to economic
success. Western-educated international bureaucrats may simply assume
that spirit is present everywhere (see Weber, 1958a: 182).

What if that spirit failed? More to the point: What if that spirit is not
present in other nations whom we honor and burden, erroneously, with the
epithet of "other cultures"? What if some of these would prefer to retain
their own traditions and their spirit? Then there is only one path open to
the Western-dominated development institutions. Bureaucrats' sense of a
religious calling now merely "prowls about in [their] lives like the ghost
of dead religious beliefs" (Weber, 1958b: 82). But that ghost may suffice
to impose a dead mechanism on indigenous ways of living. In the words
of a former chief economist at the World Bank, Joseph Stiglitz:

> When crises hit, the IMF prescribed outmoded, inappropriate, if "standard" solutions, without considering the effects they would have on the people in the countries told to follow these policies. Rarely did I see forecasts about what the policies would do to poverty. Rarely did I see thoughtful discussion and analyses of the consequences of alternative policies. There was a single prescription. Alternative opinion was not sought. (Stiglitz, 2002: xiv)

At home, too, functionaries of Western culture might try to uphold the economy by the will and discipline of external administration. Where such administration is modern, they can try to use government bureaucracy to enforce adherence to the original values.

Do we not, then, see bureaucracy replacing even the economic culture? Yes, but this does not mean that culture can be fully so replaced. A culture lives on its spirit. It cannot be replaced with a mechanism. If once we had a culture inspired by wealth as a sign of salvation, if once we had an economic culture, then today we have—without spirit—no culture at all.

Where once human beings who did well could be seen to bloom and grow (while others were exploited and destroyed), there are now only mechanisms. The mechanisms of modern organization—private and public—replace a creative culture.

In shorthand: bureaucracy replaces culture. But the culture that is being replaced is a "culture" best described by the formula: culture = economics. A "natural" culture of economics now yields to an artificially controlled one.

What is the fate of the culture of economics today? How does bureaucracy change the culture of economics? We begin with what people value, continue with what the modern experts say, and then listen to a third voice: that of post-modernists.

What People Value

Beginning the twenty-first century with a whimper, not a bang, the economic pillar supporting modern culture buckled. The modern economy had relied on capitalists understanding capitalism. The best bet for success of an enterprise was to reinvest the profits, gain market share, reinvest, and so on. Reinvestment capitalism's motto: Put the money back in! Late modern capitalism: Take the money and run!

The values that people hold are on the endangered species list. Three transitions are in progress. At home in America: from reinvestment to adventure capitalism. In the world at large: from local cultures' autonomy to economic dominance by the West. In what used to be the factory or bureaucracy: from a rational (i.e., logical) commitment to quantity to a so-called (irrational) balance of quantity with quality—without answer to who pays the cost of the actual tension between the two.

The Coming of Adventure Capitalism: Investors, CEOs, and Accountants

Investors, tempted by promises of new technology, now show not only an ignorance of what they were investing in but a fatal attraction to adventure. The new creed: take the money and run.

In the meanwhile, chief executive officers and chief financial officers engaged in creative bookkeeping to feed the frenzy. Throwing both internal and external watchdogs a bone of the action, they suborned the sense of duty. They bought those very same professionals whose jobs were created to keep capitalism safe from itself. The short-term gain, rather than the long-term investment, was pursued—regardless of what this would do to the credibility of the whole system. The flip side of entrepreneurship, lack of social conscience (so handy in business dealings with the rest of society), had finally caught up with business leaders. Knowing nothing of social systems, they appeared blissfully inured to the fact that their own private wealth-producing machine was a social system and that social systems can be destroyed by loss of faith in their credibility. In a ruthless if not mindless attack, corporate leaders risked destroying through pillage and plunder the capital reinvestment system that fed them.

In one big bubble, capitalism had violated three of its principles:

- Know your investment
- Keep at least one honest set of books
- Reinvest the profits

The Coming of Cultural Imperialism: World Citizens

A culture of corruption at home, however, did not stop entrepreneurs from imposing the principles of the old economic doctrine across the globe. As the clients revolted and street riots broke out, the lenders and their functionaries met in Washington, D.C., to argue about freedom, cultures, and the world economic order. Two leading international bureaucracies argued with one another. The World Bank accused the United States and Europe of "causing immense damage to poor countries by maintaining high barriers to agricultural imports." (Andrews, 2002). The implication was that the International Monetary Fund, charged with tiding countries over in a financial crisis, insisted mindlessly that these countries adopt Western economic principles in situations where they had already proved disastrous.

The scene was, to say the least, puzzling. As puzzling as putting the heading of "Economics" under this chapter's title of "Bureaucracy as the New Culture." Yet the sounds of a sea change could be heard in the voices of the far-flung participants locally and globally:

- Secretary of the Treasury Paul O'Neill at one point declared the United States would no longer rescue failed economies unless it could be sure the money would not simply "go out of the country into Swiss bank accounts." (Tony Smith, "As Currency Sinks, Brazil Seeks Fresh Aid," *New York Times*, New England Edition, July 31, 2002: W1 and W7; citation from W1.)
- A former presidential economic adviser, speaking of a drop in the value of the dollar, declared, "It's a sign we have lost the moral high ground. We were in the awkward position of lecturing all the countries on regulation, bankruptcy procedures, international accounting standards. In an ideal world we now would admit we had a lot of problems of our own and welcome some ideas from the rest of the world." (Lael Brainard in David E. Sanger, "The Global Cost of Crony Capitalism," *New York Times*, New England Edition, July 21, 2002: WK3.)
- A Latin American former economy minister speaking of counter-productive conditions for American aid said: "Everywhere you look, people say, 'The guys followed the model and they're in the soup. So obviously, the model does not work.'" (Pedro Pablo Kuczynski quoted in Susan Ferero, "Still Poor, Latin Americans Protest Push for Open Markets," *New York Times*, July 19, 2002: A1 and A14; citation from A14.)
- Fanny Puntaca, a Peruvian shop owner protesting the sale of electric plants to Belgians, said: "I had to fight. The government was going to sell our companies and enrich another country. This was my voice of protest." (*Ibid.*, A1.)

- A Haitian said, "We don't know when they are going to fix things. We suffer. And when you suffer enough you die." (Cited in David Gonzales, "8 Years After Invasion, Haiti Squalor Worsens, *New York Times*, July 30, 2002: A8 and A7; citation from A7.)
- The former chief economist of the World Bank blamed global bureaucrats. (Stiglitz, 2002.)

The only stable value seems to be change itself.

The Coming of Irrationality

Today organizational culture is associated with "vision." Visionary chief executive officers or administrators are held to be free to manipulate employees' values. Strikingly, economic theory today makes no assumptions about economic activity having an ultimate purpose, especially not any religious purpose transcending the activity itself. It is simply assumed that people have a natural craving for power after power that, as the philosopher Thomas Hobbes said, "ceaseth only in death." Reason writ large as the ability to choose our own purposes has become, in the words of a recent U.S. president, "that vision thing."

When we look at organizations today—whether a reinvented government agency or reengineered business firm—nothing is more obvious than radical and arbitrary changes in values. Then there is the change in ways to achieve those values. And then there are the ever again new management systems loitering just over the horizon.

There are two effects from this one same cause. Government itself is gutted. And no one in the economy seems to count the many private organizations that disappear. Both moves have the same result: in government, the loss of capacity to perform for such clienteles as the uninsured and the aged; and in the private sector, the loss of workers who might have become customers.

What is going on here? Is it likely that Reason writ large will arise again out of the ashes? Can the creation and re-creation of cultures—corporate or governmental—be simply manipulated by tinkering with values—without spirit? (See Exhibit 3.1)

The last twenty years have seen many of these attempts at organization reform, all trivial and spiritless, all of great promise and all ephemeral.

Exhibit 3.1

Quantity/Quality Conflict in Organizations

Important to Quantitative Organizations	Important to Qualitative Organizations
Bigness . . . because it gives economies of scale.	Belief in being the best.
Low-cost emphasis . . . because survivors make it cheaper.	Belief in the importance of the details of execution, the nuts and bolts of doing the job well (emphasis on the actual work well done).
Peace at all costs . . . because keeping troublemakers down ensures following the plan.	Belief in the importance of people as individuals.
Analysis as the solution to everything . . . because if you can take it apart into numbers you know what's going on.	Belief in superior quality and service (emphasis on putting things together).
Decision-making as more important than follow-through . . . because if you make the right decisions things will fall into place.	Belief that most members of the organization should be innovators, and its corollary, the willingness to support failure.
Control over everything . . . because things and people out of control introduce the unpredictable.	Belief in the importance of informality to enhance communication.
Growth as a hedge against insecurity, even in industries one knows nothing about.	Belief in and recognition of the importance of economic growth and profits (in industries known to managers).

The appeal always and again is the promise. It is a faint echo of the original call to cultivate what is deep within us and to get a chance to use it in useful work.

Global War of Values

What is going on here? What do culture and morality have to do with economics, globalism, and global bureaucrats? The fact is that when innovation and discovery must be hemmed in by rules, the spirit—economic, political, cultural—dies.

Economics: When we look at the original assumptions of reinvestment capitalism, we see its original dual driving spirit—one religious and one secular. The religious spirit that gave it meaning reached well into the twentieth century. It survives today in our work ethic. It is work that gives dignity to the late modern human being. We still tend to attribute the entire growth of Western culture, in contrast to all others, to the Protestant ethic, the spirit of capitalism. Through this ethos, capital development had found itself an ultimate meaning: wealth was read as a sign from God that you were to be saved in the next world.

Politics: The secular drive for human-made culture originated in the Enlightenment. Originally intended to free Man's rational capacity for choosing his own destiny, reason soon became merely instrumental: good at designing means but blind to choosing ends fitting human beings.

By our time, we face a capitalism devoid of religious or any other kind of ultimate meaning. We are prisoners of instrumental rationality, the belief that if only we proceed logically we will be using reason on our own behalf.

Empty of meaning and empty of humanly responsible reason, today's capitalism shows all the signs of reverting to an earlier form: take the money and run, whether on a national or global scale.

The critique of economists—that government watchdogs failed to regulate or that private accounting firms failed their professional duty to watch capitalists—sounds particularly empty. Simply taken out of the equation are religious meaning, which once served to secure a sense of fiduciary duty, and humanly oriented reason. Adventure capitalism today cannot have *any* claim to legitimacy. It simply is what it is, and the alternative is to allow bureaucracies, public or private, to take its place.

The dominant blame-seeking for the world economic crisis of 2002 focused on such bureaucrats. But this is not what was strange. Strange was the common acceptance that bureaucracy would drive capitalism instead of capitalism driving itself (as well as a need for rational administration). Would the rules of past experience now trump the risks of capital-attracting imaginations? Had the capitalist imagination gone too far or not far enough? What is a corrupt culture of capitalism?

The Standard Explanation

Without rules, greed runs wild. Despite all talk of free markets, this standard explanation for imposing rules on capital formation is, strangely enough, cast in terms of a Marxian doctrine. Without rules, the bureaucratically controlled culture of economics holds, greed will run wild: for example, the failure of private bureaucrats at Arthur Andersen to enforce accounting rules. This accusation, however, did not hold for the origins of modern capitalism. What distinguished its rise from the adventurous investments of past ages was that the investors had an ultimate internal motivation to not simply take the money and run but to reinvest it.

From the Enlightenment to Globalism

World culture today is a culture pursuing economic values. And all modern economics is an economics of capital reinvestment. The motivation for living a life is assumed to be to acquire wealth. Those who acquire wealth in business are assumed to be motivated to reinvest profits back in business. Thus a giant machine of economic development is created.

Culture, itself a modern invention, is the totality of those practices that bend the human being to engage in modern economics.

Bureaucracy—an education bureaucracy—stands godfather to culture's birth. Today a global economic bureaucracy is in place to help other peoples who are considered, if not primitive, then "underdeveloped." The first bureaucrats were *cultivated* men—as they are in a certain sense today (Weber, 1968a: 998ff.; see Oakeshott, 1991: 99–131). We can learn something about cultural imperialism from the origins of these experts and what happened to their original mission in history.

The Culture of Reason

On the secular side, one of the world's great philosophers stood up for a political reshaping of human activity parallel to what Max Weber had found in the Protestant work ethic. Immanuel Kant wrote that skill, will, and discipline needed to be cultivated. Only so could we develop our ability to set our own purposes and design our own world. Personal development was more than education, it was *Bildung*—a shaping and forming and a fitting. The goal was called personal enlightenment: *Aufklärung*—a clearing up of what life was all about.

But, to avoid antagonizing the political powers of the time, the program required a compromise. People set for cultivation would, while being gently led to freedom, also obey (Kant, 1790/1793: §83 [B 388, A 183]; and Kant, 1784). Bureaucrats who had always served kings now took on the great experiment of serving the (gradual) Enlightenment of all human beings.

Bureaucratic Culture

What awaits us in bureaucratic culture?

Our present fate is prefigured by the performance of America's "best and the brightest"—chief bureaucrats who ran the Vietnam War. Drawn from elite schools and without experience in the field, they never developed the imagination or the will to question or reset purposes. Expertise in means and methods replaced judgment. As body counts piled up, the war managers maintained the faith that a developed culture could beat an undeveloped one in war. Each body found in a B-52 bomb crater was multiplied by several more assumed to be buried. Such accounting ignored enemy tunnels and on-the-ground intelligence reporting much lower "kill ratios." One political science methodologist returning from an inspection tour announced in 1967 that, based on "body counts," the war would be over before the upcoming presidential election (Alfred DeGrazia, 1967, communication to his class). We had become, in the words of Thoreau, the tools of our tools.

Culture as economics defines the modern human being: He is an individually fully made. He works. He owns property earned by the sweat of his brow. He has reason as his tool but bows to faith as his guide. But most of all he is a he, Man, and an individual: master of his soul and captain of his fate.—and, initially at least, no women allowed.

Yet the modern human being is being made to change. How do modern bureaucracy and post-modern bureaucracy change the values of this kind of Economic Man?

What the Experts Say

Civilization-wide, culture is economics. In modern Western civilization and its colonies this showed itself originally in the form of capital reinvestment economics: the production of surplus value (profits) to be plowed back into the enterprise for continued growth. (The word capitalism may well stem from the early modern practice of investors contributing a certain amount of money per head [Latin: *caput*] to finance a ship's profit-making voyage.)

Three Types of Economic Culture

Three stages mark the history of economic development that bureaucracy was instituted to promote and protect. We can think of them as types of culture:

- *Economic culture:* If you value economic effort for itself, you have a culture that values economics: an economic culture. (Conceivable alternatives in non-Western cultures are: intellectual culture, which values achievement of the mind; political culture, which values the exercise of power; aesthetic culture, which values art, etc.)
- *Economy-based religious culture:* If you value economic effort as an indicator of the ultimate meaning of life, you have an economy-based religious culture. (This was the case originally with Western capitalism, which based its motivation on hopes of religious salvation. Eventually, though, your culture will make a religion out of economics. That the West's culture developed in this direction was argued by Max Weber.)
- *A religion of economics:* If you have an economics that loses its religious meaning, you are still left with *a religion of economics.* (And when the religious purpose of that economics dies, then you get independent or free-floating economies. These in turn give up the explicit task of providing meaning to life, though the ghost of that task may haunt the halls. We get a specifically meaningless culture of possessive individualism: where more is the chief value defined by wanting ever more. Here the technique of getting it is prized over all else. The culture of economics is specifically meaningless, irrational, and inhuman, except in its own terms. Culture and economy are held to be of equal value.)

Bureaucracy as culture—a culture of means separated from human values—implements these transformations. To show how bureaucracy changes culture is to show how bureaucracy changes economics. Therefore our title, Bureaucracy as the New Culture: "Economics."

"It is as clear as noon-day, that man, by his industry, changes the forms of the materials furnished by nature, in such a way as to make them useful to him (Karl Marx, *Das Kapital*). This is probably true of all economics at all times everywhere. But, in the West, this activity of transforming nature came to give ultimate meaning to human life. Success in acquiring its products came to be an indicator of religious salvation.

So, well into the twentieth century, the riches of property were defined as "A gift from heaven signifying, 'This is my beloved son, in whom I am well pleased.'" With time, however, a culture of economics, ever more sophisticated, is itself reduced to mere technique that knows no higher purpose. In such a culture, economics may still satisfy human survival needs but no longer takes it meaning from ultimate human values. Its link with the meaning-giving function of religion is lost, and economics becomes humanly meaningless though necessary, an obsession and a fetish where once it was a duty and a faith. (See Karl Marx on making over nature and commodity fetishism; John D. Rockefeller on riches; Max Weber on the Protestant ethic and the spirit of capitalism.)

Bureaucracy's Rationalization of Culture

The rationalization of economic culture—in the sense of the loss of a higher human reason—is a threatening development. Bureaucracy plays a key role in producing that threat. It was bureaucracy that helped modern economics advance. It is bureaucracy that still today evens out and protects the economic playing field. Global disagreements over culture today are still converted into disagreements over economics. These are decided by uncontrolled bureaucracies like the Fed, the World Bank, the International Monetary Fund, the European Commission, the Group of Eight (leading world economies), and so on. So what if this economics still resounds with the ghost of a faith, the faded Protestant ethic that once was the spirit of capitalism? So what if we have lost sight of it as a sign of the most complete extension of leading a meaningful life?

The threat is to meaning. Our culture was built originally on the meaning of economic achievement as a sign of God's favor. Even today, we still believe hard work and its results confer human dignity on an individual.

What if this, too, is to be lost? How does this work out in economic and bureaucratic practice?

The dangers need to be explored. The original source of the spirit of capitalism was traced back by the modern investigator (Max Weber) to its origins in Calvinism. The ethic survives today as a mere knee-jerk practice: "What! He doesn't want to work? Then he doesn't deserve any help." The possible disappearance of even this mindless axiom may better yield to post-modernist exploration. For example, the sociologist and anthropologist Pierre Bourdieu emphasizes the world of all kinds of practices as one into which we are silently sworn when we are born (Bourdieu, 1990).

Weber: The Culture of Private and Public Bureaucracy

The method of understanding what people do by digging down to their basic values was first and foremost developed by the sociologist Max Weber. Weber asked: Without which assumptions does the behavior of people in a given culture make no sense? He applied this question to modern capitalist enterprises. He found a specific set of values according to which modern capitalists—as distinct, for example, from ancient Roman capitalists—guided their actions and made sense of their world. Similarly, he discovered a basic set of bureaucratic values in general according to which those in bureaucracies, private or public, guided their behavior. Entrepreneurs, of course, use bureaucratic organization for some of the same purposes as do governments. Out of this research emerged imperatives of capitalism and imperatives of bureaucracy without which capitalist and bureaucratic life, complementary parts of modern culture, make no sense.

The Imperative of Capitalism

Those of us interested in understanding the conflict between bureaucratic and human values can learn something from the fact that bureaucratic norms surround us everywhere—not only in public service but in the bureaucratic components of private enterprise.

All business people at all times have always wanted to make money. But there is only one way to succeed in business today, and that is to recognize that modern capitalism is a specific way of making money superior to previous forms of doing business. The proof of the pudding lies in the fact that an entrepreneur not using modern business practices simply cannot compete against one who does. There seems to be a central set of rules—a modern capitalist imperative—which, if followed, puts the modern business person at an advantage over the more traditional predecessor.

The owners of my favorite doughnut shop on Manhattan's Fourteenth Street understand this imperative of modern business perfectly. If the doughnut shop is to stay in business and overcome slow days when income is low, the enterprise needs to accumulate money to increase its margin of security. This money can then be directed into two channels: It can be put away as a cushion against bad times, and it can be invested in another doughnut machine to increase sales and further profits. Growth and security are intimately related.

But to know how much of a cushion is needed or how much profit can be reinvested, operating costs (rent, labor, materials, depreciation of machines) must be calculated. In addition, the owners have to determine how many doughnuts must be sold to break even. How many customers have to go in and out of the shop each hour, on the average, to let them reach their break-even point?

The owners of the shop, in other words, are highly modern business people. They understand that profits are not just to be spent, but are a guarantee for the stability and growth of the shop. And they understand that sound use of investment and reinvestment can be achieved only through calculating everything—not only materials, machines, and labor, but also customers and consumption.

They have understood the imperative of modern capitalism: capital stability and growth through sound reinvestment achieved by the calculation of everything. This imperative can be analytically divided into two parts, the goal and the means. The goal is growth of capital. The means is calculation—or, to use a term with which we are already familiar from our discussion of bureaucracy, rationalization. In other words, bureaucratization of business practices becomes the means through which capital growth as the imperative of modern capitalism is achieved. The private bureaucracy of the accounting office is the first pillar supporting capital enterprise.

This is an important point for understanding the imperative of public as well as private bureaucracy. The imperative of bureaucracy, from the first, has always been control. It was through the bureaucratization of his accounting methods, personnel selection and use, and market calculations that the first modern capitalist became truly modern and therefore superior to his less calculating predecessors.

Max Weber contributed mightily to this understanding of both modern capitalism, with bureaucracy as its control instrument, and modern public bureaucracy as the control instrument of the political system. Bureaucracy in both cases is the outgrowth of a unique Western belief that everything in the world could be calculated and thereby be brought under human control. This attempt to bring the world under the command of calculating reason—rationalization—becomes not only an inner tool for capitalism but an outward condition. Weber reminds us of the rationalistic control component of the overall bureaucratic imperative, for example, in his definition of the manufacturing type of modern capitalism as "orientation to the profit possibilities in continuous production of goods in enterprises with capital accounting" (Weber, 1968a, 164).

So much for the internal norms of capital enterprise. To the extent that accounting spells control, they are entirely within the range of the list of bureaucratic norms drawn up at the beginning of this chapter. But elsewhere Weber's extensive research also establishes that modern capitalism can exist only in an environment in which general rationalized norms, including bureaucratic ones, become the external conditions of existence.

In drawing up his summary of the conditions under which modern capitalism can develop, Weber includes these three points:

1. Complete calculability of the technical conditions of the production process, that is, a mechanically rational technology.

2. Complete calculability of the functioning of public administration and the legal order and a reliable, purely formal guarantee of all contracts by the political authority.

3. The most complete separation possible of the enterprise and its conditions of success and failure from the household or private budgetary unit and its property interests. (Weber 1968a: 162)

These points summarize the dependence of the capitalist imperative—profit making through capital reinvestment—on the concurrent development of modern technology, modern bureaucracy, and modern economics.

The Imperative of Bureaucracy

The imperative of bureaucracy is control. This is true, for historical reasons, whether bureaucracy is master or tool.

Control through Rationalism. In capital enterprises, the first office to be bureaucratized was the accounting office. Rationalistic methods of accounting, embedded in regularized procedures and office structures, which are themselves susceptible to rational oversight, allow entrepreneurs to "account for" any and all operations of their enterprises and how each affects the other. The final measure of such accounting is "the bottom line"—the profit-loss statement. The bureaucratization of accounting is the starting point for bringing financing, raw-material supply, machine and labor operations, and sales into a tight relationship with profit outcome. By demanding the rationalization of the labor process—that is, its description and organization in quantifiable terms—the accounting office could demand adjusting the labor process as a means to maximize profit as an end. The logical and effective linking of means and ends in this way constitutes the very definition of the concept of modern rationality. Bureaucracy becomes the practical carrier of the rationalization process inherent in Western civilization.

But what makes this emphasis on rationalistic control the imperative of bureaucracy when applied to public service? The answer seems to be that modern bureaucracy was specifically conceived as a control instrument to be applied to public service from the very beginning. In this sense, it has always been more master than tool.

One of Weber's contributions is that he calls attention to the need that capitalism, as an economic enterprise, has for the bureaucratization of the social and legal world. The outstanding value that bureaucracy offers to capitalism is that it makes the behavior of labor, fellow capitalists, and consumers predictable. Especially in law, bureaucracy freezes into relative permanence behaviors that are in the interest of capitalist entrepreneurs to have permanent. The previous types of capitalists, with their innate tendency to play for high risks and take their money and run, come to an end when not only the methods of production but also the stabilization of the external environment make reinvestment of capital for ever-expanding growth a good risk. On the behalf of this growing class of entrepreneurs, state bureaucracies set norms of contract among entrepreneurs and marshaled the power to enforce them. They also regulated the ways workers could and could not sell their labor and began regulating markets to protect entrepreneurs from foreign and domestic fluctuations.

The central value that public bureaucracy offers private enterprise is stability against the tendency, found in previous types of administration, to allow flux through the arbitrary and unpredictable application and enforcement of policy. Such previous policy was, of course, the policy of kings, nobles, and landholders. Thus from the very beginning, bureaucracy served the purpose of limiting and regulating the exercise of political power by providing conditions of stability favorable to the exercise of economic power.

Bureaucracy ensured this relative permanence in contractual, labor, and market conditions through its structure. Instead of being left to the goodwill of individuals, policies became embedded in offices or, more accurately, became the operating procedures of permanent offices that, if followed, guaranteed the income, status, and institutional identity of their temporary occupants. By making the structure of administration inflexible, bureaucracy made an ever-changing world permanent. To accuse later bureaucracies of inflexibility is therefore to ignore the origin and nature of bureaucracy as an administrative concept.

When Max Weber first analyzed the central characteristics of modern bureaucracy, he also isolated its central values by a comparison. But his comparison was with the dominant system of administration that preceded it. Weber's famous six characteristics of bureaucracy (which are discussed below) mean little and reveal none of their value biases if they are read out of context—that is, without comparison with the preceding forms of patriarchal and patrimonial rule.

An overall view of Weber's six points shows that his theme was to contrast a new form of administration, moving toward permanence of control, against the occasional, haphazard, and often unpredictable form of arbitration associated with feudal kings and ancient empires. Each of the six points describes conditions that will prevail if a permanent and predictable administration of control is achieved. To bring out this emphasis on control through comparison more strongly, I have below taken the central ideas of each paragraph, explained them in terms of the control aim, and related them to comparisons against older forms of administration that stem mainly from Weber himself. The full text is available in a number of reprinted versions. (All quotes from Weber 1968a: 956–98.)

Characteristics of Modern Bureaucracy

1. Bureaucracy is characterized by "fixed official jurisdictional areas."

Jurisdiction literally means to speak the law. Jurisdictional areas become areas of the exercise of law. These are clearly defined, systematically differentiated within a system of legal–rational legitimacy, and assigned to specific offices. They are the beginning of a rationalistic division of labor.

In its own internal structure, bureaucracy is initially a rationalistic model of patterns of behavior that it is designed to impose on the outside world. Once the world itself has become ordered, bureaucracy is intended to reflect that order in its internal structure.

In contrast, the precursors of modern bureaucracy are patriarchal and patrimonial systems—rule by the father. Premodern organizations that survive today include the family, especially the extended family of some ethnic groups, political machines, and the Mafia. In such premodern organizations, the law is what the father-ruler says it is, within the confines of tradition. Areas of responsibility may be delegated, but not systematically, and they are subject to the arbitrary will of the father as sovereign. The vague and overlapping boundaries of jurisdiction reflect the lack of clear social organization. This is frustrating, especially to the rising classes of modern entrepreneurs, merchants, and industrialists who require stable laws and administration regarding labor, raw materials, markets, and contracts binding one another.

1.a. Bureaucracy is characterized by "official duties." Duty is defined by law and by superiors in their capacity of officeholders. A favorite saying of functionaries is, "I just did my duty; nothing personal." The psychologically compelling source of duty is an external one. Functionaries are obedient to rationally traceable, external command.

In contrast, work in premodern organization is done out of a sense of personal obligation. The source of the sense of obligation is conscience; that is, it is internal. A favorite saying of subordinates is, "I owed it to him; I couldn't live with myself if I didn't pay my debt to him." Subordinates act as if they were obeying an inner voice. In premodern organization, the reasons why someone is obeyed cannot be traced rationally by comparing actions to a list of prescribed duties; they become a matter for depth psychology.

1.b. In modern bureaucracy, authority is "distributed in a stable way."
Here Weber elaborates on Point 1: The emphasis on stability favors predictability and control. To the bureaucrats it means they can expect to see different types of orders always come from different places: The payroll department orders you to submit timecards; personnel rules on your fitness for the job; line supervisors give task commands. In a different sense, the bureaucrat learns to associate distinct forms of behavior with occupancy of distinct offices. Authority is clearly structured into permanent offices.

A further subpoint is that "authority . . . is strictly delimited by rules concerning coercive means." Rules, in other words, are in existence and are published before administrative behavior takes place. The range of sanctions is strictly limited and assigned to specific offices.

In contrast, under premodern rules, authority is centralized in the paternal ruler and either not clearly distributed if delegated, or not distributed at all. A contemporary example is the unstable fate of a White House staffer whose authority not only may overlap with that of others, but who has no permanence since the president may relieve the staffer at any time; nor are the staffer's functions usually clearly delineated or clearly understood by others. Contrast this with authority distribution in any of the permanent cabinet departments.

In contrast to the delimitation of authority by rules, consider the family as a leftover of premodern organization. Here rules may not exist until a child engages in behavior not approved by the parent. Rules are often ex post facto. Notably, the purpose of administration in the family is not primarily control but growth. The range of coercion is infinite to provide for a vast range of possible behaviors and family needs: The Roman head of household could kill the child; the parent today can torture the child psychologically to develop control mechanisms of guilt and shame even as the child grows through individuation to material independence. Any member of the family can apply psychological torture to any other member; there is no official office of torturer, though there tends to be a chief executioner. In traditional families, it is the father.

Similarly, in the political machine, rules regarding reward and punishment for graft collection or political payoffs are never published. They change with the recipient, though an ethic related to them is understood.

1.c. Bureaucracy is characterized by "continuous fulfillment of . . . duties." Such an arrangement favors the client's expectation that the administration of rules and behaviors in a functional area is permanent.

In contrast, premodern organization offers no such reliability, fulfillment of duties being dependent on the whim of part-time administrators whose interests in administration and assigned authority are ever changing. Such lack of continuity makes it impossible to develop expectations of finding the same market conditions, the same enforcement of contracts, the same administration of freedom of commerce, or a labor supply from one day to the next. This in turn makes impossible the rational calculation of means and ends for entrepreneurs or, for that matter, the rational planning of state tax levies to continue to support the administration without interruption.

Second, permanent assignment and fulfillment of duties give rise to "corresponding rights." Rights are habituated expectations on the part of people that they will be rewarded in exactly the same way for an exact repetition in their performance of assigned duties. Without clear definition of duties and guarantees of the continuous application of sanctions and rewards to ensure their fulfillment, there can be no development of rights for either the functionary or the citizen.

In contrast, in patrimonial and patriarchal systems, exactly because they lack administrative structures to continually exercise duties, there are no "rights," only privileges bestowed by the ruler and left to the holders to assert as best they can.

Third, those employed to carry out duties must "qualify under general rules." Again this provision enhances both the orderliness of administrative structure and the orderliness of administrative behavior in the environment. Functionaries picked according to their qualifications by standard rules can be expected to behave in an orderly and standardized fashion. Further, such standards can now be task-related rather than remaining ruler-related. In summary, in bureaucracy:

(1)   There are qualifications related to the task;

(2)   these qualifications are established in regulations; and

(3)   they are universally applied.

In contrast, in premodern organization:

(1)   There may not be task-related qualifications, loyalty to the ruler taking precedence;

(2)   there are no official regulations, only ad hoc rules stemming from the ruler's temporary will; and

(3)   the ruler's will varies from case to case. No way to run a railroad.

2. Bureaucracy is governed by the "principle of office hierarchy . . . levels of graded authority . . . a firmly ordered system of super- and sub-ordination."

Again orderliness favoring control is fostered. Whereas jurisdictional areas provide a vertical division of labor, hierarchy provides a horizontal division between levels of administration concerned with matters of different scope and importance. It is also the control mechanism that holds the vertical division of labor together. This latter point is of great importance to bureaucratic control: The division of labor weakens the possibility of anyone acting successfully on his or her own, especially in situations where the division has been carried to such an extent that one functionary's action completes only a fraction of an authorized administrative act. At this point the individual functionary becomes dependent on guidance from the next higher office as to when and how to perform his or her action in such a way as to integrate with the actions of other functionaries. It is this dependence, based on the division of labor, and the management of that dependence by ever-higher offices in the hierarchy, that constitute a law of causality for the immense power of modern bureaucracy. Functionaries are forced to look upward for the ultimate norms and rewards governing their actions. In doing so, they must provide a higher office with information on which sanctions can be based; they thereby surrender the management of their actions. The structuring of offices into a pyramidal hierarchy in which the highest office is the ultimate judge and manager guarantees central control over all offices.

In summary, hierarchy means the clear delegation of authority descending through a series of less and less powerful offices, the clear status knowledge of where you are located in the hierarchy, and the principle of supervision by the office next higher up.

In contrast, premodern organizations show an overlapping delegation of authority, with the formally higher office not necessarily more powerful, responsible, or authoritative. There is also uncertainty about what one's own place and authority and responsibility are from case to case. And there is a continuing struggle for power as a normal condition of office-holding, a continuous circumvention of higher-ups. Politics remains a fact of everyday work life.

Dependence on hierarchy for guidance and reward in one's own actions, and therefore dependence as a style of survival, cannot develop in premodern organization. Without the dependence, premodern organization fails to develop a means of control that is reliable over a long time and can encompass the immense vastness of geographical or demographic space covered.

The interaction between the division of labor on rational grounds and the management of divided labor by hierarchy is the basis for the scope, intensity, and controllability of modern bureaucracy as the power instrument without compare.

3. In bureaucracy, management is "based on written documents."

Written records make visible both what bureaucrats are ordered to do and what they actually do. Rationally organized administration, suiting means to ends—including the correction of such administration based on written reports from below—thus becomes possible. In private business, written methods of accounting are an example, as are computer methods, which are equally visible because they are retrievable. Examples in public service include records and reports. Administration activities are recorded and survive personal willfulness, incompetence, dishonesty, and the departure or death of functionaries. Activities are at least potentially open to supervision from above—the hierarchy—and ultimately from outside—the public. There is here the promise of administration as a politically controllable enforcer of orderliness in those areas of human activity assigned to it.

In contrast, in premodern organization, communication and command tend to be by word of mouth and by humanly fallible memory. Personal control over bias of perceptions and understanding, personal determination to put personal interests aside—these guarantee reliability. Where such honesty is absent, administration breaks down.

Without permanent records, activities are difficult to inspect and analyze for the purposes of future correction and control. Control from one center becomes doubtful given the lack of formal regulation, evaluation, and feedback.

4. Bureaucracy's office management requires "thorough and expert training."

Here Weber not only repeats his earlier observation that modern bureaucracy requires employees who qualify under general rules, but emphasizes that office management as an activity itself becomes specialized and rationalized.

In contrast, in premodern organization, the qualifications of employees are mainly the confidence and trust of the ruler—for example, the boss, the machine. The question is not so much "Can you do the job?" but primarily, "Can you be trusted?" This does not mean that a political boss, for example, will purposely hire incompetent people; rather, he or she will seek out competent people but make sure that, first of all, they can be trusted. The myth of the hack is just that—a myth—often perpetrated by professionals.

5. Bureaucracy requires the "full working capacity of the official."

Weber contrasts bureaucracy with the previous, premodern state of affairs in which the reverse was true: "Official business was discharged as a secondary activity."

Here Weber reemphasizes implicitly the primacy and continuity of administration over other, personal interests. Officials discharge administrative duties as their primary effort in life. This effort not only excludes time for personal or other interests, but suggests the development of an inner loyalty to and therefore inner dependence on the institution: Bureaucracy becomes a way of life.

In contrast, in premodern organizations, the available work capacity of the individual is given primarily to private endeavors. The office is second, at best. Officialdom is a source of private or social honor and income, not of institutional status and identity. Given such orientations, we can hardly expect officials to favor the rationalistic ordering of society according to general rather than individual interests.

6. In bureaucracy, management of the office follows "general rules."

General rules are rules codified in the interests of all or of those in whose general interest a bureaucracy is set up. Specifically avoided are rules favoring some as against others. Thus management itself becomes predictable, expectations of functionaries become regular, and a general atmosphere of orderliness and predictability is fostered—even within the structure of bureaucracy itself—with an aim toward projecting this onto the outer world.

In contrast, in premodern administration, management tends to be ad hoc, guidance occasional and spotty, the expectations of functionaries uncertain, leading them to look outside the office for security and support. A classic example of this is the type of administration that leads to corrupt police departments or academic departments.

In summary, a restudy of Weber's brilliant analysis of modern bureaucracy should place the characteristics he cited in the light of the past and the light of the purpose for which this form of administration was created. The ultimate imperative of control is reflected in each of the characteristics of structure, behavior, and implicit psychology he cites.

As it turned out historically, organizations so designed did, and still do, keep their promise. Sticking to these points produced powerful and massive control organizations such as the world had not seen before. It also produced unintended effects. With these both modernists and post-modernists are still struggling: a rationalized world is not necessarily a reasonable world. How did this become so?

Post-Modern Critique versus Modern Critique

In tracing the history of culture transition, post-modern critics skip through linear time. Dazzling footwork obscures the question of whether modernism needs to be helped by post-modernism to engage in a critique of how things stand.

Post-modernists have no trouble making much earlier critics into recruits for the cause. For example, the modern philosopher Ludwig Wittgenstein (see Chapter 6) is called to the post-modern flag. In short, either time no longer runs forward or post-modernists engage in a bit of myth-making when it comes to their own ancestry. However, two can play this game. Here is an example of self-critique rising from within modern ranks, which sounds post-modern today. Such a performance raises questions about the need for post-modern interpretation.

Take the fundamental question: How did bureaucracy, the intended tool to bring reason into the world, become the obstacle to freedom, reason, and a humane order? We begin with a modern philosopher, then we find a modern critic answering a post-modern critic *before* a crucial question is even asked. (See the "exchange" between Foucault and Loewith below.)

Kant

The Political Origins of Modern Reason

Let yourself be taken back to the Enlightenment—several centuries ago. This was a time when reason spoke to philosophers and kings. And one encounter of these led to consequences still felt in societies and organizations today. Modernization, rationalization, industrialization—all are Enlightenment products. So is Modern Man (and Woman). We are Enlightenment's heirs today.

The Enlightenment Project

In Germany, the encounter began with a philosopher's challenge. *Sapere aude!*—the philosopher called. (Folks still knew Latin then.) Dare to think! It would take courage to think for oneself. The year was 1784. And the advocates of self-thinking were calling for reasoning and disputation in public affairs. The call soon came to the ears of the enlightened (but still Prussian) king, who responded: "Reason as much as you want and about what you want, but obey!"

What a revolting development this was! "Here," commented the philosopher who had issued the dare, "there shows itself an alienating and unexpected course of things human." Freedom to reason must be won, yet order maintained.

This, he found, places us into an estranging and illogical position between order and freedom. The philosopher knows he needs to console us. When we look at the larger picture of human events, says Immanuel Kant, "almost everything in it is paradox." (All Kant references here are to the essay "What Is Enlightenment?" Kant, 1784: 53–64, except where indicated.)

Kant, the philosopher of scientific certainty and clarity, accepts a more muddled state of affairs in actual human life: human beings are fated to live in paradox. His compatriots liked order but wanted to be free. Still, Kant hoped that free citizens could slowly be cultivated under the rule of the existing order. The tension might even help develop innate human potential: the freedom of individuals being "countered by lawful authority within a whole called *civil society.*"

It did not quite work out that way. It was clear that reason, to free itself from traditional order, would need an organization to carry it forward. Frederick the Great's edict—dispute but obey—had made sure that the established order would rule—if not the future, then the day. The design of this institutional carrier would push forward the public uses of reason, but in an orderly manner (with a large army lurking in the background). Attracted to the scientific, commercial, industrial uses of reason, our European forefathers wanted to optimize reason's power.

Kant's Machine: Early Bureaucracy

Kant saw a connection between tradition and enlightenment. The one produced civil order: individual subjects' inability to think for themselves required the rule or tutelage of kings. The other tried to develop the opposite potential. Enlightenment meant freedom for individuals to grow up into the responsibility of maturity: as citizens they needed no one to tell them what to do. It would be difficult, in those times, to resolve the tension. There were too many opposites. For one, how could the structure of the traditional order be reconciled with the structure of any organization used to advance freedom of reason? Kant proposed a republic, not a democracy. And, in the same essay on enlightenment, Kant observes, hardly by happenstance and not without cunning, that an institution was standing ready and available to implement the progress of reason:

> Now some business conducted in the interest of a common life necessitates *a certain mechanism* by means of which several *links* of the common life must *comport themselves only passively* in order to be directed to public purposes through an artificial single-mindedness of the government, or at least to be kept from the destruction of these purposes. (55; my retranslation and emphases)

This administrative "mechanism," when entrusted to citizens as an office, must be obeyed: "Here it is admittedly not permitted to reason [in the sense of public disputation by raising reasoned objections]; on the contrary, one must obey." Kant himself had to live with this paradox when another king asked him to desist from religious analysis. He agreed to submit.

The king's own family motto dedicated him to serve: *Ich dien.* As servant of the king—and his professor's salary was paid by the king—Kant could do no less. He was not free to say just anything he liked, unless he was clearly *not* saying it in his professorial role. (Max Weber was later to endorse this command as an ethic [Loewith, 1970].)

Say an enlightened citizen takes public office. He must become "part of the machine." He must at the same time serve as "a link (*Glied*)" in a whole common existence. Even a learned man like Kant can be put to its service (*angesetzt*) "partly as a passive link." Everyone so employed is like an officer on duty. It would be "very destructive" if he were to dispute a superior's order: "he must obey" (Kant, 1784: 56).

(We recognize both what Max Weber said much later in his twentieth century characterization of bureaucracy and the origins of his duty ethic.)

The Kantian Paradox

The paradox has its origins in human nature and its limits. So ends Kant's famous essay. In sum: Most of what we do is paradoxical. The paradox of organizing reason's way into the world resides deep in the institutional carrier. It cannot be avoided in any attempt at developing an enlightened citizenry.

Too much civil freedom, and people tend to overreach themselves. The pursuit of the spirit of freedom goes beyond their grasp. Just enough freedom seems to make room for that spirit to spread out *within* their capabilities of the time. Hence, Kant said, enlightenment recognizes, side by side with freedom, government's need to employ "a well disciplined and numerous army to guarantee public tranquility" (61). Again we recognize an early position of Max Weber's: The state is that institution which has the monopoly of force over a given territory. Kant's words on the paradox inherent in that state's bureaucracy bear repeating:

> A great degree of civil freedom seems advantageous to the freedom of the *spirit* of the people but erects against it [this freedom of the spirit] insurmountable barriers; a degree less of that [civil freedom] achieves room for it to spread out according to all its capabilities. (61; Kant's italics, my translation)

So the paradox was built in. In the end, Kant trusted his enlightened king to carry forward the project of freeing the reason of his subjects—and thus unchaining them from the king's will. Freedom and order contesting in the production of reason becomes part of the tragedy of Western culture. What Kant described is recognized as the essence of modern bureaucracy by its foremost exponent and critic in the twentieth century.

Weber

Max Weber continues this treatment of bureaucracy as a tool for development of reason. He not only picks up on the paradox of reason but now the time had come to pick up the pieces. Reason, the ability to choose our human goals, had come under the spell of one of its sub-routines. Instrumental reason, the logical calculation of consequences of action, had virtually extruded from its own home the original spirit of reason. Choosing our way of life now stood in sharp contrast to rationalization as the development of technique to reach such goals.

The Rise of Instrumental Reason

By 1900, Weber could no longer detect the "spirit of freedom" that lived in what Kant already had called "the hard hull" encapsulating free thought (Kant, 1784: 61). Just as a pathologist identifies congealed blood of a corpse, Weber could detect only "congealed spirit" (*geronnener Geist*) of reason. This residue makes up the "non-living machine" of the factory and "that living machine, the bureaucratic modern organization."

> Congealed spirit is also that living machine, the bureaucratic organization, with its specialization of trained skills, its division of jurisdiction, its rules and hierarchically ranked relations of authority. Together with the non-living machine it is busy fabricating the shell of bondage which men will perhaps be forced to inhabit some day, as powerless as the fellahs of ancient Egypt. (Weber, 1968a: 1402)

Kant and Weber agree on the ethical implications for the person entrusted with an office. Kant: It would be "destructive if an officer who is ordered by a superior to do something were, on duty, to argue (*vernuenfteln*) about the purposefulness or utility of the order; he must obey." Weber: "An official who receives a directive which he considers erroneous can and is supposed to object to it." But: "if his superior insists on its [the order's] execution, it is his duty even his honor to carry it out as if [it] corresponded to his innermost conviction, and to demonstrate in this way that his sense of duty stands above his personal preference" (1404). Otherwise, "the entire apparatus would fall apart" (Weber, 1958b [1919]: 512–13). But where Kant was full of hope, Weber already saw trouble. We all have had experience with that kind of trouble today.

Recent Echoes of Reason's Decline

At the level of everyday experience, the paradox undergirds the depths below people's battles with bureaucracy. Experience with bureaucracy used to be excused in terms of anomaly, latent function, externality. Critical theory's exposure of a permanent dark side put a near stop to that. Pointing out the paradox allows us to accept that insult and injury to being human is as much due to bureaucracy's bright side.

At the level of critical social science, the paradox explains the critical school's findings. Bureaucracy forcefully replaces society, culture, human psychology, language, thought, and politics. Yet there is a further area of questionability. We modern critics must also ask ourselves how deeply implicated bureaucracy's paradox is in our own modern methods of studying it.

At the level of normal social science, the paradox has had its own impact: in an obsession with ordered data. Did a baby die on the floor of a welfare office, where it lay for days while workers saw it dying but stepped gingerly around it? Why, that was a statistical outlier: A well-ordered "meta-analysis" is the remedy. It shows that, in 261 surveys covering 40 states, 215,000 citizens gave health and human services almost two-thirds credit toward a maximum positive rating (Basler, 1985: B1; Goodsell 2003: 26–27). Yet ordinary human beings are touched by the anecdote. Behind every 80 percent happy with bureaucracy, we want to know what is repressed. We want to know: Who are the other 20 percent and what does their existence say about the contest of freedom and order as foundations of our "rational" society?

We now have every reason to hear the post-modern knock on our door. Do we recognize that our old concepts could use some help from the new, even as the old informs the new? Do we answer the challenge of post-modernism? Is that trip necessary?

Foucault: Human Reason without Humanism?

Venturing once again into the heart of reason, Michel Foucault warns against seeking out the usual anchorage, which "always depends on humanism" (Foucault, 1984: 44). Here the post-modern challenges both the experiences reported in this book and their modern analysis.

Modern depiction of culture tends to anchor itself in humanistic questions. What makes a human being? What is human nature? What is the nature of things? Humanism contends these can be defined in terms of the single individual self-made and at the center of the universe. Yet, Foucault points out, these definitions are products of particular times in history. The values used are the temporal, parochial, class-bound. They represent preferences of a relatively small number of middle-class Europeans in a particular historical epoch.

Humanism, with its emphasis on the equality of all its class members, ultimately imposes an inhuman order. Its norms "normalize" everybody (48). Normalization, Foucault says, oppresses differences. Normalization "can be opposed by the principle of a critique and a permanent creation of ourselves in our autonomy" (44). Here, we may recognize an Enlightenment principle: Man gives himself a law under which he finds the freedom to conduct his life. But to Foucault this is an ongoing process, to be ever and again renewed. It is ever and again to be repeated. But it cannot be a design to be frozen and dished out by the army, schools, asylums, jails, public persecution of the deviant. The task is to oppose the whole ordering repertoire of modern bureaucratic institutions and their public executions of "reason." There is no one best track to becoming human. Our task is to confront the paradoxical task of trying to produce ourselves anyway in our diversity.

Can reason help? Here the powers that be tell us: "You either accept the Enlightenment and remain within the tradition of rationalism . . . or else you criticize the Enlightenment and then try to escape from its principles of rationality" (Foucault, 1984: 43). Foucault himself recommends "transgression." He argues:

- That we must pay special attention to specific historical outbreaks of full-fledged reason through which human beings construct and cultivate who and what they are to be.
- That, confronted with slippage into the prison of order, we must take the side of freedom and spontaneity—even "transgression."
- That the power basis of mere instrumental reason must be exposed.

Yet, such analysis was already anticipated by a very modern self-critique. This was offered long before post-modernism by a modernist, Karl Loewith, who recalls Weber's own early warnings about the decline of reason.

Loewith: Bureaucracy as Victim of Reason's Contradictions

A Weberian scholar, Karl Loewith, uses Weber's own arsenal of critical concepts to expose the problem inside Enlightenment thought. The focus becomes broad. The process of rationalization in general is examined. Its effects are traced not only for bureaucracy, but for other institutions enshrining what humans consider worthwhile: the economy and religion.

Weber had already observed reason's general dissolution: its increasing submission to order. In a so-called rational culture, he observed, progress becomes identified with an increasing internal subtlety of reason. Technique rises above purpose. The ability to discern purposes declines. Well-ordered instrumental reason produces irrational outcomes. Weber had already called this "the progressive technical rationalization of *means.*" He saw this process of becoming ever more rationalistic, in the sense of logic, as getting in the way of using reason to imagine possible human ends (Weber, 1968a: 295; my translation).

Loewith now takes up this thought. Rationalization, he adds, involves an "inversion" of the relation between means and ends. Means become ends. Original ends designed to serve Man fade into the background or are forgotten. This loss leaves the very concept of reason confined to the technical refinement of the law, of politics, of the economy, of education, of government and administration, and so on. But all of these lose their connection to an ultimate human need: a sense of purpose (Loewith, 1970: 114–15ff.).

A rationalized administration supports and helps develop an internally rationalized economy. In a very specific sense, our "economy" becomes our "culture." Weber had still found in *The Protestant Ethic and the Spirit of Capitalism* the driving force of achieving an ultimate purpose—salvation—as the motivation for modern Western capitalism. In latter-day capitalism this fades. Broken is the thought that success in economic effort signals religious salvation. The break occurs, Loewith adds, not because the economy is now secularized "through a depletion of its religious contents," but because of a different development:

> "The economic temper of the bourgeois stratum of society that was religiously motivated originally, i.e., by definite human needs, becomes 'irrational' . . . by virtue of the fact that the economy becomes independent to such a degree that—in spite of all external rationality—there no longer exists any evident relationship to the needs of man as such." (115)

What uniquely characterizes everything valued in Western culture—economy, politics, education, religion—is the spirit of reason as the ability to find purpose in life. This had been Weber's argument. The culture's administrative arm of government flattens out reason so defined. Charged with educating citizens into using their own reason, the agencies of order produce an *Ersatz* function of mere logic claiming to be reason itself. That culture, its religion, and its imaginative progress, all fall victim to the fate of rationalization.

The bureaucracy is implicated in the resulting loss of purpose precisely because, from its Enlightenment beginnings, it had been thought to be capable of freeing citizens' reason through the ruler's order. The economy is implicated as it becomes more and more technically developed, but with less and less reference to human needs.

When we go back to Weber's work before Loewith, we find Weber had already pointed to this dubious progress. He saw it in regard to, among other policy areas, the development of party structures. He wrote, with specific reference to the American political machine: "According to their inner structure, all parties transit over the last decades with increasing rationalization of electoral campaign technique into a bureaucratic organization" (Weber, 1958c [1919]: 316).

Now Loewith draws attention back to that tendency. "That which was originally a means (to an otherwise valuable end)," he writes, " becomes an end or an end-in-itself, actions intended as a means become independent rather than goal oriented and precisely thereby lose their original 'meaning' or end, i.e., their goal-oriented rationality based on man and his needs" (Loewith, 1970: 1114).

The long Enlightenment trail ends here.

For reasons we call religious—the need to find a meaningful justification for the acquisitive bent of the new merchant and industrial classes—the economy became the foundation of culture. Economy remains the culture of our day.

Bureaucracy's concern is for reason of the well-ordered, but not imaginative, kind. This concern has led both economy and bureaucracy itself into developing mere technique without purpose. The tradeoff was to cut lower instrumental reason off from the higher task of meeting human needs.

In the narrow history recounted here, a philosopher and a king had given a mission to policy and its administrative instrument: they were to develop people's ability to think for themselves. A new class—the solid first citizens of the modern era (the bourgeoisie)—had sought meaning in this secular quest. But a hidden linkage intervened. In Western civilization, a link developed between culture, economy, and religion as the ultimate source of meaning. In this context, the rationalization of means to which each of these was subjected also disconnects each from its human purposes. Does post-modern analysis add anything to that?

The Economic Culture of Bureaucracy

Culture as the great Enlightenment experiment collapses when means take over from ends. What contribution does Foucault's work make to our understanding of this outcome? How does he explain the inversion of purpose and method in the functioning of both bureaucracy and economy?

His individual studies—of prisons, mental hospitals, armies—expose the pervasive bias toward the ordering power of our institutions, even as government claims to be doing this for the well-being of citizens. In each of these studies he shows how freedom and reason are subverted by order.

But do we need post-modern analysis for this insight? Weber saw rationalization in full flood as early as 1904–5. His student Karl Loewith reiterated his points in a journal article in 1932, just before the Nazis closed down the *Archiv für Sozialwissenschaft und Sozialpolitik.*

Take a post-modernist, placing himself at the end of modernity. You might not think that he would have much concern over the birth of modern misshapen rationality in the marriage of order and freedom two hundred years ago. Yet in his own commentary on Kant's "What Is Enlightenment?" Michel Foucault takes up the paradox. Something has to be done to dissolve the fatal intertwining of freedom and order that led to full reason's being stillborn. Foucault focuses on the idea of order itself. Hidden inside this concept he finds yet another, subordinate paradox. This he calls "the paradox of the relations of capacity and power" (Foucault, 1984: 47). In so defining the problem, he already offers a solution to the forces that fight each other in modern culture.

The Enlightenment paradox pits order against freedom, our mental maps of how things are against how they might be seen to be otherwise. This ordering enchains reason. Free reason as the ability to imagine human ends flattens out. It becomes rationalization. At best it enables us to engage in mere decision-making about the most efficient means to reach ends mysteriously treated as given. From the beginning, this is a reason of power. Reason, as the ability of fitting means to human ends, now is spoken of in terms of the power of reason.

Foucault sees the origins of this paradox in two experiences we have of order. These are experiences arrayed against themselves. One tells us that, by ordering their lives, we can enable others to stretch their minds and muscles to enhance their capabilities: By enabling her, I enable myself. The other experience tells us that ordering can foster growth, not for its own sake, but as a reflection of our own power: I made her the way she is. Here the temptation of power seduces me away from enabling her. Foucault sees the solution in disconnecting what is humanly fitting about order from its seductions.

Order does make and maintain room to foster the growth of our capabilities. Order can enhance freedom. For example, a well-ordered hospital can free a surgeon to do his best. This tendency is to be supported. But when order intensifies relations between human beings that are power relations, this temptation must be resisted. The scrub nurse perceiving the surgeon's order to be a power gambit, may resist the order and, in doing so, weaken the order's enabling power. "What is at stake, then, is this: How can the growth of capabilities be disconnected from the intensification of power relations?" (Foucault, 1984: 48)

Order, the guard dog outside the house of freedom, needs to be defanged.

Order would lose its tendency to exacerbate power relations between the people it had helped grow. As freedom would be enhanced by order's capacity to foster growth, reason would lose its bias toward power. Reason would regain its status as human reason. Reason *for* human beings.

A Foucaultian "bureaucracy" would be occupied by a new sort of officeholders. It would never occur to them to use power as a means to advance the projects and rules of reason. Their clients would be enabled to use reason for their own sake. Unrealistic as this may seem without a proper budget, the principals of New York City schools would value the shaping of cultivated individuals more highly than the typical vice principal's need to keep order.

If bureaucracy is a state of mind, we need to find what made that mind for the sake of changing it. Foucault: "The thread that may connect us to the Enlightenment is not faithfulness to doctrinal elements, but rather the permanent reactivation of an attitude." This attitude demands "a permanent critique of our historical era" (42). There is a danger leaving such examination to mere modern self-critique. We may slip into facile generalizations about the nature of human beings—that is, into a humanism found in a specific historical era of a specific class: the era of the early bourgeoisie.

The critical question, says Foucault, is to be receptive not so much to what order shouts at us but what freedom and deviation whisper. In what is given to us, let us pay attention to the question "what place is occupied by whatever is singular, contingent, and the product of arbitrary constraints?" (45) In sum: "The point, in brief, is to transform the critique conducted in the form of necessary limitation into a practical critique that takes the form of a possible transgression" (45).

Transgression is the key: not opposition against the existing order, but a constant going out of bounds that finds new spaces for a human being to stand for its own sake. This, to Foucault, calls for a fundamental change in what we look for when we engage in underlying explanations for how things are: "Criticism is no longer going to be practiced in the search for formal structures with universal value, but rather as historical investigation into the events that have led us to constitute ourselves and to recognize ourselves as subjects of what we are doing, thinking, saying." The task is to give impetus to "the undefined work of freedom" (45–46).

Each one of us makes him- or herself freely in making a world for him- or herself—and then taking responsibility for living in it. Foucault in the end saw himself as "preparing—with a rather shaky hand—a labyrinth into which I can venture, in which I can move my discourse, opening up underground passages, forcing it to go far from itself, finding overhangs that reduce and deform its itinerary, in which I can lose myself and appear at last to eyes that I will never have to meet again. I am no doubt not the only one who writes in order to have no face" (1972: 17).

In the end, Foucault sees it as our task to resolve the paradox of reason. It still works its hidden will upon us. Whenever we practice what he calls "the technologies" of today, the paradox is at work: whether these are the productions of economics, or institutions for social regulation, or techniques of communication (Foucault, 1984: 48).

What counts is not what human beings think they are doing or kid themselves into thinking they are doing, "but rather what they do and the way that they do it" (48). The study of metaphysical foundations of human behavior is replaced by the study of human practices. (See also de Certeau, Bourdieu.)

For a culture of bureaucracy, the critique is trenchant and to the point. One-size-fits-all culture of bureaucratic values may still dominate. To fight this, we need to become deviant to become free. There we need to reclaim reason as a servant for the sake of defining and growing ourselves. And there we need to do what opens up opportunities for freedom and beauty, rather than foreclosing them. So speaks the post-modernist Michel Foucault.

One set of commentators points to Foucault's "genealogies" of reason. These focused on the rotting of reason in institutions that discipline and punish. They exposed the mistaken use of one aspect of reason, instrumental reason, to substitute for imaginative and creative possibilities in reason. "When this in turn reveals its procedural emptiness," say the commentators, "modernists are driven to substitute for the true order of the cosmos the true needs of the self and society" (Dreyfus and Rabinow, 1983: 259–60).

But, they continue, "Foucault has already shown" that the use of reason to discover an alleged deep truth about ourselves and society is a "historical construction." This leads to the use of science to look for that truth. And this reliance on science and its ordering imperatives, in turn, leads "to the very normalization one seeks to avoid"—a cookie-cutter model for Man.

We may see that the argument on the uses of reason between modernists and post-modernists is a continuing one. The post-modernists, however, can claim an advantage despite their undue denial that modernists can critique themselves: They have an easier time accepting paradox as a natural condition of human beings. If Kant was right in saying that much of what Man does is paradoxical, their acceptance of the paradoxical in the redesign of culture may bring post-modernists closer to life rather than to logic.

4

The Psychology of Bureaucracy: Organization as Psyche

The bureaucratization of all administration very strongly furthers the development of . . . the personality type of the professional expert.

—Max Weber

Wo Es war, soll Ich werden.

—Sigmund Freud

Man's desire is the desire of the Other.

—Jacques Lacan

Bureaucracy replaces the psyche. Psychological functions of knowledge and judgment once owned by the individual are now taken over by parts of the organization. Feeling and emotion are exiled.

The modern way of organizing people at work tries to give form to the formless. It tries to fit into the bed of reason: imaginative thought in its boundlessness, feeling in its elusiveness, emotion in its subtlety and wildness. To the extent that thought, feeling, and emotion can be rationalized, modern organization designers extract their functions and distribute them across structures of the organization.

Bureaucracy *is* the new psychology. What does this mean? Words almost fail us. Or is it we who are the ones who fail to get the word?

Psyche was the ancient word for *soul; logos* meant the *word by which the inward thought is expressed. Psychology* gives us word of our inner

95

spirit. But, before the spirit of any one of us can express itself, we must adopt the preexisting language of those who came before us.

Here lies an essential difference between modern and post-modern psychology. Modern psychology saw an active, self-making, language-creating individual—the Bourgeois Man of the Enlightenment. When we looked at what happens to that individual and his or her psychic structure in factory or bureaucracy, we saw major parts of the psyche being ripped out and transferred onto organizational structures (Hummel, 1977). Post-modern psychology sees the individual as a chimera, the function of a deficit between what we need and our ability to express it, the uncloseable gap between what we try to say and what existing language allows others to hear. As a post-modern psychoanalyst said to his students: "There is no reason why we should make ourselves the guarantors of the bourgeois dream" (Lacan, 1997, 350–51).

The modern insight sees a distortion of the psyche, suggesting therapy: a move toward healing what modern organization has ripped asunder. The post-modern insight sees an ineluctable fate sealed in the foundations of the human psyche: therapy now can amount to little more than getting people to stand up and face their fate; it cannot mean reconstituting the individual.

An interesting question presents itself: does the post-modernism view of the psyche allow us to be more or less critical than modern self-analysis?

Bureau refers to *office*; *kratos* means *power*. When we accuse bureaucracy of replacing our psyche, we are saying in several languages that bureaucracy claims the power to shape our soul. Modern psychology, making assumptions taken over from early modernity, set up and still defends a standard. It still tries to express what our soul is like under the influence of modern institutions. The practices—mindful of what is being done or mindless—of late modern institutions themselves aim to substitute organization design for psychology. Where does post-modern analysis stand in defense of the individual, the psyche, the human being autonomous in and of itself? Is it a psychoanalysis that no longer defends the core of its own focus: the psyche? During the transition from early to late modernity, we get word of our psyche in a language already edited by the power of superior offices. Can post-modernism find any problem with this?

Structuring the Psyche

Psychology seems to stand under the sign of power. From the modern self-critical perspective, it is the power of the bureaucracy that attacks

Figure 4.1 **Topology of the Psyche**

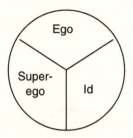

the individual psyche; from the perspective of post-modernism, it is the lack of an individual psyche to begin with that disables a psychology built on that dubious foundation from being an effective advocate for the human being in late modern situations.

Do we experience bureaucratic power as misshaping our very being—who and what we are? Our experience on the job can leave us with no doubt. Try to bring your conscience into the workplace. Try to bring in your own way of working. Pause for a second and weigh what will happen to you. You will be asked to check any such weapons at the office door or the factory gate. The organization will tell you how to master the work, and whether doing it is morally right or wrong.

The most subtle form of modern psychology—psychoanalysis—identified in the individual psyche specific functions of mastery and morality. Its word for mastery over ways of working is *ego*; the function of knowing right and wrong is *superego*. If we accept these terms, we can say that the modern organization takes over from our inner order the functions of ego and superego. Leaving us with what? Traditional psychoanalysis knows only one other function that has a place in the order of the soul: the *id*, with its largely unconscious drives and energy.

The word among psychoanalysts is that a complete soul or psyche requires all three, as seen in the constellation in Figure 4.1. We recognize that in bureaucracy two of these functions—ego and superego—are surrendered by the worker to another level of hierarchy. If hierarchy is part of the organization's structure, the handwriting is on the wall. Within the walls of the organization, two human beings, the manager and the subordinate, now must work out the truncation and externalization of part of what the worker used to call his or her own soul—or psyche. We now owe our souls, not so much to the company store, but to management,

Figure 4.2 **The Work Bond**

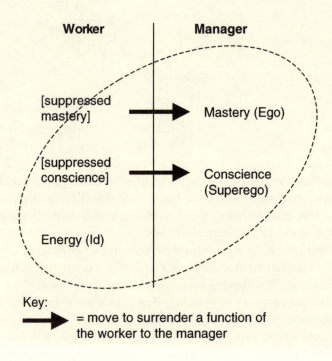

which operates large chunks of it. I have called the resulting relationship "the work bond" (Hummel, 1977; see Figure 4.2).

Only once the three functions are brought together can we speak of a unified psyche in the old sense. There may be advantages in avoiding this and giving a new phenomenon a new name.

Post-Modern Analysis

The concept of the work bond still is modernist. It uses modern assumptions. We assume there is or was such an entity as an individual. It is this presumed individual that the work bond perspective shows as being destroyed by bureaucracy. This is not a post-modern analysis, which assumes there is no autonomous individual to begin with.

However, we must now bow to such additional analysis. Postmodernism's new perspective cuts deep into old assumptions we make about nature and human nature. It opens up these possibilities:

- that there is no natural psychology,
- that the psyche in every age is shaped by institutions,
- that even the most sophisticated knowledge of that psyche is itself shaped by the *words* of that age: by language.

At best, psychology now turns into a particular way of getting word of the inner organization of human beings, in language that is itself suspect. At worst, psychology yields to organization design. (Though the responsible psychoanalyst will not go quite that far, refusing to throw out the psychoanalytic baby with the modern bathwater.)

This is the point in history at which post-modernism picks up the problem of the psyche: the point where modern and post-modern experiences of the psyche overlap. It asks: *What* is the client really saying that can't be said? Early modern psychology did not ask this question, which refers psychology to the barrier of language. It still held the belief in the natural individual:

- belief in individuals as free actors,
- belief in the individual's ability to reason for himself,
- belief in the individual's potential of speaking truth to power.

Here we still had confidence. Straight talk was possible. The human being could show itself in its full nature. Here, in short, stood the assumptions of the Enlightenment: freedom, reason both freely imaginative and logical, freely reasoned-out order. Once we began to question these legends—and ask what organizations really do to us—we grasped just how individual psychological functions are taken over by the organization.

Now we also can begin to suspect the role of modern psychology in modern organizations. It cannot lie in healing any breach of the soul of the individual if there is no individual. What can it achieve? To this the post-modernist gives a disturbing answer: From infancy, we are *all* trapped in an intolerable condition. Our needs must be expressed in the language of a parent, that is, of someone who potentially can fulfill these needs. But this language, these words, this grammar all preexist us. They are not our language. Only coincidentally do they allow us to give word to how we feel. We are dependent on this language and those who own it: our predecessors, our parent. Their understanding per force is limited—until we express ourselves in their language. And even then the best we can do is approximate their language. Since perfect mutual understanding of what we say in terms of this language is not possible, fulfillment of our needs always falls short of what we feel we need. This gap, this lack, this vacancy, the desire that cannot be fulfilled drives us all of our lives.

In short not only our conscious reason but our unconscious is structured by the language we are born into. There is no original Adam. There is no irreducible and indivisible individual. We as human subjects are an effect of our language relationships. What we take for our psyche, soul, and spirit is an effect of these relationships.

The implications are clear. Nothing untoward is happening to the psyche in modern organization—except disproval of the thought that there is a natural psyche. The organization simply reaches into us, takes us apart (analysis), and puts us back together to suit organizational purposes. See personnel tests, selection procedures, organization "development," and other frauds pretending to access or restore the "natural" psyche. We are simply reconfigured to fit the prevailing organizational structure. (See below, "Post-Modern Critique: Lacan.") A result is a different approach to organizational consulting.

A Dis-Ease of the Soul

Under modern psychological examination, bureaucracy appears as the replacement of individual psychology, the external power of the office shapes the order of our soul. In that interpretation, bureaucracy confronts us with two problems. The bureaucrat is seen as sickened with an infectious dis-ease of the soul. And healers appear who claim they can help us repair the injury. (Under post-modern assumptions, those who claim to be healers are seen as falling into the trap of perpetuating the illness by exacerbating its cause: the dominance of reason.)

Sigmund Freud already gave us the tip-off to the nature of the disease that modern psychoanalysis attacked. He spoke of our being ill at ease in culture: *das Unbehagen in der Kultur*. The result in English was *Civilization and Its Discontents*. The translation of the title successfully covered up Freud's original thought: that culture—contrary to Enlightenment hopes for cultivating reason—had not produced a comfortable home for Man. (The word *Kultur* was erroneously translated not as "culture" but as "civilization." And *das Unbehagen*—the feeling of being ill at ease—as "discontents.")

Originally, Freud found the cultivated world a place where every human being would, in some sense, feel vaguely discomfited. No specific "discontents" could be expected to rise up among the population (Freud was not Marx), but there was that miasma of a vague feeling: We are not at home in culture.

If the cultured modern individual lacks a sense for his or her true position, the bureaucrat is twice insulated. The bureaucrats, who so jealously guard their position in the organization, *have* no sense for position in life: a sense for the situation one (literally) finds oneself in. In Max Weber's words, the bureaucrat is not only headless (without reason) but soulless (without heart). And the heart is, as the psychoanalyst Michael Maccoby reminds us, the seat of judgment.

When we say that the bureaucrat is sick to heart—or when a retired bureaucrat says of his kind: "The bureaucrat has a hole in his heart"—then what are we saying? In self-critical modern analysis, we are saying that:

- Reason as mere logic detaches the modern individual from life—the full experience of being in the world, feeling in touch with it, being moved by our relation to it.
- Half-reason (logic alone) detaches us from reason as being able to imagine different worlds with other purposes.
- The cure—turning unconscious hurts into conscious insights analyzable by reason—worsens the problem by treating with more reason a problem caused by a surplus of reason.

Bureaucracy favors purposeless reason as against sensibility and emotion and the purpose-making of imagination. Ironically, modern psychology tells us that any falling away from this view of being rational is the cause of our dis-ease. It tells us that to fight this dis-ease of reason, we need to apply more reason. The patient in psychoanalysis—as well as the client in an intervention or consultancy—is told to bring the unreason of the unconscious to consciousness—where it can be examined by reason. The patient or client is promised discovery of the cause of being ill at ease in modern culture, including the rationalized organization. But what if that cause is reason itself? (Kramer, 1996)

How People "Feel"

Patrolman Williams

A story illustrates how bureaucracy produces a psychology that distorts and challenges the life of those working in it. It is the story of a police officer tasked with applying the law while setting aside all but the most rational tools of human judgment. This story displays the resulting distortions of the psyche.

The modern psyche is supposed to work best when mastery, conscience, and energy are thoroughly integrated. Such integration is, however, systematically denied to those working in the modern factory or bureaucracy. Judgments of ego (mastery) and super-ego (conscience) are to be left to the manager, leaving the worker with the task of letting his or her energies be guided by the judgment of others. Evidence of such a division of labor as pure energy unmediated by the working man's or woman's judgment is lost in the complexity of daily work. But there is one place in which the division is made clear: in the application of law. Those who know the law best are, in a modern system, not those who enforce the law. Judges do not patrol the highways of the nation. Yet those who know the reality of these highways best, officers of the police, are usually called to task by judges to give an account in rational-legal terms. A quickly decided arrest, done in all the uncertainties of the situation by feel and sometimes with emotion, is expected to justify itself in terms of pure reason. The officer on the scene is expected to act so as to produce what one court called "the cold sterile record" that, on appeal, "speaks with clarity and certainty as to the realities of the reason for the detention" (*State of New Mexico v. Bloom*, Court of Appeals of New Mexico, 90 N.M. 226; 561 P.2d 925; 1976 N.M. App. LEXIS 664-March 16, 1976).

Needless to say, this never happens. The officer has at his or her actual command reason based on logic but also imagination and sensibility: a feel for the situation as it is and how it might develop. When that feel lets an officer down, the results may be fatal, as they were nearly so for the patrolman in our case. That emotion can be totally held at bay is a legal fiction also. In fact, emotion may help fit a judgment to the situation at hand. In short, conscious ego mastery consists of more than instrumental reason; it also involves imaginative reason, feeling, and emotion. Even the sense of right and wrong, not in the legalistic sense but as conscience, may be an essential presence, even a motivator, for the judgment on the scene and the energy to act on it.

The kind of action of the police officer is a perfect example of the influence of modern action on individual psychology precisely because—while that action always demands and is enhanced by the ability of the officer to integrate mastery, conscience, energy, even feeling, and even emotion—it is ultimately judged in the courts according to only one of these: reason. The institutional division of ego from all other human faculties, and the claim of judicial management to a monopoly over such judgment, puts on the record what often is lost as the echoes of managerial/worker dialogue fade away. Let us turn to the judicial record as an example of such dialogue, and then bring to bear the understanding of modern and post-modern psychoanalysis.

Dialogue in a Courtroom

The witness is Patrolman Williams of the New Mexico State Police. The record of what he says was laid down in the trial court and is now being read in the appeals court. Here is what the judges see.

Two men appealed their conviction of marijuana possession in a traffic stop. Frank Bloom was convicted of possession of marijuana, aggravated assault upon a police officer, and escape from the custody of a peace officer. Ralph Mikorey was convicted of the same count of possession of marijuana and escape from custody charges, and also of battery upon a peace officer. Both defendants appealed, asserting: (1) the trial court erred in refusing to suppress the marijuana seized because the seizure was a result of an illegal stop, arrest, and seizure; (2) the police officer was not in the lawful discharge of his duties when he arrested the defendant; and (3) the marijuana conviction should be reversed for failure of the state to disclose.

In considering the motion to suppress, the Appeals Court viewed the following testimony from Patrolman Williams at 3:00 p.m. on January 27, 1975, in reference to a roadblock he had set up to check driver's licenses and registration certificates.

Cross-examination of Williams by defendants:

Q: Okay, now, at the time that you stopped the Mikorey vehicle, did you have any reasonable cause to believe that that vehicle was unsafe or not equipped as required by law?

A: No, I knew it was hauling marijuana, or something, there was something wrong with it.

Q: Okay, did you have any reason to believe that its equipment was not in proper adjustment or repair?

A: No, I'm not a mechanic.

Q: Okay, did you have any reason to believe that the driver did not have a valid license or registration?

A: That's why I asked him, to see if he did have.

Q: I see. Did you have any reason to believe that the automobile was stolen?

A: No, I knew it was a rent car, a rental car. I suspected it, being a rental car.

Q: Then why did you stop it?

A: Why did I stop him?

Q: Yeah.

A: Because I figured he was hauling marijuana.

Q: This is before you, before you even approached the car?

A: Yeah.

Q: Now, you said that you do not search all the cars unless you have reason to, right?

A: Right.

Q: And that day did you search some of the other cars?

A: Yes, sir.

Q: I see. What were the reasons that you searched those other cars?

A: Like one I thought was a stolen vehicle, which I had run it through on the computer, but it come back that it wasn't stolen, but like California, they don't enter their vehicles until 24 hours after they have been missing and they can be further than here in 24 hours and not ever be entered in the computer, and I check them, see if their spare tire and stuff are in there. You know, usually, somebody steals a car, they got no money, so they take the spare tire out and jacks and sell them.

Q: Well, did you have any reason to believe that any of the cars that you searched were, in fact, stolen?

A: Yeah, I just said I did.

Q: Okay, what led you to believe that they might have been stolen?

A: By the way the people act, by the car they are driving. You take a 'skroag' driving a Lincoln Continental, a ten thousand dollar car and he don't even have shoes to put on, something wrong.

Q: A what? What did you call—

A: Hippie, skroag, whatever.
    . . . [appellants-defendants' attorney]

Q: (continuing by Mr. Rosenberg) Did you encounter any vehicles like that that day?

A: Oh, yeah, I encounter a lot of them.

Q: Did you stop them and search them?

A: Oh, some of them I did. I can tell whether they are hauling dope, usually.

Q: So, then the reason that you signalled to Mr. Mikorey to stop at that roadblock is because you suspected he was hauling dope?

A: Uh huh.

Q: And what was it about that car, its appearance as it approached you that led you to believe it was hauling dope?

A: Rent car. Nearly every car we pick up hauling marijuana is a lease vehicle.

Q: I see. Do you ever encounter any leased vehicles that don't have marijuana?

A: No, I haven't.

Q: Or do you just stop the lease cars that have marijuana and let the lease cars that don't have marijuana go by?

A: Well, yeah. Why would I want to stop the ones that didn't have marijuana?

Q: What was it about this car that led you to believe that it was a lease car before you stopped it?

A: I can tell a lease car.

Q: What is it about a car that—

A: Well, all of them has got a little sticker in the window, and some of them has got them up behind the mirror or on the bumper.

Q: I see. And where did this car have its sticker?

A: I think it was on the left or right side of the windshield up at the top.

Q: And what did it say?

A: It's just got numbers on it.

Q: And that's what led you to believe that it was a rent car?

A: Uh huh.

Q: And that it was hauling marijuana.

A: Yes, sir. That, and then the two people in the car.

Q: What was it about the two people in the car?

A: They just looked like dope haulers.

Q: Okay, what do dope haulers look like?

A: Just like that.

. . .

Q: Would you tell the Court, would you describe to the Court what their appearance was on the day in question that led you to believe that they were dope haulers.

A: I just told you.

Q: What was it?

A: Well, they just look like dope haulers.

Q: Okay.

A: I got my own way of telling.

The Court: How would I know what to look for if I were looking for a dope hauler, Mr. Williams?

The Witness: Well, your Honor, you would have to go through the State Police school and be out on the highway and know, you can tell these people. I mean, you have to do it with experience, you just, you couldn't just jump out there say that guy, I think, is hauling dope.

The Court: Go ahead.

Q: (continuing by Mr. Rosenberg) When in your State Police school did they tell you how to identify dope haulers?

A: No, like I said, it comes with experience.

Q: I see. Was it their age?

A: No, I didn't know how old they was.

Q: Okay, was it their length of hair?

A: No.

Q: Was it the clothes they were wearing?

A: No. It was by the way they acted. Like I said, I got my own way of telling which you wouldn't have.

Q: Okay.

A: You know, I can't explain it to you.

Q: So you, you knew before that car even came to a stop, you felt in your own mind it was hauling—

A: No.

Q: —dope?

A: I had a good idea it was when I found out it was a rent car, lease car.

Q: And there was something about the people in the car that you can't really describe to us that you knew?

A: Sure.

Q: Okay.

A: Nervous.
Q: Who was nervous?
A: Mikorey.
Q: He was nervous?
A: I never did talk to *Bloom* [second suspect] at the initial contact.
Q: What would you have done if Mikorey hadn't let you look in his trunk?
A: What would I have done?
Q: Yeah.
A: I would have probably brought him to town and obtained a search warrant.
Q: Did you tell him that?
A: No, he never did tell me I couldn't look in there.

Modern Analysis

From the modern perspective, which knows the externalization of mastery and conscience in modern organizations, the officer, while psychologically under attack, shows a surprising integrity. He defends his mastery on the basis of experience and feel, grounds he knows will be discounted. And he refuses to lie when given the chance to lie. He persists in crediting experience and judgment when he simply could have pointed to a legal-rational justification for a stop. He travels in good company. Thus did Immanuel Kant observe that many judges know the law but show lack of judgment (Kant: "stupidity") in being unable to recognize an occasion in which to apply it. Kant, too, says the only remedy is experience and example. There are no rules for applying rules (Kant, 1781/1787: A134,135/B173,174).

Post-Modern Analysis

Patrolman Williams's testimony looks different under post-modern interpretation. Here the foundation is not an integrated psyche of ego, superego, and id but an empty center seeking recognition of its being: a lack in being, a gap. This marks the distance between what we want to express and what others can hear. It is the black hole that opens up when we try to get others to understand what we are trying to say and be. In this de-centered center lies the problem of what Lacan calls "desire"—the empty center of an insatiable want and need of the soul.

The gap denotes that each of us is dependent on an other, each is defined in the language of the other, each of us is denied being who and what we are or would be given a full understanding by the other.

Patrolman Williams experiences this gap. Counsel for the State and counsel for the defendants open it up. There is what he says he did and what they want him to have done. There is the abyss between what he is able to say and what they want him to say. In the modern legal system this gap is institutionalized; that is, it is immured in the rules of procedure, the ritual of recorded routine, the structure of courts.

Judges will tell you whether you did right or wrong, and whether you used the proper tools to do it. Mastery and conscience are externalized and embedded in the institution. But aside from substance, the legal system demands you communicate in its language. The choice is: Speak in our language about what you did or have your case thrown out of court. But speaking only the language of abstract reason while living and working in action is *never* possible!

In modernity, what the post-modernist calls desire is the gap frozen into institutions. And here is a new paradox. The gap, produced and exaggerated almost beyond human tolerance, may be the necessary space in which each one of us "finds" himself or herself as a human being. Desire may be the only evidence I ultimately have that I exist as an individual among others, precisely because the gap shows the difference in our identities.

To the extent that Williams is aware of this human condition and is able to stand up to it and come back the next day for another traffic stop, to that extent will he be the being that post-modern psychoanalysis respects. He is the human being who knows its fate and comes back anyway to stand up to it. All cops know this gap.

Difference between Interpretations

Two different kinds of human beings are seen in modern psychoanalysis as against post-modern psychoanalysis. The modern posits a being of a certain nature that is actualized through development. When the integrity of that individual is broken—as it is in factory or bureaucracy—it may be repaired. (Strangely, however, modern psychoanalysis has until recently ignored such a need when it comes to dealing with workers.) The post-modern posits a being with "a hole in his heart," to apply the words given us by a former bureaucrat. This is a hole in the center of the self. When such a hole is made wider and deeper in working practice —what can the post-modern analyst offer? Which type of analysis is the more radical and critical? Where there are standards there we can measure the distance to performance. But what if there is only the gap inside ever-growing desire?

For now, we can anticipate this: the post-modern analyst is aware of the source of power. It is brought into the world as twin to the baby. The parent has it if he or she understands to seduce the baby into substitutions and surrogates for what it wants; for example, to sleep on parent time, not baby time. The parent who understands the baby's gap knows that all satisfactions are substitutions and thus knows the origins of power. And so the manager who, due to her or his position, knows the emptiness in the soul of the subordinate—and fills it with surrogate satisfactions: recognition, advancement. The politician's power also rests on the reality of an unsatisfied hunger within citizens—easily and ever and again suitable to being filled with promises. Modernist analysis, by contrast, has a record of hiding the origins of power.

For a fuller answer to this we may look to the more thorough discussion under "What the Experts Say."

What the Experts Say

Psychoanalysis seeks to heal. Therapy is to repair damage that disables full functioning today due to an injury of childhood. Full functioning is modeled as the integrated meshing of ego, superego, and id: mastery, conscience, and energy. In psychoanalysis applied to organizations, old injuries are exposed that have become hardwired and inappropriately transferred to a present problem. The aim is to "free" the adult to fit into the organization. With the best of humanistic intent, the individual is nevertheless normalized to accept the prevailing order.

Here is where post-modern analysis provides a challenge. In the words of a post-modernist: "There is no reason why we should make ourselves the guarantors of the bourgeois dream" (Lacan, 1997: 350–51).

Historically, Sigmund Freud's psychoanalytical model of the psyche is a product of his time. The model of an integrated and "normal" psyche owes much to Enlightenment assumptions: for example, that unknown forces can be brought to greater consciousness and subjected to the insight of reason. This is the dream of Rational Man. It neglects the working conditions of the modern organization under which that psyche is actually formed. Full damage is revealed only when we consider the obvious answer to the question: What happens to the assumptions of psychoanalysis in the actual workings of modern organization?

Modern Critique: Sigmund Freud

The most striking event of the bureaucratic age is the disappearance of the individual. This becomes clear when we juxtapose Sigmund Freud's image of humans against today's reality.

Elevating the Ego

As Freud saw the history of the psyche, it developed through two stages. In the first, the *communal* stage, the individual was submerged in the mass. His or her psychic structure, to the extent that separate components could then be considered as already differentiated, consisted of a dominant superego, a weak ego, and a repressed id. Graphically, the constellation might be depicted in this way:

Superego

Ego   Id

This constellation asserts the supremacy of communal norms through the superego. The ego, as autonomous integrating center for the individual to adapt to reality, is weak: all the allowable patterns of adaptation have already been worked out by the community and are dictated through the superego. Similarly, the superego of the community sharply represses or punishes any asocial attempts by the instinctual drives, death-dealing and life-loving, to assert themselves. The id can gain satisfaction through tightly circumscribed, culturally approved social channels.

In contrast, we may observe, as Paul Roazen has done, that in applying his psychology to the people of his time, "Freud's whole therapy is aimed at liberation and independence" (Roazen, 1968: 247). The concern of Freud is with the maturing of the individual into an autonomous source of intelligence and power from whom society in turn draws its strength. Gone is the idea of each member's subjection to the community. Here also lies the difference between society and community, the form of social life that preceded it.

In the second stage of development, the *social* stage, the psychology of the single human being is restructured. The ego rises to the top, pushing the superego aside when its socially derived norms get in the way of individual survival. And the id is freed to express itself in channels approved by the ego in its attempt to mediate between the outer and the inner world. This is not total freedom, but individuals in modern society did radically make over the world in their own image. The psychological structure of individualist man can be depicted as follows:

Ego

Superego   Id

Here ego is dominant. "The ego has a unifying function, ensuring coherent behavior and conduct. The job of the ego is not just the negative one of avoiding anxiety, but also the positive one of maintaining effective performance" (Roazen, 1968: 234). And what Freud did not do for the dominance of the ego his successors did. With the ego dominant, society's standards, as enshrined in the superego, were subject to revision and adaptation to the needs of individuals. In contrast to the communal era, the superego now becomes dominated by the ego. The id remains often repressed, but when its needs are fulfilled, they are more likely to be channeled through the ego than through the superego. In fact, the major concern of Freud—how to free individuals from the pain of neuroses—attributes their origin to a repression of drives, for example the sex drive.

Speaking in Enlightenment terms, Freud considered the growth of the individual not only crucial to the individual himself or herself but essential for society at large:

> The liberation of an individual, as he grows up from the authority of his parents, is one of the most necessary though one of the most painful results brought about by the course of his development. It is quite essential that that liberation should occur and it may be presumed that it has been to some extent achieved by everyone who has reached a normal state. Indeed, the whole progress of society rests upon the opposition between successive generations. (Freud, 1955: 237)

Exactly for the reasons that politically Freud was a European liberal and that scientifically he made the individual his unit of analysis (Roazen,

1968: 248), his ego-dominant image of humans stands in stark contrast to our age. There, the individual person created himself or herself in the company of other humans. Often the individual would be, in the words of Thomas Hobbes, alone, alive, and afraid. But then freedom was defined in terms of being left alone by others to work out one's own fate. On this definition both the political philosophy and the theology of liberalism met. Today the prevailing political and social reality is that of the corporation and the government agency. The unit of analysis now is the disindividualized individual at best.

Fragmenting the Ego

With the separation of the superego from the rest of the psyche and the fragmentation of the ego, the possibility of the individual resubmerges into the mass from which it only recently emerged. The concept of the individual derives from the Latin word *individuus*—"indivisible." The individual as such did not exist in the world of community; he or she was molded too much by the social environment. The individual arose only with the development of modern society, owing his or her existence to the idea that humans could grasp hold of their world, including the social world, and reshape it in the individual's own image. This was the idea of early modern science, technology, and industry, and it carried over into the early social sciences.

Freud's psychology, despite its group context (which he did not at all deny), was an "individual psychology" (Freud, [1922?]: 1). The task of Freudian psychoanalysis and therapy to this day remains, at least avowedly, the reestablishment of the functioning individual. If analysts or therapists are asked to whom they owe their direct obligation, they reply that it is to the individual whom they analyze or attempt to heal.

But man or woman the indivisible is now no longer so. Especially not in bureaucracy. He or she is man or woman the divisible. Whether or not he or she is still a human being in some absolute sense need not be asked here. All we require is an understanding of why the bureaucratic human looks so inhuman to us as outsiders. He or she looks inhuman from our perspective to the extent that we still operate under the definition of "individual" that emerged with the rise of society, the form of social organization within which we still perceive ourselves to live apart from working hours. Similarly, the more our own perceptions reveal the penetration of bureaucracy's human-concept into society at large, the less surprised we are at the divisible human.

In contrast to both preceding pictures of the structure of the psyche in other eras, perhaps this is the best that can be done for the image of the bureaucratic human:

Externalized Superego

Fragmented Ego

Id
(in the service of the organization)

While this image has a faint resemblance to the communal psyche, under the dominance of a superego, it bears no resemblance at all to the structure of the individualist human. The individual has simply disintegrated under the immense power of bureaucracy and his or her need to make a living in it because one cannot make a living elsewhere in the shrinking arena of society.

Freud Applied: The Work Bond

Take any human being. Now remove his or her ability to judge what is socially responsible. The result is a sociopath. Then remove the ability to master challenges from the environment. He or she does not survive. Yet modern organization strips the human being of control over both these abilities. How does the functionary so deprived nevertheless survive?

The functionary survives, socially and physically, exactly because bureaucracy exercises the functions of superego (conscience) and ego (mastery) activity on the person's behalf. As long as the individual remains inside, the same agency that takes away the use of certain individual psychological capabilities also exercises them *for* him or her.

The functionary exists as long as he or she establishes strong bonds with managers or offices, into whose hands two-thirds of the original individual psyche has been placed. This may be represented in Figure 4.3.

After the externalization of superego and ego, the functionary must identify or bond with the hierarchy and division of labor or their representatives: the functionary's superiors. If not, he or she ceases to exist. Since the manager is the closest representative of the powers of hierarchy

Figure 4.3   **Externalization of Superego and Ego**

I. PSYCHE IN SOCIETY

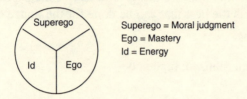

Superego = Moral judgment
Ego = Mastery
Id = Energy

II. PSYCHE IN ORGANIZATIONS

A. Superego Externalization

Test Question:
What happens to an
employee who brings
personal values
(conscience, judgments
of right and wrong) to
work?

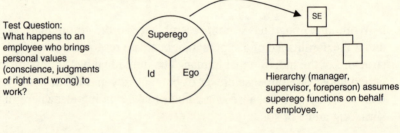

Hierarchy (manager,
supervisor, foreperson) assumes
superego functions on behalf
of employee.

B. Ego Externalization

Test Question:
What happens to an
employee who insists
on using own tools or
methods at work, or
who attempts to
experiment?

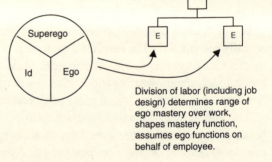

Division of labor (including job
design) determines range of
ego mastery over work,
shapes mastery function,
assumes ego functions on
behalf of employee.

and the division of labor—externalized superego and ego functions—the manager becomes the object for such bonding. Identification and projection establish the bond.

Bonding also derives from the organization's need to get work done. Under the imperative that only the responsible manager shall judge the propriety of a piece of work and the methods and tools to be used, which leaves functionaries with little more than their id energy, the organization itself welds the manager and functionary into one work unit.

Figure 4.4   **The Work Bond**

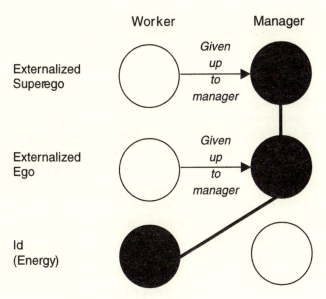

The functionary cannot work without the manager, and the manager is similarly dependent on subordinates: Without their energy the work cannot get done.

The new unit of analysis comprises both the manager and the functionary in a work setting. Psychologically, I have called this the "work bond." The work bond refers to the structure that is the simplest unit of the modern organization that can get work done. This structure is welded together not merely by external reinforcements but actively by a psychological bond between manager and subordinate. The bond stems from the positions of mutual dependence into which the manager and functionary have been placed by the organization. The bond is the very human attempt to salvage lost personal integrity by placing portions of what was lost in one other person and identifying that person as part of one's self. The manager and the functionary in the work bond become, together, a reconstructed self. What does human nature in bureaucracy look like? Investigate the work bond. Pictorially, the work bond can be depicted as in Figure 4.4.

Workers who do not integrate themselves into the work bond may engage in a misplaced narcissism: the desperate search for a lost self conducted in the wrong place—within the self. But from the viewpoint of individualistic psychology, the psychic activities necessary to maintain the work bond are similarly pathological. Identification with the manager is regressive, reawakening early childhood ways of bonding before the capacity for loving existed. Projection is the attempt to bridge the gap between the self and a lost object in one great subconscious leap of faith; when the lost object is one's own ego or superego, an entirely new form of projection must be developed. The relation between functionary and manager is hardly one based on any sense of reality. It is, from the bottom up, a projected relation constantly subject to sudden, unforetellable, apparently irrational corrections from above. People who fit well into the bottom part of the work-bond dyad are those trained in society to be masochists. They love punishment and the power of the punishers. Those who fit into the top half had best be sadists.

Visions of the snakepit open up when the lid of organizational structure is lifted. From the viewpoint of an organization psychology looking at the new bonds and psychological processes with cold and "neutral" eyes, what emerges are entirely new concepts of what a psyche is—along with an entirely new view of what psychology is.

Modern Consulting: Michael Diamond

Since the psychology of organizations was refounded in the 1970s, the most developed new model for exploring such questions, in both the public and the private sector, has become an organization-structural variant of psychoanalysis: psychoanalytic organization theory (Schwartz, 1990: 8). This is also the least understood approach. It is subject to the easy popularization that the psychology of Sigmund Freud has suffered in general; it is easy to make fun of, evoking concepts like sex, mother, and childhood. For both these reasons, this section not only reports some of the findings of this approach but tries to show how organizational consultants use it.

Psychoanalytic Organization Theory

What makes people in modern organizations tick? This question is treated in psychoanalytic organization theory as both a question of personality and a question of the prevailing conditions that shape it. Much is known about how organizations impose values and what pathways they construct for social relations. Until recently little was known about how the individual unconsciously processes such values and such structures—or how such processing then feeds back into organizational values and structures. In the words of psychoanalytic organization theorist Howard Schwartz: We knew little about how the emotional "snakepit" related to the idealized "clockwork" of organizational structure. Worse yet: We did not *want* to know anything about it! (Schwartz, 1990: 8) What is probably the most advanced of psychoanalytic organization theory explores this question of the unconscious life of individuals in organizations—*but in relation to a theory of organizations.*

How this type of analysis works is depicted first in a case involving a consultancy. Then we can evaluate the power of insights produced by application of a single one of its concepts. And then we can summarize some of its findings.

A Case of a Psychoanalytic Consultancy

How does a psychoanalytically oriented organization consultant work on what goes wrong in an institution? In the case below, we can, up to a point, fantasize that as we read its facts we could do a social or a cultural analysis. What happened in one state's department of human services can be explained to some degree as a function of hierarchy and the division of labor. To some degree it can be seen as a conflict of values. A restructuring might be the solution. Or a good dose of the proper values, announced by the director and trained into staff. But this is not enough to right the wrong.

The psychoanalytic approach does not merely add depth to such analyses; in this case, at least, it provides an insight without which social or cultural reconstruction would have failed. In order to make possible the reader's concurrent evaluation of the case according to social or cultural insights, the psychoanalytic insight is presented only toward the end. The reader is asked for patience in following the case step by step. The case (from Diamond, 1993: 193–210):

A state department of human services acquired a number of new programs to administer in addition to its own. The new director, Jack Smith, wanted to draw up a department-wide mission statement. However, he ran into departmental problems: "inadequate sharing of resources, poor communication between agencies, and a general lack of vertical and horizontal information-sharing." Subordinates expressed widespread acceptance of Smith, saying "Jack has background with the department,

and that makes a difference!" or "He's one of us." Yet their unwillingness
to share resources and information persisted.

In group sessions, the psychoanalytically oriented consultant looked
for feelings. He found them. The stories people told were full of suppressed anger and resentment toward two previous directors. The directors
had called staff members "stupid" and "incompetent" in front of others.
They were remembered for shouting at them. One director, it was recalled,
derided managers of staff for perceived disloyalty and insubordination.

The harvest of discontent persisted into the reign of the new director. Instead of focusing joint efforts on a man they liked and a mission they could
themselves design, staff kept on complaining about the past. At a retreat,
program divisions complained that support divisions were too preoccupied
with control and, consequently, were unresponsive to the needs of the
programs. Support divisions felt programs were withholding information,
were uncooperative and ungrateful, and tended to pin blame for problems
on them. One head of a support division put it this way: "Programs go
around with the attitude: What have you done for me lately?"

The consultant identified the cause of the problems as the fact that
the two prior leaders were still present in the minds of employees. Bad
feelings and defensive reactions stimulated by the previous directors had
become institutionalized and got in the way of working with the new
director they liked. Projecting their previous treatment outward onto the
environment, staff referred to themselves as "survivors" of an unapprecia-
tive and often hostile public and victims of sadistic leaders.

The consultant interpreted this behavior in terms of the technical concepts of *projection*, *object loss*, and *persecutory transference*. Surface
self-examination by the participants could not reveal a psychological
truth: You must mourn even someone you hate. Furthermore, the psychoanalytic approach expects resistance to such mourning. The consultant
explains:

> *Projection*—the psychological tendency to reject bad feelings and place
> them outside oneself, and, then, to act as if they belong to someone or
> something else—makes grieving hard to do. With each group session and
> during the retreat itself, participants criticized and told painful stories about
> the previous two directors. "They were buddies of the governor," some said.
> "They lacked leadership skills, and they misunderstood the program divi-
> sions," others proclaimed. "Polk was corrupt and Holmes treated people
> badly," they agreed. Finally, and most pointed for the consultant, "Jack
> Smith inherits the baggage of Holmes and Polk," several suggested.

The consultant's conclusion: "Mourning the loss of someone loved and cared for seems understandable, but grieving for someone despised is unimaginable to many. . . . DHS members had to confront and let go of these negative feelings from the past, which affected their relations with one another and with the new director. They had to undo the *persecutory transference* that left them cynical and with little hope of positive change."

The technical terms used here may, like all professional language, exclude the noninitiated. However the terms remind the expert that one phenomenon such as anger or grieving is embedded in an entire psychological dynamic that must be understood to make a diagnosis and suggest a solution. A cultural approach might simply have focused on getting members to discover shared values for a mission statement. The psychoanalytic approach discovered deep-seated injuries that had to be healed first. Only then could reasonable discussion of values and missions ensue: "*Mourning the loss* of a despised leader was essential to their constructing more realistic (and less pessimistic) perceptions of themselves as an agency, and to repairing emotional injuries . . . that influenced their view of the current leadership."

Without psychology—in this case, a psychoanalytic understanding—of the mental processes of people involved, it is not possible to understand oft-cited paradoxes and pathologies of modern organizations. This can be illustrated by pointing to the power of a single concept.

Ritualistic Behavior as a Key to Bureau-Pathology

The power of an approach can be evaluated by the depth of its insights. In the case of psychoanalytic organization theory this can be shown by exploring how a single concept—that of *ritualistic behavior*—can explain how bureaucracies become their own worst enemies (Baum, 1987; Diamond, 1993; Schwartz, 1990).

Begin with a simple question. What sustains the surface equanimity of the bureaucrat—his or her constant display of even-handedness? A cultural interpretation trivializes how this is created and maintained. It says simply: They act without fear or favor because these are their values.

When we look at the psychology of the bureaucrat, we are pointed in a different direction: down into the realm of feelings. Is even-handedness simply due to an iron discipline? Is it due to reason, which "controls" any outbursts of feeling? On the contrary, we find that feelings themselves are working and writhing just below the surface to maintain the image of instrumental rationality we observe when we see the cold and neutral bureaucrat. These are exposed in psychoanalytic organization theorists' concept of ritualistic behavior.

Since Max Weber is it well understood that government bureaucracy's original purpose was that of stabilizing the economic environment. We will understand if this value of stability is echoed in the orientation of the functionary. Just as the organization attempts to stamp out all instability in the environment, the organizational operator is asked to focus on stable practices such as the habitual observance of an established form or process for doing things and the repetition of such acts. But in terms of the health of the individual—his or her own ability to gear successfully into the reality of the environment—excessive devotion to such habits is what Michael Diamond calls *"dysfunctional and obsessional practice"* (Diamond, 1993).

The practices mentioned function as a defense that allows the individual to evade normal anxiety. But normal anxiety is very much part of human existence. It arises from confronting the great life dichotomies of life and death, love and hate, stability and growth, and the resulting juxtaposition of meaning and meaninglessness, self and dissolution. To sidestep confrontation with these leads to a greatly curtailed life and personality. Yet, as the study of bureaucratic culture has shown, bureaucracy tries to place its inmates clearly on one side of these life dichotomies.

The mission of bureaucracy explicitly devalues the conflict and uncertainties that these existential dichotomies create in the world. The method of bureaucracy is to raise to primacy in our attention the *means* to flatten out such instability.

Ritual in social life affirms the dichotomies and confronts them in celebrations such as a christening or a b'rith, a rite of passage from puberty into adulthood, a wedding or wake. These produce a feeling of completeness—"a whole act, a finished sequence, the achievement (at least for a while) of satisfaction, satiation, perhaps serenity" (Diamond, 1993: chap. 2). *Ritualistic behavior* denies the dichotomies of life, repressing the ambivalent feelings they create that threaten one's self.

We may say that the bureaucracy is an appealing workplace that attracts people already inclined toward ritualistic repression of healthy feelings toward life's openness and contradictions, and we may also say that it will train newcomers in such repression.

The concept of ritualistic behavior as typical of bureaucrats' emotional state also gives us insight into bureaucracy's intolerance for healthy conflict in the environment it was created to stabilize. Given its selected operators' trained intolerance for ambivalence in the life status of the self, it is unlikely that their imagination will be able to tolerate such ambivalence in their field of endeavor. Economic growth and entrepreneurial innovation, in an environment which the bureaucrat has strict orders to stabilize, are perceived not only as a threat to the mission of a regulatory agency but as a personal threat to the individual operating it.

There is here an explanation of one of the great conflicts of organizational culture: between bureaucratic values and social values. The bureaucratic values include those of formal rationality, formalistic impersonality, and discipline. These serve to repress healthy concerns with one's fate as expressed by social values: justice, freedom, violence, oppression, happiness, love and hate, and ultimately salvation and damnation. The result is that "exaggerated ego defenses and ritualistic actions perpetuate the organizational culture by encouraging resistance to insight and change" (Diamond, 1993: 45).

Diamond, in his case studies, goes on to show that the entire range of values, actions, and personality formation of people is tainted by distortions of reality relations such as *ritualistic behavior.*

But there is an even larger lesson to be drawn from exploring bureaucracy through the concept of ritualistic behavior. As already pointed out, some of the effects of such distortions reinforce the modern organization's mission. But it would be superficial to conclude that a mission of enforcing environmental stability can be reinforced by simple parallel rigidity in the thinking and feeling of the enforcers. Carrying out such a mission may require much personal sensitivity and flexibility. With these tools the enforcer can respond to challenges emanating from control operations and adapt his or her tactics. A rigid controller may in fact be too inured to what is going on to produce the desired rigidity in the environment. Thus personal pathologies stimulated and home-grown by the government bureaucracy's mission and methods end up being counterproductive.

The bureaucratic personality subverts the bureaucracy!

The exploration of bureaucratic pathology exposes not only the incompatibility of government bureaucracy with healthy personality formation among its clients but the incompatibility of the bureaucratic personalities it produces internally with its own mission. This is not a minor insight.

Toward Post-Modern Critique

Sigmund Freud and his heirs have demonstrated that modern critique can handle modern problems. Freud's critique does what critique is supposed to do: it lays bare the assumptions undergirding ways of life. The question remains: To the extent that Freud himself was caught up in early modern times, was he able to lay bare his own assumptions or the assumptions of the discipline he founded? Is modern critique adequate to the critique of late modern life? Post-modernists say, No. But what do they have to offer that is better? For an answer we take a look at the post-modernist psychoanalyst Jacques Lacan.

Post-Modern Critique: Lacan

Post-modern analysis turns up new word of the modern soul. It digs up the foundations on which modern analysis was built. What does this digging contribute to the psychology of organizations? Take the most serious challenger, the psychoanalyst Jacques Lacan. (The following interpretation is based on the work of the commentator Jonathan Scott Lee, 1991; and Lacan, 1977 and 1978.)

Lacan's work is both helpful and, at the same time, manages to miss the point of a critique of modernity. In focusing on individual psychology, Lacan gets to the bottom of what makes up modernist's concepts of the individual psyche. He does not, however, look at relations at work that keep the worker in bondage. Taking apart the modern construct of the psyche (deconstruction) does not in and of itself produce a concept that relates the psyche to the social: that is, to working conditions such as hierarchy and the division of labor.

A Difference in Foundations

How, speaking of social relations, would Lacan read the work bond? How would he treat managers' taking over workers' functions of mastery and conscience? What does his psychology make of the resulting dependency? How would he react to consultants using traditional psychoanalytic theory to heal "sick" organizations?

The foundation that Lacan digs up, and sets aside, is Sigmund Freud's theory of the Oedipus complex. Lacan digs deeper than this theory that focuses on hidden injuries of sons struggling with the father for love of the mother. Lacan's theory replaces this model of a childhood struggle to be repeated in adulthood, where its injuries must be exposed to be healed.

Lacan finds that as infants we are *all* trapped in an intolerable condition. Fulfillment of our needs always falls short of what we feel we need. This gap, this lack, this vacancy, the desire that cannot be fulfilled, drives us all of our lives. (We might add, in application of this theory, that of course the modern manager's position in response to a worker's needs gives him or her the power to reenact this scenario.)

As the infant develops, Lacan continues, it finds there is only one road into the company of others who might satisfy our needs. It is language. But language is always the language of others. It has been constructed by the others who are there before us. Our needs can only be expressed in *their* terms.

Sisyphus Redux

The model is Sisyphus condemned. Ever and again upward do we roll the stone of our fate, only to see it roll down again. Each attempt to say what we really want has the effect of opening the gap that then again functions as ever-more strengthened desire. And Lacan would agree with Albert Camus, the author of *The Myth of Sisyphus*, that in the end we must imagine Sisyphus happy.

It is exactly because Sisyphus collaborates in his fate that he has to some extent hold himself responsible. Mental health for Lacan is to face up to our fate, and to do so *because* we are condemned to it. There is here no "therapy" in the sense of again making well what has fallen ill. Life just isn't fair.

With Sigmund Freud we would see the work bond in terms of insult or injury to the functions of the ego and superego. But Lacan's emphasis differs. While he shares Freud's picture of the psyche in which ego and superego and id have their place (topology), Lacan finally leaves him, making desire the center of his psychology.

What Lacan accepts, but ultimately rejects, is Freud's early structuralism. We are not born with a human nature hardwired into our soul and body. We are the function of energies that flow through our nerves. (We can still see the hardwired early position of Freud's in the electrical diagrams of his early volumes.) Lacan here takes a step toward the broader context of the society into which we are born. Psychic energies are now seen to be given their sense only in the context of language. In this innovation, Lacan does not tear down the house that Freud built, but in a sense takes Freud's structuralism with its origins in neurology out of house arrest.

Psyche as Language

There may be a structure of the psyche, but it is not a physical structure, it is a structure that looks like a language. The move actually solves a problem Freud glosses over: how does the flow of psychic energy become meaningful? No longer will Freud's magical transformation of the physical into the intelligible be allowed to be hidden. The myth of the translation of matter into word—of the wordless id giving rise unto an intelligible self-reflective ego—now looks to be just that: a convenient myth.

Freud himself had raised the issue. How can matter (though the living matter of biology) become mind? He imposes his answer as if by fiat: *Wo Es war, soll Ich werden.* Where an "it" was, there shall be an "I." (The literal translation avoids the later the terms "id" and "ego" originally chosen for the English translation.)

Lacan follows Freud, but the whole idea of the psyche—its forces, drives, structures—is now to be taken as something that becomes intelligible only against the background of language. Lacan is re-theorizing Freud but within a language substructure. No wonder orthodox Freudians went crazy and kicked Lacan out. They must see betrayal even in a move that gives psychoanalysis a defensible theory of knowledge. Lacan revisits the problem of how matter becomes mind—how electrons become human self-awareness—and he may be on safer grounds in placing all of psychoanalysis within one single framework.

In sum, with the gap of desire left insatiable, the gap perpetrated by the work bond would be considered perfectly normal, and no therapy possible—except that which gets the individual to stand up and face his or her fate.

Lacanian Analysis and the Consultant

So what's an organization consultant to do? How would a Lacanian consultant to organizations work differently from a traditional Freudian?

Recently, the field of organizational consultation using a psychoanalytic orientation has been extended to the field of public service (Michael Diamond, Michael Maccoby, Douglas LaBier, Howard Schwartz, Howell Baum, et al.). Traditional Freudian analysis of the worker allowed us to speak of an externalization of the psyche's structures onto structures of the organization (Hummel, 1977). We could observe the diffusion of one single psyche's structure over two people: the manager and the worker. The problem seemed obvious: It was defined by our observation. The consultant needed to restore full functioning of ego, superego, and id to each of the individuals participating in the work bond.

This, however, is not necessarily what happens. The psychoanalytically oriented consultant aims to make the work group functional for organizational purposes. If there is anything seriously wrong with a boss, they would do what Harry Levinson said he would do when asked about a consultancy with a banker: What if the guy who hired you were seriously ill? "I would refer him to an analyst," Levinson said. (Repartee at a conference of psychoanalysic organization consultants circa 1985.)

To begin with, though he later amends this, Lacan is agreeable to seeing a psyche distributed across organizational structures. He does not see a structure of the psyche as confined to one individual. Each of us is always dependent on the other. A human being is not given at birth. We become human as we experience unquenchable desire and learn the language and routines of society in vain attempts to quench it. Here he agrees with Martin Heidegger that the human's way of being is in essence open and unstructured, yet amends Claude Levi-Strauss to say that eventually there is a structuring. Lacan ends up reconciling the two: An open being is captured by language, just as for Heidegger that open being is captured by society and goes on an endless quest for authenticity.

Lacan sees a self ongoingly constituted in the "in-between" of biology and language. The individual is the product of the way it is thrown into the world as a biological entity; this entity is allowed to become itself only within the prevailing language it finds there. But that means it can never wholly become itself.

"Therapy" as mere remaking of the individual so as to fit into the organization becomes suspect. What can justify a move to reconstruct a disintegrating or injured configuration of ego, superego, and id? Less suspect is a move to get the adult individual to face up to his or her situation: namely, that there is no such natural structure except the artificial one that society and its language construct.

Where Freud listens to what the client says (speech) as the means of accessing given structure (ego, superego, id configured as "psyche"), Lacan suspects language as the *source* of such structures. He is thus consistent in using only what is available to him in terms of what the client says instead of making assumptions about hidden structure.

Where Freud sees in the client a speaker (subject, *der Sagende*) who makes a statement (*enonce*; *die Aussage*) about the tripartite psyche's handling of the world, Lacan would focus on desire: the lack, the gap. The work bond pulls us apart. For the orthodox, this is to be corrected. The structure is to be made functional or healthy. Yet this is never totally possible. In Lacanian terms: An identification of the speaker with what is spoken would transform a fragment of the real, the speaking body, into a signifier, an element of the system of the symbolic, language. But "we cannot put ourselves totally into language saying everything is forbidden (*interdire*)" (Lee, 1991: 139). Representation always leaves something out. That may be okay for the seeker of separate scientific knowledge superior to pre-scientific knowledge. But it is not okay in psychoanalysis, which takes an interest precisely in those half-baked, dark, marginal ideas and feelings that are to be brought to the surface in practice.

A Critique or an Echo?

When we look at the structure of desire, we now begin to see a new basis for the human bondage. In the work bond, the desire of the Other—in this case, the language of the manager—must become, to the worker, his or her own desire. We are now defined by our desire as want of being, and not through the wholeness of an integrated ego, superego, and id (Fuery, 1995: 20).

Our desires are the other's. Our fate is no longer decided by the ego as judge of an appropriate satisfying object. It is decided by an elusive unknown, an unconscious that is neither my own nor the other's: "Man's desire is the desire of the Other" (Lacan, 1977: 264).

The work bond is made to seem, by Lacanian analysis, not so much destructive of the psyche but, in its extended form, as perfectly normal. Just because we don't like this result as humanists, are we permitted to discount it?

Here we encounter a new question. Post-modernists especially subscribe to this axiom: All representations we make ourselves in social science tend to be products of the age in which they are made—as we ourselves are. Should Lacan's concepts be exempt? What about Lacan's representations of the psyche? Is it coincidence that he speaks of a diffusion of the psyche that is also evident in the working dyads of the modern organization—as these are exacerbated by false post-modern moves: quality circles, and the like? In the spirit of both Lacan and Immanuel Kant, maybe there is no problem. In all ages, human beings have faced a paradoxical fate; so again do they today (in the work bond). Face up to it!

At the least a challenge has been issued against the orthodox foundations. The individual psyche is not the be-all and end-all of all analysis. Admittedly, the individuated psyche has a great record in exercising control. It controls everything in the world—from splitting the atom to the making of antibiotics. Except it lacks control over itself. In its death-dealing tendencies, the psyche so defined is a failure.

History will answer whether the socially distributed psyche will do any better. We already have the suppression of individual mastery of working skills, to say nothing of individual responsibility and morality. Will their absence be fatal not only to the organization but to civilization as a whole? Minimally, the post-modern approach at least raises such questions. It opens up a whole new field of insight into the internal workings of manager-worker relations: the organizational psyche that treats two as one.

The Psychology of Bureaucracy

Among innovations in organization psychology, Lacanianism offers a profound example of new insights that can be found when we take post-modernism seriously.

Power is the unresolved issue in the traditional psychoanalytic treatment of the human being in the modern organization. A neutral stance of *any* kind of analyst draws a veil over the fact that all relationships, even the relationship of psychic functions, involve hierarchy and therefore power.

The normal external relationship of individuals is one of three: being equal, being superior to, and being treated as inferior. In the highly functional organization, which set of relationships we belong in is determined by our real or alleged equality, superiority, or inferiority of knowledge.

The Unanswered Question

No psychology of organizations has yet answered the key question these divisions raise: How can a power relationship (analyst-analysand), with its constant disclaimers of a power differential in its own operations, give insight into another power relationship (manager-worker)? How can even the group analyst or consultant keep from him-herself the fact that he or she is looked to as having greater wisdom, and therefore as a power that must be obeyed?

Worse yet: we must ask of any specific psychology—for example, psychoanalysis—whether the therapy does not simply polish the worker's psyche to fit better into the manager-work power bond—by, for example, getting rid of emotional baggage.

Language Therapy?

Not only the work bond but the larger psychological frame of bureaucracy appears in Lacanian analysis as structured by language. The range of language determines what managers actually can say. Within language it is that they must attempt to justify the separation of the worker from mastery or from morality. To accomplish this, management creates a whole separate and artificial language that becomes the matrix shaping possible behaviors and personalities (organizational identities). This prevailing language in modern times is the language of scientific management. The worker and we others, to the extent that we are excluded from such language making, sense as our closest experience the void this creates in our human core: in desire.

The advantage that Lacanian analysis adds to our observation and analysis of the work bond is two-pronged: besides whatever aspect original Freudian focus on the psyche reveals, there is now the all-encompassing force of language. Taking language seriously, as the organization theorist Jay White (1999) has put it in the title of a book on the theory of knowledge in organizations, enables us to simultaneously consider both the soul and the word. We can begin to weigh what might be gained in human health by changing the underlying language structure of the modern organization: that is, what it is possible to know and say. Negatively, this is a task of recovering what is forbidden: in French, the *interdit*—that which is said unspoken between people, that which goes without explicit saying. Transgressions of the language boundaries may not be a mere luxury. Transgressions, in the sense of Michel Foucault, may be necessary if organizations are to remain open to discovery—that is, to avoid becoming bureaucratic in the worst sense.

The modern organization imposes a matrix in which instrumental reason is in authority at the top. However, only the science-based mid-manager can have actual knowledge of the overall rationality of operations in the sense of coherence. Only he or she both knows the goals of the organization and is acquainted with what management science can extract from the know-how of workers. The worker, of course, possesses the actual know-how. Each of these levels in the pyramid of knowledges has its own language. There is the language of authority. There is the language of science. And there is the language of practice.

As executives, managers, and workers are all forced into interdependency, their differences both create a sense of individuality and guarantee the amplification of desire. At each level, members will feel a growing estrangement from those in other levels. The more sophisticated the knowledge at one level, the more alien to those at other levels: comptrollers do not know what middle managers know, workers have more know-how than engineer-managers, and so on.

Reducing the linguistic alienations of these divisions of knowledge would remove a major burden. This burden is on individuals' psychic ill health. It is produced by institutionalized sadism, masochism, unnecessary power plays, and the like, that far exceed the curse of mere fate. But there is also the impact on the cost of doing business. There is an impact on the cost of running government. At key points and key times, language development might also involve preventing the development of a dangerous personality: the kind that would kill the organization or society.

The point of Lacanian analysis is this: it retains the option of individual therapy but makes possible an alternative. This alternative reduces the void in organizations' members through means outside of individual therapy. Linguistic organization therapy becomes conceivable.

Practically, take the example of unnecessary use of power. The psychoanalyst Douglas LaBier, specializing in pathological bureaucrats, writes of his own experience with high-level bureaucrats in the federal government:

> For the sample studied, it appears that at the highest levels of the federal bureaucracy what is valued most is the ability to appear and act tough, to put others down and humiliate them, to constantly test others, and to produce a flurry of activity on demand—memos, decisive talk at meetings, "firefighting," and so on. (LaBier in Hummel, 1982: 144)

This analyst treats such people when they develop individual symptoms of pathology. The question he asks a new patient is always, "Has anything changed at work lately?"

In orthodox analysis—the talking cure—language is from the beginning implicated but is not itself at issue. The Lacanian approach makes language the central focus for analysis of trouble on the job. The question becomes: What won't they let you say at work? This puts in question the authoritative interdict: what is said between two people but cannot be spoken. What is questioned is control over language as a tool forbidding innovation and maintaining a divisive structure of language.

Orthodox psychoanalysis can be used to put organizations on the couch (to cite one book title). But is this true of the language variant? Can we change the language structure underneath our very way of thinking and speaking?

This question also points beyond psychological costs. Narrowly defined these are hidden costs. But we can expect that bureaucracy's psychological interdict—its limited matrix of the permissible—creates distortions of language and thought. Of these in the next two chapters. In the meanwhile we can say this of post-modern psychology (the Lacanian version presented here in abbreviated form): It can serve as yet another way of explaining the breakup of the individual psyche. But this would be to miss the point of Lacan's challenge.

The point is that Lacan is locating the center of our experience in desire. This experience of an unfillable need, rather than the subject (as the little man who sits in the brain and steers), questions the foundation assumptions of those of us modernists who have observed the loss of individuality and psychic integrity in the workplace. Because Lacan sees the inequality of the power relationship between manager and worker as just another example of a condition we are born with, his solution, however, is neither reconstitution of lost integrity nor resurrection of the supposedly autonomous individual.

The individual subject is seen as itself a product of modern language. Any intervention at the psychological level would at best be only temporary. The restrictions of the language we swim in will reassert themselves. Exposed as reflections on a humanist illusion in the larger culture are concepts of the work bond (Hummel), organizational identity (Diamond), narcissistic identification with the organization ideal (Schwartz), double identity (Baum). Furthermore, what appears to the Enlightenment psychologist as escape from freedom might now be viewed as simply adaptation to changes in the meaning of reason (reduced to logic) and our understanding of what constitutes a natural order in technological society.

More narrowly it should be clear that the set of relationships we call the modern organization has begun to function, at the smallest unit-of-analysis level, as a psyche. If this is difficult to accept, a further consequence may be insuperable. Post-modern thinking asks us to at least consider this possibility: Assume as true that different parts of the modern organization now operate and enforce a psycho-logic. Certainly they can be seen to carry out what we used to consider psychic functions of the individual human being. Is it not reasonable now to look at the human being as merely the product of these organizational operations?

Whatever modern industry has been manufacturing, has it not been manufacturing modern Man? Has government not produced the citizen?

In late modernity, with the aid of hindsight we can open up the smallest unit of analysis of late modern organization. It is the relationship between manager and worker. In it we can see the externalization and diffusion of mastery, morality, and energy over two hierarchic levels. Whatever has been the product of late modern organization heading into the post-modern practices of industry, business, and government: Have we not been manufacturing, selling, administering post-modern man?

We can thus speak of bureaucracy as psyche. Bureaucracy practices the logic of an artificial soul. In effect, bureaucracy replaces psychology. Are we willing to consider the implication of such transformation? We can return to the humanist ideal—if we want to stuff and baste a world already brimful of illusion. Or we can face up to the transitional question: Who or what is post-modern man (and woman)—and are they still on speaking terms?

5

The Language of Bureaucracy: Virtual Words

The bureaucracy's supreme power instrument is the transformation of official information into classified material by means of the notorious concept of the "service secret."
—Max Weber

The executive branch seeks to uproot people's lives, outside the public eye and behind a closed door. Democracies die behind closed doors.
—U.S. Court of Appeals, Sixth Circuit.
August 26, 2002

If lions could talk, we could not understand them.
—Ludwig Wittgenstein

Bureaucracy silences language. We are born into language. It determines what we can say—and not say. Language is the schema within which we talk. It shapes not only how people talk, but whether *what* they say can get heard. Modern bureaucracy, public or private, is at war with language. Its aim is to silence speech by making language inaccessible. By attempting to control language, bureaucracy attempts to control the actions of the people who speak it—without, however, revealing its grammar or its dictionary.

Modern understanding of language as tool plays right into this attempt, leaving no opening for escape. Seeing language as a tool to grasp hold of things in the world with certainty, and once and for all, is possible.

Modern critique merely suggests the fee: loss of the constant rebirth of meaning and a kind of "freeing" ourselves from the commitments to a common way of life. Nowhere does this quest for certainty show its fatal inclination more than in the extreme: when we try to speak the unspeakable.

Speaking the Unspeakable

Say you are told that uncounted human beings were placed in an unspeakable situation. Then someone comes along and says it never happened. Those who would ascertain the fact, now face a choice: If witnesses do speak about it, it is no longer unspeakable, but only a very small and superficial part appears before us. Briefly. Like an uncertain wraith. A soundless sound. Ghostlike. If witnesses don't speak about it, they leave us ignorant and the field open to those who will say anything.

Can the *way* we say things truly represent *what* needs to be said? I put this to a Vietnam veteran after seeing the movie based on the book *We Were Soldiers Once—and Young*.

"It wasn't right . . . ," he said.

". . . but the fighting was okay," I said.

"The fighting is always okay. Over there, there is no bullshit about it. You have to come home where there is *only* bullshit. You have to come home to a world that is just corrupt. Things didn't end that way. Things ended the way they were: nasty, dirty, and unfinished."

Jean-François Lyotard tells of an unspeakable world. Of millions who were there, none is now able to speak about it. "Most of them disappeared then, and the survivors rarely speak about it. When they do speak about it, their testimony bears only upon a minute part of this situation." Then he asks: "How can you know that the situation itself existed?"

He is speaking about Auschwitz and the gas chambers. The question is not his but that of someone other: a doubter (Lyotard, 1988: 3–6).

Here the victim is asked to speak what cannot be spoken, to call up the proof of damage done where all witnesses are struck silent because they are dead or our ears are deaf to them.

Now, if you can bear it after recalling the death of millions, recall the quandary of the workers in our introduction. They were workers at the sewage treatment plant burdened beyond capacity (see Chapter 1). Will they speak? The life and death of a population downstream may depend on it. If they speak, they may convey the impression that they know something that can be done (though the issue of capacity is beyond their abilities); if they don't speak, we get the sense they know something they haven't been telling us. In both responses—victims of an outdated plant—they are seen as complicit.

"They're in a terrible situation," says the consultant. "If they speak up, they might get hurt; if they don't, they might get hurt. But there is [another] enormous risk in not speaking up. If you don't tell the truth, your standing as people falls away" (Anonymous management consultant personal communication).

Am I saying being gassed at Auschwitz, being killed in Vietnam, and working at a sewage treatment plant are the same? I am not. I am trying to speak the unspeakable. We are the being that has the word (*zoon logon echon*). Whoever takes the words out of our mouths kills language—and us. Now what is the fate of speech when life meets the modern organization?

How People Speak

Let us take a look at "normal" speech situations.

A Native American

Each December, Tex Hall's father would get a check from the government. Just the check. No explanation. Just the check in the yellow government envelope.

The father would call the Bureau of Indian Affairs. A voice at the other end of the line would say, "We'll get back to you." They never did.

All Tex Hall's father wanted is expressed in a shout startling his eight children: "I want an accounting!" He never got it. Tex Hall's father died some time ago. "To this day," says the son, "when I get my check there is nothing that shows what tract of land it's for. Isn't that crazy?" (*Washington Post*, National Weekly edition, April 29–May 5, 2002: 30)

What is this story about? At issue is the lack of a government accounting for Indian land taken in trust more than a century ago. Lacking is a statement reconciling the payments and the piece of land they are for. Without it, no member of the Mandan-Hidatsa-Arikara tribes in North Dakota can tell whether he or she is being cheated—by the U.S. government. But there is something in the story for the rest of us. It shows what language and speech are reduced to by a bureaucracy. The fact is we may have to talk to the government, but the government does not have to talk to us. Surely this is an exaggeration? Consider the next example.

Other Citizens

On March 31, 2002, the *New York Times* published a picture of an almost blank 8½ by 11–inch sheet of paper. Left on it were the words "I hope this information helps" and the initials PJD. The rest of this page and numerous others had been scrubbed clean by government lawyers. It was the government's way of talking back to a court that had ordered the release of 11,000 pages of Energy Department documents related to secret deliberations of Vice President Dick Cheney's energy task force (*New York Times*, March 21, 2002, Week in Review section: 10). Conclusion: You can make the bureaucracy talk, but you better accept that talk is silence.

Judges versus Bureaucrats

None of this is to say that the government bureaucracy won't talk. It will, but in its own sweet time and on its own terms.

Bare-facedly ignoring the fact of judicially established breach of fiduciary responsibility in the Indian land case, the head of the Interior Department claimed that "Indian trust asset management is a very high priority for the department. The tribes, Interior, and the Congress have to reconcile the competing principles associated with trust responsibility and self-determination" (*Washington Post*, National Weekly edition, April 29–May 5, 2002: 31).

Here is how the Indian Bureau responded to a judge's order to shut down its trust fund websites because of the ease with which they could be hacked into. The department pulled a version of a traditional defense against budget cutting, the old closing-the-Washington-monument trick: It shut down all websites, even those for non-Indian clients. The expectation was clear: upset the tourists trying to make reservations for campgrounds and mobilize them against the judge. (In passing: 300,000 trust accounts are at stake.)

Bureaucracy will talk, but it will define the matrix within which the conversation will run. In short: the essence of bureaucratic talk is silence, the power not to talk. At best, bureaucratic talk is monologue, a one-way conversation, where in society conversations are two-way: dialogue.

Because it is given the power to do so, bureaucracy also does not have to give reasons for its actions. Its speech is acausal. It does not reveal why the organization is speaking at all, nor is anyone in the organization charged with tracing where the rules come from and what was their intended meaning. Bureaucratic speech may thus be detached from anything human to refer to—except the formalistic standards into which an action with real-life referents is translated by bureaucrats themselves. Whether there is such a referent, we listeners simply cannot know. When the bureaucracy yells "Fire!"—is there really a fire? When the bureaucrat says "priority," can we expect anything to happen soon? Interior's head, Gale A. Norton, said the issue had a very high priority. This may even be true in terms of improved internal processes, but, even if these improve, the results will be measured only in systems terms, not in human terms. Her words are writing checks her actions (and the Indians) can't cash. (Later a judge held her in contempt of court.)

Workers

And yet, the farce of an organization determining what people can say is sometimes uncovered by humor. See, for example, Exhibit 5.1 on alternate ways of combining well-known organizational clichés.

If *any* combination of phrases is meaningful, then *no* combination is meaningful. Meaningful speech is finally determined by the last phrase you utter with your last breath, not by an elite or a hierarchy or an idea that claims the authority to define language from the top down.

Pasquale Plescia

A story from the first edition—the story of Pasquale Plescia—is dated now, but remains the archetype of citizen interaction with government. Pasquale Plescia went by bus from California to Washington, D.C., to find out about delays in his Social Security checks. Here is what he found:

> Well, I'll tell you something about this town. They got a secret language here. You know that? Bureaucratese. Same thing we used to call double-talk. These government people, they don't hear you. They don't listen. You start to say something and they shut you out mentally, figuring they know right away what you're going to say before you say it.

Exhibit 5.1

Empty Talk in Organizations

Column I	Column II	Column III	Column IV
Gentlemen,	the realization of the program's goals	leads us to reexamine	existing fiscal and administrative conditions.
Equally important,	the complexity and diversity of the committee's areas of concentration	have played a vital role in determining	areas of future development.
At the same time,	the constant growth in the quality and scope of our activity	directly affects the development and advancement of	the attitudes of key members regarding their own work.
Still, let us not forget that	the infrastructure of the organization	requires the clarification and determination of	a participatory system.
Thus,	the new shape of organizational activity	ensures the participation of key members in	new proposals.

Source: James R. Killingsworth, "Idle Talk in Modern Organizations," *Administration and Society,* vol. 16 no. 3 (November 1984): 346–84; chart from p. 352. Originally produced as a satire by Polish students.

I knocked on doors here for two weeks but everyone's so busy with paper-work, they got no time for nothing else. I go to see one Congressman—a priest, so I figure he's got humanitarian interests—and his aide says I got to write him a letter first. Another one won't let me in 'cause I'm not in his constituency. Another gives me a press release and says, "This is the Congressman's position on Social Security." No kidding, that happened. So I go down to HEW [then the combined Department of Health, Education and Welfare]. They've got 180,000 people working for HEW, and you know what? They've got nobody to make a complaint to. (Reported in the *Los Angeles Times*, reprinted in *New York Post*, July 29, 1975: 62)

Bureaucratic Language

Pasquale Plescia captures what bothers us most when we try to communicate our needs to bureaucrats. He asks, Why won't they listen to me? They tell him to write a letter or fill out a form. If you want something from bureaucracy, or even from a congressional staffer acting bureaucratically, you've got to say it on their terms. Write a letter, fill out a form. Bureaucrats don't seem willing or able to think themselves into our language: we are expected to think ourselves into theirs.

Bureaucracy also has its own way of thinking. This is what enables bureaucrats to "shut you out mentally." At bottom it is this that prevents us from being understood by the local neighborhood bureaucrat in his or her capacity as an official, though the person inhabiting the bureaucratic role may understand us very well. The typical demand: I'd like to help you, but the rules say you've got to answer a few questions for us first.

The answers to such questions determine the basic judgment as to whether you are real to the bureaucracy. Yet this judgment seems to be made by reference to some abstract and hidden standard that is not of this world. In a way, these standards are more real than you are. The bureaucrat looks up to them. He or she compares your situation to the standards for action. Through such *reasoning by analogy*, the bureaucrat determines whether you qualify for attention—and ultimately for the program's benefits.

What happens to a person who, like Pasquale Plescia, acts out of the ordinary, sidesteps the local office, and takes the bus to the top of the hierarchy, thus failing to follow normal procedures? He does not fit the normal profile of a client deserving action. Result: "They don't hear you." For the bureaucrats you don't exist.

In short, language and thinking in bureaucracy strike us as strange because they seem designed to prevent understanding, which is what speech and thought are basically for. Understanding, bureaucracy seems to tell us, is a one-way street: If your behavior or your speech doesn't fit our program, there's nothing we can do for you.

As a result, the words that bureaucrats utter seem to be directed *at* us ("Talk our way, or die!") rather than being a bridge that both sides construct to serve as a medium *between* us. Instead of being two-way or reciprocal, bureaucratic language is one-way or *one-directional*. And, because we don't know its source in bureaucratic thinking, there seems to be no rhyme or reason for it. Such language seems to be arbitrary. Its challenges are peremptory. And ultimately there seems to be no willingness to admit to an original cause or present context that can give such language its sense: It is context-free or *acausal*.

These are observations that can emerge out of the most cursory of contacts with bureaucratic language and the thinking that lies behind it. Pasquale Plescia clearly has discovered two outstanding characteristics of bureaucratic language: *one-directionality* (the speaking without listening) and *acausality* (the contextless detachment that makes bureaucratic language seem a secret language).

What the Experts Say

Modern Critique: Wittgenstein and Searle

Wittgenstein

In bureaucracy, we may be moving in a direction where language is not language at all. Language is communication, what goes on in bureaucracy is not communication but information. Communication is a two-way construction of meaning between at least two human beings; information is literally the molding and shaping of one human being by another. In fact, information does not necessarily involve human beings: machines can "inform" one another. One of the strongest arguments on behalf of the death of language can be drawn from the philosopher Ludwig Wittgenstein:

Communication and Information. Language originates in the common life that human beings share as members of a community, Wittgenstein seems to argue. Within this communal context, we engage in "language games." That is, we engage in mutual interaction through language that is based on taken-for-granted rules silently agreed upon among ourselves. The fundamental agreement of the game is agreement on "what we do" (Vesey, 1974: 133–38). We might think of such agreement as a result of convention: "Okay, Joe, let's agree on not killing each other in this game by calling this a head and we all know heads are easily injured." But before I can even begin to agree with you on such definitions, I must already have an understanding of what a head is and what it means to be injured. That is, I must share with you my humanity. "If language is to be a means of communication there must be agreement, not only in definitions, but (queer as this may sound) in judgments" (Wittgenstein, 1953: §207). As a Wittgensteinian commentator said, "Unless people agree in their reactions to colours they will not have the concept of colour they need to have to see certain behavior as 'agreement in reaction to colours.' Unless they agree in their expressions of, and reactions to, pain, they will not have the concept of pain they need to see behavior as 'pain behavior'" (Vesey, 1974: x).

In summary, what makes language as a means of communication possible is the shared experience of being human. This shared experience Wittgenstein called "forms of life" (*Lebensformen*). Forms of life are specific expressions of behavior among human beings that rest on the organic peculiarities of the species. In the words of another Wittgensteinian commentator:

> Language, and therefore the higher forms of consciousness, depend, logically, for their existence on the possibility of common "forms of life." Hence, also, they depend, as an empirical matter of fact, on the existence of human beings regarded as members of a (fairly gregarious) species. To assert the existence of *such* forms of consciousness is in part to assert the existence, not of a single person, nor even of several separate persons, but rather, of people, that is to say of groups of individuals having not only common characteristics but also common (mutual) responses, interactions, etc. (Teichman, 1974: 145)

The relevant question to be asked about life in bureaucracy is whether such life still maintains the characteristics of human "forms of life" based on our biological characteristics as a species.

Specifically we can address this question to two kinds of "communication" within bureaucracy: (1) "communication" between bureaucratic structures and individual functionaries, and (2) "communication" between computers and individual functionaries or clients.

One of the leaders in modern organization theory, Herbert Simon, considers bureaucratic structures to be frozen decisions (Simon, 1971). In other words, the office of the sales manager in a vacuum cleaner company is set up to perpetuate the decision that whenever a customer comes in to buy a vacuum cleaner there will be adequate sales staff to effect the sale. Setting up this structure once—the structure of the sales manager's office—for all time hence, or until another decision is made, obviates the need to have unqualified and ill-informed personnel run around, when a customer comes, searching desperately for vacuum cleaners, price lists, and the proper procedures for recording the sale so that inventory can be brought up to date, new machines ordered, and so on. In this sense, the office structure is not simply one frozen decision—the decision to sell—but many frozen decisions: on how to sell, what price to ask, how and when to reorder.

Nonhuman "Language." The question that arises here is: Are the instructions contained in the frozen decision—that is, the sales manager's office—really communication? That is, are they language? Or are they something else?

Let me tentatively suggest that the instructions so frozen are neither communication nor language in the traditional sense, but information. That is, for the very good reason of achieving predictability of behavior by the sales staff, the instructions encoded in the sales manager's office are not subject to mutual agreement from below. They are one-directional. They shape behavior from the top down. As soon as, and because, it becomes detached from the original decision makers, who then become inaccessible to communication from below, information of this technical sort loses an essential characteristic of human language. The office in question is not a living thing, although it might be argued that it is usually inhabited by a living thing—the sales manager. But what characterizes the bureaucratic office is that its frozen decisions (functions) exist no matter whether there is a sales manager or not and no matter who he or she is. Even when the office is temporarily empty because the manager has been fired, the office "exists" and even "talks." It "talks" because many of its frozen decisions are encoded in price lists and work rules, which serve as external stimuli to my behavior as sales clerk.

But does the office talk and exist the way human beings do? As a sales clerk, I am quite aware I can never talk back to it to inquire after the original decisions under which it was structured. One of these decisions was to have an office that would talk to me without having back talk. But, more important, in bureaucracy the office is specifically not the human being who fills it. Rule is impersonal. This means that even if I were to try to engage in back talk, I would be addressing a "partner" of intended communication that very specifically, and by design, lacks experience in the human condition. The office, after all, is the attempt to mechanize and automate both perceptions of what goes on in the sales process and instructions based on such inputs. Lacking human experience, the office as such can never become, under Wittgensteinian concepts of language, a partner for mutual agreement about a language game called "sales." Because the office is inhuman, it can only impact me as a thing like itself. I, who think of myself as a human being, am "thought of" and treated as an analogue to the machine—another machine. I can understand it only to the degree that I accept the functions it imposes on me, that is, to the extent that I become mechanical not only in my behavior but also in my conception of what language is. At this point whatever "talk" goes on between me and the office is no longer "language" in the Wittgensteinian sense. As Vesey notes, with tongue-in-cheek, about similar situations: "Arguments from analogy haven't a leg, even *one* leg, to stand on" (Vesey, 1974: x). This is, of course, because offices, unlike humans, do not have legs. Given such a handicap we might, under Wittgenstein's premises, have assumed from the beginning that neither communication nor language is possible between human beings and the structures of bureaucracy.

But something does go on between the two, and if it is not language in the traditional sense, what is it? Here we may look to what Herbert Simon considers the ideal structure of modern organization, the computer, for an answer. Don't computers speak to us? Don't programmers "program"—that is, "speak" to—computers? Would you say that hitting a key is "speaking" to your laptop?

Before proceeding to an answer, let us emphasize that the above argument on the linguistic relation between office structure and functionaries already demonstrates our main point: Language in bureaucracy is radically different from language in society. Wittgenstein's argument in fact suggests that language is not only different in bureaucracy, it is abolished.

Nowhere does this become clearer than when people freeze business or public-service decisions into a computer and then make other people subject to the computer's instructions. Like the relationship between organizational structure and functionary, and for exactly the same reasons, the one between computer and functionary is not one of communication. The computer provides us with an especially clear-cut example of the difference between communication and information precisely because the last human element has been squeezed out of the computer, seen as an organizational structure into which decisions are frozen. An office, on the other hand, still seems to be occupied by a human manager, giving the impression of a human–machine symbiosis. In general, computer–human exchanges can no longer be understood in terms of how language used to link humans because a computer is not part of the human species.

A computer is as different from humans as humans are from dogs or stones. As one Wittgensteinian put it: "Why can we not intelligibly say of a dog or an infant that it is hopeful? Or of a stone that it is in pain? Why can we not say that a computer calculates?" (Dilman, 1974: 165) Pointing out that Wittgenstein himself asked this last question, the same author summarizes Wittgenstein's reply:

> A computer can reel out unimpeachable answers to the questions we feed into it. It may be tempting to think that here is exemplified the kind of competence that makes us speak of thought and intelligence in a mathematician. If the mathematician differs from the computer in *other* respects why should that undermine the similarity in their mathematical performance? Certainly if a man or a child writes down the answer to a mathematical problem this, in *itself*, does not prove that he has intelligence. To think of him as having mathematical ability we want him to be able to solve *other* mathematical problems. Whether or not his present performance exhibits ability and intelligence depends on what he does on *other* occasions. But when we call a man who solves a wide range of difficult mathematical problems intelligent, we take it for granted that the symbols, formulae and simple operations he uses have meaning for him, that he understands them. We cannot take this for granted in the case of the computer. Merely responding to the problems fed into it with the correct answer does not show that the computer understands what it prints. . . .
>
> In short, if the computer is to calculate it would have to have something like the human body, with arms, face, eyes, and enter into various activities in which the symbols and formulae it prints play a role. It is their role in these many activities, in shopping, measuring, accounting, engineering, that gives them the sense they have. (Dilman, 1974: 166)

In other words, without participation in the human experience, the computer is not capable of something like understanding. For the same reason, we can argue that the interaction between people and computers can never fully partake of the characteristics of communication, because one of the basic requirements for communication, the capacity for understanding on the ultimate grounds of sharing the human condition, is not available to the computer.

Similarly, the more human beings, who are dependent on modern organization for employment, adjust to the machine, the less likely they will remain capable of communication. As Wittgenstein points out, if a human responded to mathematical questions with the quickness of a computer and always came up with the correct answer, could carry out complicated formal transitions, and could work out involved mathematical proofs, but was "otherwise perfectly imbecile," then he or she would be "a human calculating machine" (Wittgenstein, 1956: Pt-IV, section 3). In yet other words:

> A person who produces such answers, whether in words, writing or print, is performing an activity in which thought and intelligence are displayed *only* if one lives a life in which this activity has a point and a bearing on other things we do, *only* if we have other interests—interests independent of producing these answers. In the absence of such a life, even a being who is alive is not a human being. (Dilman, 1974: 166–67)

As we move from the society of human beings to the bureaucracy mix of functionaries and machines, we thus experience a sense of strangeness in the kind of language spoken there. According to the Wittgensteinian explanation, this is because structures of the bureaucratic type are incapable of producing human language, human communication, and human understanding.

Searle

There is a very basic experience in bureaucracy in which we sense that speech there is radically different from speech in society. We reflect this when we call an institution's press spokesperson a "mouthpiece." We encounter a similarly strange experience when we see computer specialists "talk" to their machines. In both cases we sense that something strange is going on, but we don't understand why. In both cases we are right.

Detaching Meaning from Message. What we are observing when bureaucrats or bureaucratic structures (including computers) speak, or are spoken to, is often something unparalleled in human history—the separation of meaning from the message. It was of such language that bureaucratic practitioner and critic C.P. Snow (1964: 371) wrote, "It was a curious abstract language, of which the main feature was the taking of meaning out of words." Marshall McLuhan may glibly tell us that the "medium *is* the message," that the form of a message is its meaning; and he may be right: All communications media shape what they are capable of saying. But what is happening in bureaucracy is very specifically the separation of the message from both its content and its context.

Press secretaries of government institutions are very specifically understood by reporters *not* to be involved in what they are saying. They do lend, as the derogatory but very descriptive appellation of "mouthpiece" suggests, the mouth as tool to the conveying of the institution's message; but his or her personal meaning is detached from what is said—the impersonal message. This is the function of the "good" bureaucrat's detachment from his or her acts. It is a sign of insufficient bureaucratization that news reporters held President Nixon's press secretary, Ronald Ziegler, personally responsible for the misinformation he distributed. On the other hand, Ziegler showed he understood the functionalist nature of official speech when he chose to characterize previous statements exposed by the press as falsehoods as "inoperative" instead of as "lies." A lie is a concept that belongs to the world of social language in which individuals are held responsible for what they say, and their intentions are expected to be congruent with their words. Within the world of bureaucratic language, "inoperative" is a perfect term for a statement that no longer functions in the bureaucracy's overall attempt to impose its will on its environment—that is, in a world where means and meanings no longer matter but program integrity does.

Nevertheless, those of us coming to bureaucracy from society are right in feeling there is something very strange going on in the way bureaucrats use language, though perhaps our sense of strangeness should be resolved through understanding rather than outrage. What can explain our sense of strangeness when confronted with bureaucratic language? For something to be strange, it must differ from what we are used to. How does bureaucratic language differ? If we could answer this last question, we could also understand our sense of being strangers in a strange land.

But first another example. Our sense of strangeness reaches a peak when we are spoken to by computers. Computers interest us here because they have replaced large segments of bureaucratic structures, and are in fact often used *as* bureaucratic structures. A computer can, for example, replace a large section of a business's or civil-service institution's accounting or payroll office. To a large degree it is, in effect, the accounting or payroll office, and it is more bureaucratic in Max Weber's sense than any structure that preceded it. Precomputer structures are mixtures of people and machines in which people still visibly dominate even if, for the sake of bureaucratic control and stability, they are supposed to act like machines. For the segments that the computer takes over, this duality is resolved: The structure in which formerly twenty accountants performed calculating operations on a payroll is now a computer. The computer *is* the ideal bureaucracy.

When such a structure speaks, as we have said, the speech seems very strange to us—because all human components (for example, intention) have been removed from the speaker. What is left is myself and the IBM terminal, myself and the printout. Here, because the computer presents us with an extreme or "pure" example, we begin to see clearly the nature of bureaucratic talk—machine language—as opposed to people talk—human language.

The difference, as we have already indicated, is that in bureaucratic talk the message has to be so encapsuled and protected against the personal interests of its human carriers that it can stand by itself—apart from, and even despite, these human carriers. With the machine language of the computer, the designers of bureaucracy have finally reached that goal. There now is an impersonal language. And it is free from human interference. It is this fact that is unique in human history. No wonder we feel strange!

At this stage we may call upon the services of an expert linguist, John R. Searle, to deepen our understanding of just how serious this difference is.

A Retreat from Language. In ordinary human discourse, Searle argues, what is said (language) is never separate from the intentions of the person who says it (the speaker). The purpose of language, in fact, is to have the listener recognize the intention or meaning of the speaker.

Now, one of the strangest things about observing people who program computers—that is, who work with what computer specialists call "machine language"—is that they "utter speech," or construct speech, which the machine will then be able to use, without having in mind anything specific that they want to communicate. They are simply laying down the *means* of communication without reference to any specific *meaning*. Someone who wants to use the computer to communicate will come along later and use the means laid down—I hesitate to call it language for it is nothing of the sort in traditional terms—by attaching a meaning to it. This process of attaching meaning to the means of a language is one of the strangest experiences in which humans have ever engaged. Not that definitions have not been imposed from above for millennia. But the permanent, and very visible, separation of what is said, the signs and symbols, from what is meant has been experienced only for short spans at most, as when a child or a newcomer to a country uses a new word before learning the meaning attached to it. In the past such separation was always a handicap, a barrier to communication, but now the computer promises that separating means from meaning will encourage communication and make it more certain.

Some further exploration of Searle may deepen our understanding of this difference between what is said and what is meant. He writes:

> Human communications has some extraordinary properties, not shared by most other kinds of human behavior. One of the most extraordinary is this: If I am trying to tell someone something, then (assuming certain conditions are satisfied) as soon as he recognizes that I am trying to tell him something and exactly what it is I am trying to tell him, I have succeeded in telling it to him. Furthermore, unless he recognizes that I am trying to tell him something and what I am trying to tell him, I do not fully succeed in telling it to him. (Searle, 1969: 47)

That is, in ordinary human life the act of telling and the meaning attached to what is told are usually inseparable. In contrast, the computer, and to a lesser degree the thoroughly bureaucratized bureaucrat, separates the two. Computer "language," as a pure example of an ideal bureaucratic "language," is not fully language until it is applied *by someone* to a *particular case.* That is, it requires someone to come along and put what is a highly abstract and detached system of signs into a human context.

Linguists, who take language apart in their day-to-day work, have of course encountered language in this amputated form before. But, as Searle says, in real life "speaking a language is everywhere permeated with the facts of commitments undertaken, obligations assumed, cogent arguments presented, and so on" (197). Those of us toying playfully and naively with computer "language," and the "language" of bureaucracy in general, might well be forewarned by the caution Searle addresses to his fellow linguists:

> The retreat from the committed use of words ultimately must involve a retreat from language itself, for speaking a language . . . consists of performing speech acts according to rules, and there is no separating those speech acts from the commitments which form essential aspects of them. (198)

While Searle does not address himself to what we have observed—that people in ordinary bureaucratic life are now playing games with a language that involves the separation he fears—it is perhaps not too impertinent for us to read into his specific caution a general warning for ourselves as speakers, as listeners, and, above all, as human beings. The fact is that in everyday life we have begun to use "language" in a way that heretofore only linguistic analysts have encountered in their scholarly analyses that take living language apart. Modern use pries language out of its communal context of human beings sharing a common way of life (Wittgenstein) and reduces it to a mere tool (Searle). In modern organization, the consequences of such distortion appear in the clearest and cruelest form. But what makes such distortions cruel does not become fully clear until we ask what, in using language in such ways, we do to ourselves as human beings.

Modern Summation

In modern life, language is the patterned result of agreement between people that certain sounds are signs of similar experiences. In the modern world, the word is in between two people. It gives mutual meaning—by referring to shared actions. It is meaningful when both attach the same meaning to it.

In bureaucracy, it is our experience that, more often than not, what a word means is not what it says. It is not subject to reciprocal construction. For example, workers among themselves are not permitted to create new official language. Managers believe they get a power advantage every time they demand—as they well can—that an employee use the official language.

Yet, we begin to observe several ironies. In our ordinary modern experience, we assume that a word means something: that is, the symbol stands for a thing, an act in the world. Words orient us toward the world. Such words have us in their power. We are allowed to express only those orientations, feelings, attitudes for which there are words. In bureaucracy this demand is taken to the extreme: you can't talk about stuff for which in the official language there are no words. What a word can mean is detached from the fullness of human experience.

Modern analysts attribute the disconnect to a separation of word from experience (Wittgenstein) or the separation of message from meaning (Searle). These are products of bureaucracy also observed by post-modernists—but to different effect. Where modern critics look toward greater clarity and coherence to "fix" speech, post-modernists claim that such fixing makes things worse. Clarity and coherence are seen to play into the hands of control—though, paradoxically, also opening up the space or escapes.

Post-Modernist Critique: Derrida, Lyotard, Bourdieu

The giving of orders is a major problem in administration (see Follett). How can we give orders so they will be understood, sent on as intact, and acted on as intended?

Managers and organization designers have never tired of the problem. Searle seeks to protect meaning. Even Wittgenstein considers the problem of language repairable. Jacques Derrida, the post-modernist, disagrees. The modern critics of such systems, Derrida points out, seek what the bureaucratic designers seek. They, too, place their hope in clarity and coherence.

Derrida: The Myth of Total Control

Derrida derides the quest for the perfect language where everything is under control. He sees such an aim as part of the failed project of modernity. If we were to accept his argument, there would be profound consequences for politics, government, and administration. There would be no hope of ever fulfilling our longing for perfect understanding and reliable communication. Bad news for managers.

Good news for the hopeful citizen. As human beings we are always searching for the freedom to start a new business, bring about a new policy, choose new leaders—all while bucking the existing order. So there is good news for us in the failure to communicate. Good news—*in a way*. Why? Because attempts to use language as an instrument for social control now can be seen to produce the spaces for saying something original. Control produces its own lacunae, blank slates, uncovered realities—opportunities for escape. That also applies to making new starts: such starts always have unintended consequences. We are *never* totally in control of our lives, because we keep on living it by leaping ahead into the unknown. Language has no fixed origin or end.

The Myth of Control. In what way and with what consequences can bureaucracy use language to control behavior? A post-modern answer is offered in Derrida's *The Post Card: From Socrates to Freud and Beyond*.

Postcards are sent everyday. For anything to be sent—a postcard, an order, a man on a mission—there has to be a system. But as Derrida's translator says, Derrida's examination of the source of anything that is sent "and the principles operative in any 'sending system' (e.g., the postal system), reveals a certain indeterminacy intrinsic to the concept of *sending*" (Bass, 1987: xii).

So far all of us—newfound experts on bureaucracy and old—get what he is talking about. It's the old problem of getting people to obey orders. And there is an old answer: You make them clear, shout them loudly to be sure they are heard, train people to pass them on correctly, allow for a minimum of discretion. In short, we have here the problem central to modern organization: How can it all be held together?

We all understand the danger of any deviation in the postal system. But do we see the hope in this danger? "What if this system necessarily contained a kink, so that despite the absolute authority of its usual sequences (like the absolute authority of alphabetical order), somewhere it contained the subversion and reversal of its own progression (L before K)?" (xii) Why then, this must be fixed. So say the fearful and orderly among us. Unless the kink is taken out of the system, postcards will go to the wrong address. The cards might get stuck somewhere or even come back marked "Return to Sender." Let's design so we don't get a halt of the flow or even a reversal of the cards' progress, and, if anyone particular is at fault, let's get that subversive out of there.

This is precisely what Derrida himself says is not possible. In an astonishing literary performance in *The Post Card*'s main text, he exposes the reality of all systems: any sending system has its kinks, its twists, in fact the subversion of itself built in. There are "delicate levers that pass between the legs of a word, between a word and itself," he writes (Letter of 9 September 1977 in Derrida, 1987: 78). In short, there *is* hope for the citizen seeking islands of freedom from which to launch new undertakings in the midst of the ordering stream.

The Postcard. The story of the postcard is this: In a visit to Britain's Bodleian library, Derrida comes across an old postcard. It shows two philosophers at work: Socrates is writing while Plato is dictating to him.

Derrida of course noticed the reversal: Socrates was the one philosopher who never wrote; Plato did the writing for him. But Derrida went beyond noting this. It occurred to him, in a series of free associations or even inspirations, that in one regard at least Plato was worse off than Socrates: the problem of being misinterpreted. Derrida first speaks of this card when he writes on the back of one sent to a former lover:

> Have you seen this card, the image on the back [*dos*] of this card? I stumbled across it yesterday, in the Bodleian (the famous Oxford library), I'll tell you about it. I stopped dead, with a feeling of hallucination (is he crazy or what? He has the names mixed up!) and of revelation at the same time, an apocalyptic revelation: Socrates writing, writing in front of Plato. (Derrida 1987: 9)

What does Derrida make of this?

Philosophers, like the rest of us, are always misunderstood, misinterpreted, literally mis-taken by others. Yet, in a face-to-face encounter with a student, the philosopher could always defend himself: this is not what I meant, that is, what I meant to say, and so on. However, once writing comes on the scene, the philosopher's thought can be widely disseminated. His writing is a seed that goes out into the world—perhaps by the postal service.

We can make ourselves an example. A postcard with a philosopher's saying arrives, perhaps with the words: *Illegitami non carborundum!* The recipients are free to take this writing any way they want. In fact, the more widely disseminated the writing becomes, the more likely it is that someone will discover the above is pig latin (Don't let the bastards grind you!) but also that, in the case of a serious philosopher, misinterpretations will multiply. (This is one of them.)

But being misunderstood runs counter to everyone's intentions. We have agonized over making our thought as clear and distinct in writing as possible. We want to be able to pass the thought on. We may here anticipate the fate of the orders of a top bureaucrat: the more the orders are circulated, the more likely it is that someone will mis-take what the order said.

To Derrida, the postcard's reversal of who speaks and who writes is itself an example of what he is talking about: The designer of the card is an interpreter in a medium that sends messages around the world. Perhaps the artist has mis-read somewhere, erroneously, that Socrates was Plato's student. Perhaps the artist had been mis-taken about the ways of communicating of each. Perhaps the artist had mis-thought that Plato was teaching his old teacher the lesson that writing allows thoughts to be made more clear and distinct.

The Message. Whatever the case, mis-reading, mis-taking, and mis-apprehending can now be expected to be a consequence of writing. The greater clarity and distinctness that written control over our words gives us does not produce the complete order we seek. Disorder, not order, can be and must be the result of writing disseminated. That is one point Derrida leads us to.

The more elaborate the postal system, the greater the chances of a letter being sent to and delivered at a place unintended. Does anyone remember the fate of a memo sent by a local FBI office up the hierarchy before a certain September 11, warning of strange activities of strangers taking flight lessons?

This is in fact the fate of modern complex systems. Take accidents in nuclear plants. The normal response is to write more elaborate instructions and tighten their enforcement. The result is: more accidents. In contrast, plants where the problem is informally talked out witness a reduction in accidents.

Derrida is giving us an insight into why this might be so. The incident of the postcard also might serve as a warning to administrators that clear and distinct orders broadly disseminated will at some point yield not only action but a reaction. As Michel Foucault would say, the exercise of power creates its own counter-power.

If Derrida is right, the dispute over full control versus discretion in organizations is resolved: discretion is unavoidable. Citizens should expect their expectations to be interpreted by politicians. Lawmakers should expect legislative intent to be interpreted by, say, the courts. Managers should expect their orders to be interpreted by workers (and authors by editors). The wider the range of distribution, the more variation. One of the premises of the Enlightenment experiment is undercut: clarity in reason—and speech—does, in modern times, produce reactions contrary to the message's aim.

This gives new meaning to Max Weber's comment that fate in modern times is the consequence of Man's actions contrary to his intentions. The problem of meaning is a particularly modern problem. With his attack on the myth of control, Derrida gives us a reason why this might be so.

Writing—being asked to write a memo—*may* be a concession to freeze our thoughts into "normal" categories. Thus encapsuled, what commitments we imply in our speech are just as certain and frozen as dictionary entries. But writing also opens possibilities. It can "reveal the unlooked-for possibilities latent in all communication" (Norris, 1987: 191).

Here the post-modernist begins to boggle our minds by pointing out this: The essential aim of writing—seeking to be clear in conveying thought by making marks on paper—is always already there when we first make sounds in the air; that is, when we speak. Writing, in trying to secure what we mean, simply suggests the presence of the opposite: the insecuring of meaning. Rather than foreclosing discussion of what an author meant, his or her writings actually serve as an invitation to interpret—and thereby open up language. Writing, the tool of control, evokes the antidote to control.

Lyotard: The Myth of the Single Narrative

Control slips through the fingers of the controller in various little-suspected ways. The quest for order through pure reason is, if not fundamentally mistaken, lopsided in result. An example is the argument of Jean-François Lyotard about the disappearance of the Grand Narrative.

Pure reason would have all human beings speak with a single voice: the voice of Rational Man. As hopes for a single univocal language fail, so does control slip through bureaucracy's fingers. We do not all sing from the same hymnal. No single way of telling the stories of human beings, so argues Lyotard, can claim to speak for all humanity. To Lyotard the rise of other stories that other cultures tell signals the end of monolithic Western culture. He focuses our attention not so much on values as on language: the stories communities tell (Lyotard, 1984).

Believers in progress have believed in a single story: that of Western history exported as *the* model around the globe. The belief is captured by Max Weber's comparative histories tracing how we, the people of the West, got to be who and what we are. (Not that Weber approved of us!)

To critically examine this supposed "highpoint" of Western civilization, of which he was deeply critical, Weber wrote a series of comparative histories of world cultures and their utmost attempts to capture the ultimate meaning of life in their religions. These histories covered Hinduism, Buddhism, Confucianism, Protestantism, and, in the case of the West, our own development from the day of the Judaic prophets on.

Lyotard also sees the emergence of many stories. The Grand Narrative is dead. Modernity—the rule of order through freedom and Reason (see Chapter 3)—may not be the be-all and end-all of all peoples. What is the difference between Weber and Lyotard? Perhaps we can argue this: Weber still wrote out of concern for the Western culture he lived in, specifically for its dehumanization and disenchantment of the world. Lyotard seems to suggest a change in locale: the concerns of every other culture are as valid as ours; history is always many histories; these are the histories of what cosmopolitans used to call "the provinces"—the provinces are as central as the metropolis.

This shift in point of view from which history is told has serious impact on bureaucracies at the global level. There, international bureaucrats encounter the narratives of other cultures. Yet Lyotard, as other post-modernists, still stands on the shoulders of modern giants. From what position does Lyotard announce the meta-narrative's demise? Is he not himself speaking a new Grand Narrative?

But perhaps he is Nietzsche's "over-man"—the bridging human being. This super-being not only discovers but crosses the abyss between modernity and so-called post-modernity. In that case, Lyotard misses the grounds of the abyss (*Abgrund*) as he crosses it sanguine in the belief that this lack of grounds is a simple void.

One figure revered by post-modernists as belonging to their pre-history has already charted the bottom that lies beneath this sea of sanguinity. Edmund Husserl calls those grounds "technique." Technique issues from a tendency of reason to refine and refine and refine measurement. It also is a seduction of the mind. This seduction attracts us to the ever more detailed and more finely measured. It takes us as human beings from our initial concern of taking the measure *of* something *for* our sake to reducing that something to ever finer and more detailed measures. For the sake of what? For the sake of technique itself. The means becomes an end. We seek refuge in what the mind can handle: ever smaller segmentations of the universe—yet all in the service of eventually charting the organic whole. Husserl is still a modern critic. Does Lyotard add anything new?

Lyotard never tells us where he finds a place to stand. Where is his home? In what kind of a story, the Grand Narrative, or a *petit écrit*? But he sees the problem of post-modernity as one of finding ways to show what modernity cannot show. And that is presenting the unpresentable. Instead of finer and finer rules to master reality—what an artist might call art's *petite technique*—Lyotard reflects another human need: bursting out of the rules of the game.

Bourdieu: The Myth of the Word

Just as post-modernists have attempted to undermine the further *extension* of modernity's universalizing language, they have looked at the increased *intension* of modern speech. Turned inward on ourselves, modern speech "colonizes" our own experiences by telling us that these are no good, or not valid, unless they can be put in explicit words. With this imperative, language imperatives penetrate our thought and speech. The result is the suppression of sensibility and judgment. The myth is drummed into us that the word is superior to action. The parallel to how bureaucracy speaks can hardly be missed.

Some things go without saying. Some things *only* go without saying. For example, once I start thinking about how I am able to say what I say—the mechanics of moving the tongue this way or that—I stutter.

There are other things that only go without saying. Like reading this line from left to right. or capitalizing the beginning of sentences. Or how my fingers touch the keyboard as I type this. Or what style of words is appropriate (not just grammatical) for this kind of book. Or that most of these words will be in English, considering the kind of reader I hope to get.

These are not matters for reflection or discussion. They are not matters of following rules. (In fact, if I follow all the rules given to me by the production editor, I probably will be so locked into them as to be able to express nothing at all.) These are, says Pierre Bourdieu, matters less of consciousness thought and language than matters of the practical sense of our *practices*. The question for bureaucracy is what to do with worker practices, which run silent and deep, are not responsive to being named, and therefore run the danger of being a permanent unknown with which the manager must deal.

"Practical sense," Bourdieu says, "is a quasi-bodily involvement in the world which presupposes no representation either of the body or the world, still less of their relationship" (1990: 66). In short, practical sense short-circuits our assumptions that there is a worker over there and our managerial world over here and we must somehow bridge the gap by communicating with the worker. If bureaucratic talking and doing are all about rules, ordinary talking and doing for the most part function in the absence of rules. This means they function not merely to bridge the gaps; it is the gaps that make the rules possible.

For it is in the gaps of what we can know and say that we first experience new events. And it is there that imagination runs rampant. Reality is what happens between what the rules lead us to expect and what emerges. Experience is not conscious of rules.

This is perhaps the most cutting indictment of your old grade school teacher's claim if you can't say it, you don't know it. This is not a statement about what you know; it is a statement about who has power in the classroom. Exposing such statements exposes modern language use as a grammar that serves as a straitjacket for experience. In the formally administrative context, we can say the same for bureaucratic language. The indictment comes from a scholar who did not consider himself a post-modernist. Yet in his critical remarks he is often associated with the post-modernists.

We already know that modern language use, and more so the language of officials, assumes that in order for something to become known it must be said. And saying must consciously follow a form or grammar, which the language underlying speech provides.

Bourdieu now shows that most of what we do involves not language or conscious cognitive thought but know-how. Know-how is our being involved in things that enable us to change them. Separate conscious thought and words may follow. What we do may not rest on a formal logic at all. The hinge of judgments cannot itself turn on an explicit grammar of rules.

This has fatal implications for managers' claims of being able to "cause" workers to turn this way or that. No one is able to dictate operations on the basis of controlling speech unless he or she has the cooperation of the one spoken to. The entire dictatorship of bureaucratic speech collapses when faced with the fact of pre-speech practices that follow no rule, no concept, no visible grammar.

Bureaucracy therefore denies the existence of know-how. For example, a judge will throw out a police officer's testimony that justifies an arrest based "on a feeling I had." (See Chapter 4.)

The rationalist basis of bureaucracy fears such know-how. It contends that only if the *logic* of speech can be abstracted from the speech *act* and formalized in someone's head, can that someone claim the authority to tell us what goes on. And only then is the agent considered able to know something and be able to say something of and about what we know and do.

For us critics of bureaucracy, the question becomes: Which came first? Was it knowledge of grammar, of the categories of what we can say about what we do? Or was it practices, a feel for what we do? Bourdieu opts for the second.

His argument restates an earlier one of Martin Heidegger: that we have a silent sense of where we are in a situation. He calls it our "foundness" in that situation: *Befindlichkeit*. We have an understanding of that situation before we can say anything about it. We engage in a silent discourse with people and things *before* we say anything out loud. We are already a *part* of the whole before we participate.

Similarly, Bourdieu shows how relations between people rest not on rules (the bureaucrat's preference because workers can be held to them) but on unspoken sensibilities. These involve a sense much like our sense for beauty. They are more aesthetic than logical—in the ancient Greek meaning of the word (*aesthesis*—a sensate feeling). They capture a feel for situations, people, and things that is continually constitutive of on-going social relations—without being spoken. Yet they communicate; they communicate in what we do: our practices.

Say, for example, someone gives you a gift. It is understood that you will give a gift in return. But when? Where? How much? It cannot be an even gift of the same value. That would put too much of a calculation into gift-giving, changing the practice into a mere exchange. It cannot be too soon; to reciprocate too soon would again seem too calculative. Nor can it be too late; for a reciprocation too late implies at least a memory lapse and at worst a lack of a sense of what is fitting. Furthermore, none of these arrangements is spoken; they are silent sense.

"Practical sense," writes Bourdieux, "is what causes practices . . . to be *sensible*, that is, informed by a common sense. It is because agents never know completely what they are doing that what they do has more sense than they know" (Bourdieu, 1990: 69).

This statement evokes some of the positions of post-modernists. For one, I do not always know the sum of what I am doing, because I do not, in all my doing, say to myself: Now I am doing this, now I am doing this, . . . ad infinitum . . . and then add it up. I do not always reflect: that is, take a position outside myself to look back at myself and my doings. Lacan's "je" is distinct from the "moi."

Another example. Say you intentionally go to the ballpark to play a little baseball. Someone hands you a bat. Someone shouts, "Play ball!" You swing . . . and you miss. You do this three times. You are called "out." You walk off the field. You stuck to the rules. But was that the game? Or was the game what went on between all the skills you brought with you and the facts of the rules everyone else plays by? Is the game not something that emerges between your subjective experience and the objective opportunities—your sense for the ball and how the ball is pitched?

"If it's not in the day report, it hasn't been done," a police officer may be told by a sergeant. Or, more fatally, the comment of a NASA official regarding the history of experience with O-rings that failed in the space shuttle *Challenger*: "It's all been documented." "If you can't answer *my* questions," a nurse once told me while I was down with an undiagnosed illness, "you're not saying anything."

You need a "feel for the game," says Bourdieu. When you have it, you get "the almost miraculous encounter between the *habitus* and a field, between incorporated history and an objectified history, which makes possible the near-perfect anticipation of the future inscribed in all the concrete configurations on the pitch or board" (66). Or for that matter on the field of work. Similarly in the game of life in general: "One does not embark on the game by a conscious act, one is born into the game, with the game" (67).

Bureaucratic Language

The best way to learn how bureaucratic language works is to experiment with your own personal home bureaucracy: the computer. Or any gadget swarming with tamed electrons will do. Can you program your VCR? Can you ever find out all the functions of your Bose radio? Can you ever learn all the permutations in the gadget? What allows you such learning? Are you independent of the computer while operating it—or is it operating you? Certainly you can get it to do what you want only if you adjust what you want to the way it is programmed. And, of course, the suggestion that most of us can reprogram our computer is met with—silence.

As the post-modernist Jean Baudrillard has pointed out, the outside of the computer or gadget confronts you as a faceless test. This interrogates you. However the gadget itself, on the face of it, does not give itself away by any—or, at best, only minimal—cues. Its archetype may be the monolith whose black polished impervious face appears without a clue in the movie *2001*. It kills or stuns the first humans to touch it. Only later (and in its own sweet time) does it open up, giving a vista onto a peremptory gift: an infinity of stars. Even then we must guess whether this is an invitation for humans to explore and live there. Or—? There is here an endless array of choices for human beings. None of which are the humans' own, each of which is "given" by . . . —what? We don't know. Note the choices, although seeming infinite, are the choices *provided by the monolith without any participation of a human.*

This has a direct impact on human freedom. You are free to select from any of the choices built into the monolith—but you have no way of knowing what these are. (Jacques Lacan would say this is an issue of recognition: such a partner in dialog as the monolith does not reveal whether it recognizes us or not.)

When the computerized gadget of our day—like an advanced radio—first comes into your home, you experience that same initial helplessness in the face of an object that invites but doesn't give a damn whether you take the invitation. It is a constant reminder that there are things in this world to which your being (or not being) is totally without concern. In the face of objects that hide any lawfulness, our freedom is only apparent.

But, you say, at least here there is an instruction booklet. It gives you more choices or permutations of functions than you can shake a stick at. You can do anything with it that the designers want. The multiplicity of possible instructions to follow, however, simply causes a confusion. This multiplicity gets you to confuse infinity with indeterminacy. The infinity of programmed choices allows you to immerse yourself totally in the possibilities built into the gadget, and thus to dive deeply into technology. None of these possibilities, however, are yours: they are first the machine's, and can only secondarily be made yours—within the limits of an alien program whose scope you may never know.

To crack the monolith means first to break yourself and your indeterminate possibilities on the functional shores of an illusive infinity. Just as to speak to bureaucracy, as the living machine, means learning the language of those who animate it, you now need to learn the language of the program.

The makers of such home bureaucracies complain of consumer "resistance" to having to read a 450-page instruction manual to operate a car. The issue, however, is not user resistance—after all, who is more motivated to get the thing moving than a user?—but the fact that electronic gadgets are increasingly produced without a handle to lay a hand on. The faces of faceless gadgets are a mystery to us for exactly the reason that Ludwig Wittgenstein foresaw. Computers, he said, would never be able to engage in human actions. They would never be able to "calculate"—in the sense of strategizing a human course of action. We can never expect a computer to act purposefully the way we would ascribe "calculation" to "a calculating man or woman."

Lacking hands, eyes, ears, arms, and legs—knowing nothing of human activities such as shopping, measuring, accounting, engineering—no computer can be said to enter into the various activities in which the symbols and formulae it prints play a role (Dilman, 1974: 166). The trouble is that the electronic device, unlike the older machine, does not mimic human form—or, if it does mimic it, mimics it only at an invisible level. Such things may fit into a hand. They may be designed to communicate, "I am handy." But they lack visible "handles" by which to grasp them (physically or intellectually). They *look* handy but they are not, in fact, handy. As one respondent on this issue, a schoolteacher, said, "I'm a hands-on person; I learn by doing" (Pam Grainer of Fairfax, Virginia, quoted in Mayer, 2002).

Jean Baudrillard speaks of *simulacra* (see Chapter 2). These are what used to be known as representations (mental images) of things, except that now they have no thing that they represent. Language has begun to use these signs without referent as a conscious tool. Simulacra become bureaucracy's tool. It is a tool without commitment behind it, and yet paying attention to it can be enforced. It is all bark and arbitrary bite—without the dog.

The Word also becomes a self-referential simulacrum: It looks like a word, sounds like a word, is spoken like a word—but it is the quack without the duck. By now we are all acquainted with virtual reality games. They communicate. But what do they communicate? There seems to be something, but in back of it is nothing. Sort of like the stock market.

In short, bureaucracy's language has entered the most intimate corners of our lives. Devices that don't look like a bureaucracy or even a machine demand we approach them in their terms to achieve our goals. After a while, it becomes easier to take the means they offer and to perfect them—immersing ourselves in technique—rather than pursue the ends for which they were designed to begin with.

To the post-modernist, there is closure in this, but perhaps also opportunity that opens up. The closure comes if we fall into the temptation of immersing ourselves in language as technique; then we become ever better sophists, able to argue anything, without aiming at something. But since these devices also force us to guess spontaneously at the meaning of the invisible text they offer, they will—over time—also produce unanticipated and unintended openings.

Yet our immediate experience is not so hopeful. As we submit to the language of the computer, we all become bureaucrats. Is there still room to speak up? (See Dreyfus and Dreyfus, 1988.)

6

The Thought of Bureaucracy: Failure of Imagination

Thinking is a thanking.

—Martin Heidegger

For reason has no dictatorial authority; its verdict is always simply the agreement of free citizens.

—Immanuel Kant

Do androids dream of electric sheep?

—Title of a story by Phillip K. Dick

Bureaucracy replaces thinking. It trains us to look at ourselves as means, not ends. It enframes our thought. Whatever happened to imagination?

Does bureaucracy think? Do bureaucrats think? Do computers think? Such questions focus us on the final stage of modernity. So-called thinking fails to be for the sake of human beings. It is turned into "thinking" *without* human beings: universal use of the computer as the bureaucracy without bureaucrats.

Do computers dream? Would you say your laptop thinks? As a friend put it: Why, no. It computes. It does what it's told to do. It follows orders. We say: Yes, it follows orders—but only if properly saluted. First we must convert human thinking into terms the computer can accept. To dream and to fully think, both require imagination. And don't we hope that the computer doesn't start "imagining" things? Why, that would be for the computer to crash. But aren't we told the brain is like a computer? And don't most of us believe that?

These issues are not academic ones. Computers reach around the globe, and they reach into our minds. Each one of us carries a computer around or is wired to one. We get to surpass the thought of our best thinkers only by going through that thought. What kinds of thoughts can we think through computers? What can't we think?

When we compare bureaucratic thinking and computer thinking, we find they are the same. Bureaucratic thinking now has expanded beyond institutional walls: to the world and to ourselves. The three domains of bureaucracy now are:

- Traditional bureaucracy: The home of live bureaucrats.

- Laptop bureaucracy: The exodermic brain. You carry it with you.

- Global bureaucracy: It greets you wherever you go.

Thinking

One of my favorite cartoons shows two groundskeepers at work at a college. They are picking up paper using pointed sticks with a nail at the end. It is a college because you can see, in the background, people in caps and gowns looking professorial, and students looking not. The one groundskeeper says to the other: "Now them professors. They think we don't know nothin'. But some of them don't even *suspect* nothing."

For modern human beings, to think is to combine, but to know is to think with content. So writes the great philosopher of modernity Immanuel Kant. Thinking as combining calls for logic; thinking with content calls for sensibility to the world. But both, Kant says, have their root in imagination. For it is when we put our imagination to use that we construct the schemas within which what we later come to know is allowed to appear. Such schemas must allow for both logic and for sensibility to have their say. When sensibility is muted, logic tries to determine the world (Kant, 1781/1787: A 124; Heidegger, 1973: 196; Arendt, 1982: 81).

In this last move lies the fatal attraction of bureaucratic thinking: if only our logic could think the world into existence, then we would have control. But then we would be God. "What is wrong with that?" the bureaucrat says.

The Beginning of Thought

What we combine when we think is ideas. These are about ourselves and our human world. Note that it is a *human* world. We take an idea here and an idea there, combine them, subtract them, add them, to see what new ideas the combination gives us.

All such thinking, however, is empty. It is a rearranging of our mental furniture: statements *in* logic, statements *about* how to grab hold of reality. In batting about these statements of logic, our mind—the powerful engine that creates the certain knowledge of science—is in neutral and idling. Unless we fill such statements with content *from* reality, we may be thinking, but we are not engaged in an act of knowing at all.

Knowing

To know is to combine logic with content. In coming to know things— what is out there, how matters stand—we combine our way of thinking with material from reality. Because our tool for grabbing hold of reality is always "our way of thinking," because we are merely human, the resulting knowledge is always only knowledge *for us*. It is not how a god would know, nor is it how a Martian would.

Computer "Thinking"

For whom does the computer think? On behalf of whom does the bureaucrat claim to know? The two questions now come together. For the personal computer now makes bureaucratic demands on us; it is a bureaucracy without bureaucrats.

Mostly none of us as yet believes that a computer knows, though we sometimes slip in that a direction. We do not as yet believe it knows reality the way a human does, or that it knows what it is doing. The best we can say for computers is that their logic may provide the pigeonholes which when stuffed with data may show some kind of pattern. It is still we—human beings—who must judge whether and how the pattern has meaning *for us*.

But there is another, more dangerous alternative. Believing computers are somehow superior to us (faster, more efficient, and so forth), we may dumb down our knowledge operations to resemble the "thinking" operation of computers. While this may seem farfetched, we already have in front of us two well-established examples: our grudging submission to bureaucratic thinking and our unawareness that computer thinking is equally bureaucratic.

Bureaucratic thinking operates on behalf of human purposes. These, however, had to be converted into the terms a formalistic system could handle. In converted form, they are now the system's own purposes. So justice is converted into law, faring well into welfare, peace into permanent readiness for war, psychological health into normalcy, and so on—as has already been shown in Chapter 3. These are well-established machine purposes—whether of the bureaucratic machine or the computer as bureaucracy without bureaucrats. Our purposes, by the time they are translated into systems terms, are no longer ours. Successful application of a program has standards, but these are systems standards, and the resulting knowledge (of success or failure) is no longer knowledge *for us*—unless we start to think like computers or bureaucrats.

The parallel between computers and bureaucratic systems is evident: for both systems human purposes have to be converted into terms the program can handle. The full spirit of reason is reduced to mere instrumental logic. Only then can the system proceed to process what are now data *for it*, and produce outputs that are successful *for it* but are no longer *for the sake of* human beings. Where the freedom to imagine frameworks of human purposes is itself enframed in systems ordering our thought, reason dries up, and logic runs rampant. This truncated reason itself reinforces the order that constricts our thought (Figure 6.1). Reason now weighs in on the side of order instead of the side of freedom, where human beings find liberty to formulate their own order freely and without external compulsion.

In short, programmed reasoning of bureaucracy is made even more programmed in the computer. While thinking and knowing in the first still require some sensibility as to where to apply the program (according to its own criteria), in the second all sensibility is left to the human operator. To make this clear let us begin with how bureaucrats think.

How Bureaucrats Think

How do bureaucrats think? Knowing this would help many a citizen trying to get the goods. It would also help the politician charged with exercising oversight, the manager figuring out what functionaries are up to, functionaries trying to read the mind of the manager.

Figure 6.1   **Pendulum Swing of "Reason"**

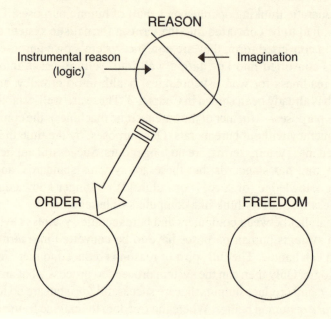

In the constellation . . .

REASON

Instrumental reason   Imagination
(logic)

ORDER   FREEDOM

. . . the weight of reason now shifts toward order.

Bureaucrats and Citizens

Is there such a thing as bureaucratic thought? What for example was the bureaucrat thinking who caused the story of the bureaucrat and the batboy? (See Exhibit 6.1.)

Here we can see the bureaucrat reasoning. Noticeably, when we look at his or her mental exercises, we will observe that the bureaucrat thinks but does not know. He or she applies a finished program standard to a reality, but does not allow reality to speak for itself. The business of monitoring reality is equated to a picture of it. But will the business of creating a picture of reality stand the test of reality?

In short, the reality of batboys and baseball does not have any say at all in bureaucratic thinking—except as they become raw material for a case. We simply lay a program rule alongside the given information.

Exhibit 6.1

Batboy Is Called Out;
U.S. Is Reviewing Law

ATLANTA, May 27—Facing accusations that insensitive bureaucrats were trampling on the national pastime, the United States Department of Labor says it is reconsidering the case of a 14-year-old Georgia batboy who was sacked after his employment was found to run afoul of child-labor laws.

Shortly after a local newspaper published an article about the Class A Savannah Cardinals' new 14-year-old batboy early this month, a Labor Department official told the team that their employment of Tommy McCoy violated child-labor laws, which state that 14- and 15-year-olds must not work past 7 on school nights or 9 during the summer.

The club reluctantly dismissed the boy, who had papered the walls of his room with pictures of team members even before being hired, and put a 16-year-old in his job. Other minor league clubs, many in the same situation, ducked for cover amid fears of a nationwide crackdown.

The article set off a blizzard of local and then national publicity, and Labor Secretary Robert B. Reich issued a statement Wednesday that termed the application of child-labor laws to batboys "silly." A department spokeswoman, Mary Meagher, said today that the Department of Labor will not enforce any hourly violations in organized baseball pending a review of the law.

Mr. Reich said: "The application of child-labor laws in the case of 14-year-old batboys does, at first glance, look silly. It is not the intent of the law to deny young teen-agers employment opportunities so long as their health and well-being are not impaired."

The Cardinals' general manager, Ric Sisler, whose team has a 32–14 record in the South Atlantic League and a nine-game winning streak, seems to be making the best of things. The dispute has been a publicity windfall. Tommy threw out the first ball at the Cardinals' Wednesday night game, and Friday has been designated as "Save Tommy's Job Night" at the Cardinals' 8,500-seat Grayson Stadium.

The aim is to see if the case can be subsumed under the rule. It is the bureaucratic ethic, and the organization's strength, that nothing in reality can be allowed to bend the rule. Were something to do so, this control institution would fade away. It would lose its consistency, its predictability, its rationality as an instrument. It would lose its purpose—part of which is to allow us to know ahead of time what is allowed and what prohibited—a handy thing to know, for example, when you are transporting a thousand pounds of frozen fish across state lines.

The bureaucrat is not in the business of knowing. That was supposed to have been taken care of by lawmakers when they looked at reality and made a rule for it. The politics/administration dichotomy may have been long buried—certainly there is politics in the creative sense in bureaucracy—but to the extent that competing political interests pervade a bureaucracy, it ceases to be a control instrument for those in nominal control.

For the most part, the bureaucrat is expected to reason by analogy. Analogic reasoning applies a rule the mind uses to reflect from one object to an entirely different object. So, for example, we may propose:

Children are to work

as

Batboys are to baseball

This kind of reasoning may give some insight into both baseball and work. It focuses on their differences and similarities. But it cannot say, baseball is work. Just because the same *relation* exists between terms of the two statements, we cannot therefore infer that baseball and work are the same reality. That both are the same, or not, is determinable only empirically. Yet the bureaucrat assumes that the two are the same, and that therefore the same rule applies.

Bureaucrats and Nations

Every country is pretty much like any other country. If you have just returned from Paris after visiting Hong Kong, you will know this statement is false. It is, however, treated as true when the International Monetary Fund decides whether to give support to one country rather than another. The rules of capital reinvestment economics are thought to apply everywhere. That they don't has been exposed by former world finance bureaucrats themselves (for example, Stiglitz, 2002).

The Thought of Bureaucracy

The world is the product of freedom. Reason can fix this product by drawing on its power to order, but it can make itself a picture of what that product might be only by drawing on the imagination. In short, reason cannot *determine* reality, but it can *regulate* our thought of it. This was the thinking of Immanuel Kant two hundred years ago. It has changed the way we think of the world. We no longer view the world as either a product of our ideas or the imprint of sensations stamped onto our mind. The world is a synthesis of reason and the empirical.

Bureaucracy's use of reason takes us back two centuries. Bureaucratic reason tries to tell us what our world is like. It seeks to determine where it has legitimate power only to regulate. Modern organization, in other words, has turned into a latter-day form of idealism—a way of knowing the world that reduces us to functions of an idea—shadows on the wall of Plato's cave.

Kant himself encountered this threat to human experience. He found himself in a situation in which idealists claimed ideas could determine what was in the world, while empiricists claimed sense impressions could determine what was in our mind. By asking each side to leave some of its claims behind, he created a new domain—a second nature—in which both ideas and the empirical could play a role. If they wanted to get the certain knowledge offered by this synthetic reality, both sides would be asked to leave key claims behind.

The empiricists would be asked to bring with them from out of their explorations of the world only those aspects of things that could be sensed (phenomena) and leave behind what they could not know (noumena, the things themselves).

The idealists were granted their claim of having direct access to things in themselves, but these now were restricted to the higher reaches of the mind—and would be confined there. They would be asked to abandon their claim that the categories of thinking derived from them could *determine* the world. Instead, they would have to be satisfied with the restriction that ideas might help reason *regulate* the acquisition of knowledge (in the understanding) but could not *determine* that knowledge.

To return now to the previous state of the theory of knowledge would also mean to shrink our picture of what it means to be human. Yet this is exactly the state to which modern organizations would have us return. It is at this root level that post-modern philosophers make a difference because they freely question what has distorted the original perspective of modern philosophy on who and what we are and can be. We begin with the original modern view (Kant) followed by the self-criticism of two philosophers born into modernity but seeking a way out of it through it: Edmund Husserl and Martin Heidegger. Only then do we turn to a post-modernist.

What the Experts Say

What does it mean to say bureaucracy replaces thinking? Thinking is about something. A danger is implied. Just what is the danger, and to whom?

Modern Critique: Kant, Husserl, Heidegger

In thinking, as in speaking, we may be heading in a direction where thinking is no thinking at all. Instead, those who have thought most deeply about thinking—philosophers—suggest an inherent tendency in modern thinking to remove itself from ordinary life. Initially this is the source of the legitimate power of science. Beyond this it is the source of the power of elites.

By looking at the world through the lenses of only a few factors at a time, science wins clarity and coherence in forming a picture of how things work according to its assumptions about the world. Ultimately, however, playing with such pictures—analyzing them, reassembling them—becomes a technical preoccupation. The result is neglect of the problem of how applying such pictures helps us lead a more human life.

There is, from the beginning of modern science applied to management, a split in thinking. There are those who play with abstract pictures—in bureaucracy: managers. There are those who have to apply such pictures in real and complicated contexts for human purposes: workers.

Increasingly we recognize a disadvantage that the division into purported thinkers and mere doers gives us: in the aggregate, less knowledge than an organization is capable of. The claim of elites to power rests on the basis of having acquired a trained monopoly over thinking. With this monopoly comes a trained arrogance that casts a long and darkening shadow over the full reality of things. A mighty effort separating thinking from the immersion in doing was necessary in the early stage of science.

People turned to science because of problems they had with controlling the conditions of daily life. Their task was to raise themselves out of the confusing manifold of sensations that constitute the ongoing flow of living; they sought to win a clear view. This was offered by the scientific perspective, which takes a look at only a few well-defined factors at a time. Today that clear perspective, but also its detachment from the flow of life, is dominant.

The problem now is how to rejoin science's findings back to the problems of real life. This is also the problem for bureaucracy: How can its functioning be brought back into how we live life?

To answer this question, we draw on three philosophers who probe the relevance of science—and its form of thinking—to life. Their insights fail to justify the obstinately recalcitrant knowledge elite that today dominates not only science but technology and modern organization based on a division of labor between those who think and those who do.

Immanuel Kant is the first to be critical of a split between the function of being in touch with reality and the function of analyzing what we are in touch with: the split between knowing and thinking. His insights challenge today's division between a management that claims it thinks while workers merely do. Thinking, Kant shows, is not possible without content that comes from doing.

Edmund Husserl, writing 150 years after Kant, gives us a further insight into what is wrong with our modern thinking. Accepting Kant's critique of thinking, Husserl predicted the current crisis of quality as the inevitable product of the conversion of science into technique.

In turn, Husserl's student Martin Heidegger suggests how we can rethink our thinking to escape from the modern preoccupation with technique that functions to the detriment of getting good work done. All these critiques are also critiques of the thinking of modern organization.

Kant: Thinking and Knowing

The most clearly recognized problem of today's organizations is the inability to produce products and services *for* human beings despite ever more sophisticated quantitative controls. This is the crisis of quality. It is ironic that this was anticipated as a result of modern thinking by a philosopher looking at the rise of science more than two hundred years ago.

At first this is a story of the liberation of the mind: enlightenment. With the successes of the first modern experiments, wrote Immanuel Kant, a

light dawned on all researchers into nature (B xiii).* Like the early geo-
metricians who inspired all modern science (B xii), they understood the
need to lift a clear picture of things out of a turgid and chaotic manifold
of sense impression. The researcher achieves this not by leaping into the
fray of things but by making clear to himself first what he is looking for.
Instead of trying to read off all possible properties from things before
him, he studies only those properties that his own preconceptualization
(the hypothesis) alerts him to (B xii).

Only in this way would the picture, also called the concept, be totally
clear: for the researcher, backed by empirical tests, could make it so. He
is like a fisherman who constructs a net from factors that promise good
fishing. The net is the searching concept the researcher dips into the sea
of reality. The shape of the net determines what objects he catches. But
for the net to prove itself, it finally must be dipped: It is good only when
it is full.

Besides clarity, the scientific procedure got a good grasp on those parts
of reality it was designed to net. The experiment demanded that every
concept be tested out against actual data given by reality and captured in
the conceptual net. Pursuing the metaphor of the net, we might say, with
today's commercial fisherman, that a net woven to precise specifications
makes sure that only the fish for which the net was designed stay in it.
Kant himself used the metaphor of the courtroom:

> Reason, holding in one hand its principles, according to which alone
> concordant appearances can be admitted as equivalent laws, and in the
> other hand the experiment which it has devised in accordance with these
> principles, must approach nature in order to be taught by it. It must not,
> however, do so in the character of a pupil who listens to everything that
> the teacher chooses to say, but of an appointed judge who compels the
> witnesses to answer questions which he has himself formulated. (B xiii;
> Kant, 1965: 20)

Fans of the television series *Dragnet* may recall Sgt. Friday's injunction
to witnesses: "Just the facts, ma'am, just the facts." He did not mean all
the facts but only those that were relevant to a picture of the crime that
was already in his mind, either confirming or disconfirming it.

---

*The form of references in this section is the standard one for Kant's *Kritik der reinen
Vernunft* (Kant, 1781/1787), with A referring to the first edition followed by the page
number and B referring to the second edition.

By keeping a precise and clear construction of reality in mind, and forcing reality to respond (or not) to it, and measuring the degree of congruence, the modern scientist avoided the complexity, confusion, and fuzziness of being fully immersed in reality. (Soon, impressed by those things science could do successfully, society itself shifted its values to honor those things. Things that science could not do were devalued by society also.)

The scientist had separated from the worker, who did have to face the problems of tracing out the moves specified by a blueprint in all the fuzzy complexity and confusion of reality. Even and especially today, the management scientist can promise the worker, "If you precisely follow the procedures we have outlined for the limited set of factors in the blueprint, you will achieve the conditions of coherence and variance among those factors that we predict in the blueprint." But no management scientist can know the moves a worker needs to make to bridge the gap between the clear scientific picture and the complex reality.

Kant anticipated this in distinguishing between thinking and knowing. Today, in our organizations of strict hierarchy and division of labor, we believe the engineer or scientifically guided manager thinks while the worker *does*. Kant knew better and would contend the worker *knows*.

"To *think* an object and to *know* an object are thus by no means the same thing," Kant concluded in his *Critique of Pure Reason* (B 146). "Knowledge involves two factors: first, the concept, through which an object in general is thought (the category); and secondly, the intuition, through which it is given."

Clearly, since today's managers are cut off from direct sensory organizing (intuition) of reality, they only *think*, they do not *know*. In fact the problem often is that they think they know.

By the knowing of intuition Kant did not mean what today we popularly mean by a sudden flash of insight. He meant the way the mind organized and looked at sense data within the categories of time and space. This initial on-looking provides a view (literally, *Anschauung*) that makes a flowing reality stand still long enough for specific objects to be broken out of the complex flow. The objects then can be brought before the cold eye of reason to be analyzed into their component parts or related to one another according to a model or hypothesis.

But, unless the thinking part of the mind (reason) provides a picture ahead of time, what is broken out of reality cannot be organized for the purpose of further analysis. For this reason Kant concludes that, for anything to be understood, reason and intuition have to work together, for "thoughts without content are empty, intuitions without concepts are blind" (A 51–52; B 75–76).

Because of this does Kant "distinguish the science of the rules of sensibility in general, that is, aesthetic, from the science of the rules of the understanding in general, that is, logic" (B 77; A 52). The former makes knowing possible, the latter is thinking—at least as far as modern science is concerned. Unless the two work together no reality-related knowledge is possible.

Splitting thinking and knowing has serious consequences in modern organizations. There it is indeed the assumption that managers think while workers. . . . Well, what do workers do? Workers *do*, don't they? With the crisis of quality recognized since Japanese management, quality circles, Theory Z, search for excellence, and total quality management, we realize what Kant had already tried to alert us to: In the search for quality, those with the aesthetic sense—who can say, "This feels right"—have a great advantage. But these, in the hierarchically split organization, are: workers.

Only those who approach reality directly through their senses *know* directly, that is, have the sense or the feel—Kant would say an intuition—of it. Quality understood as *what* something *is* in relation to the working human being presents itself to that human being first. And that understanding can be communicated to management only in terms of words, concepts. Since concepts are considered clarified by numbers, worker knowledge tends to be qualitative while manager thinking tends to be quantitative.

Modern organizations separate the thinking function radically from working. Kant had already damned such a result. Management is confined to exercising "a faculty, therefore, which by itself knows nothing whatsoever, but merely combines and arranges the material of knowledge, that is, the intuition, which must be given to it by the object" (B 145).

If management, therefore, is dependent on what is communicated by workers about what they do, then management is truly in the dangerous position of being isolated in pure reason. Research may fill managers' concepts. But what can such research tell them about instructing workers in the handholds of implementation that only working experience can give them knowledge of?

The problem for workers is that managerial minds, empty of working experience through which alone objects can be known, give them the orders as to how to do their work—and evaluate their success.

To understand our crisis in the effective production of private goods and public services, we needed to go no farther than Kant to find the causes. In organizations that split thinking and knowing, our managers live in a never-never land of concepts, while workers are desperately trying to take blueprints, based on those concepts but irrelevant to working itself, into a recalcitrant but very real reality. But, oh no, why bother with philosophers?! They, after all, are so irrelevant to real life! Aren't they?

Husserl: The Thinking of Science, Technique, and Bureaucracy

Another way of understanding the thinking of modern organization comes from a second warning about the split between science and life issued toward the beginning of the twentieth century. The mathematician and philosopher Edmund Husserl had begun to investigate how the split worked itself out in everyday life.

In the chaotic world between the two World Wars, it could escape no one that science, in becoming ever more sophisticated, had become increasingly irrelevant to basic concerns of leading a meaningful human life. Amazingly powerful and historically unique as a way of producing and controlling the material world from the outside, modern thought as epitomized in science did not, as Husserl pointed out, address such questions as the inner meaning of life, the reason or unreason of human beings, the human being as free subject.

Today we might say that science, in all the things it gives us, cannot answer the question "What's it to me?" In other words, science cannot demonstrate the necessity of the things it produces to being human. Only the human being can testify to any such need. But in our day that human being has surrendered its judgment to science: Anything science can produce we want. And so it is that the human being adapts itself to science rather than science being adapted to human needs.

In his book *The Crisis of the European Sciences*, Husserl pointed out the paradox in an ineluctable though somewhat Germanic question:

> Can the world, and human existence in it, truthfully have a meaning if the sciences recognize as true only what is objectively established in this fashion, and if history has nothing more to teach us than that all the shapes of the spiritual world, all the conditions of life, ideals, norms upon which man relies, form and dissolve themselves like fleeting waves, that it always was and ever will be so, that again and again reason must turn into nonsense, and well-being into misery? (Husserl, 1970 [1937]: 6–7)

Science's role in these failures needed to be explained, especially in view of its influence on the design of modern organizations.

Husserl's critique can be put this way: We are committed as a culture to declare real only that which science can establish. But every time we conclude a scientific experiment, there is a pause. During this rest from science, ordinary human beings get along perfectly well without doing any science. In fact such pauses constitute the vast majority of the moments in which we live. Even science takes its point of departure from such ordinarily lived moments. And its findings, to be useful, must be capable of being translated back into the world of ordinary human life. Science therefore is far removed as a way of thinking about the world from the way we actually live in the world—and so is any organization designed on scientific principles of understanding work.

But, how do these judgments about the existence of different types of thinking relate to the critique of bureaucracy?

How Do Ordinary Folk Think? We have already observed a conflict between bureaucratic thinking and the ordinary thinking of everyday people, even of bureaucrats when they put on civilian clothes and empathize with clients. Husserl's work suggests this conflict can be understood if we understand science and everyday thinking better. First, ordinary everyday thinking must be understood.

While thinking in the everyday world, each one of us experiences things from his or her own point of view. Things look different from the perspective of each one of us, though we assume that what we see are aspects of the same world.

These are two constituent assumptions about the nature of the world. Inasmuch as these assumptions—about perspective and the given oneness of the world—determine our thinking, ordinary thinking differs sharply from scientific thinking.

Scientific thinking grants no validity to subjective thinking. It insists on objective thinking as a necessary procedure for doing something the rest of us take for granted. It aims at *proving* the coherence of the world. And, with a vehemence the rest of us consider unnecessary, it seeks *total certainty.* Of these differences later.

Here the point is that ordinary folks have their own way of thinking. Science deprecates such thinking as lacking validity. We ourselves often subscribe to the idea that our thinking is more secure if it is scientifically tested. But daily life does not wait for science. Somehow we manage to open doors, grab coffee cups, walk—without engaging in a hundred experiments of scientific testing of our perceptions, observations, conceptualizations, and conclusions and prescriptions for action.

It surprises the scientist in us that we do not simply kill ourselves as we go barreling around the next curve of our immediate future, without scientific test or rationalistic plan. But the fact that we survive proves that our ordinary way of thinking is just good enough for our purposes. This is exactly Husserl's point when he speaks up on behalf of the experience and thinking of ordinary people.

Not only does such thinking exist but it has its own legitimacy. Such thinking, he concludes, has its own standards of validity, "which are just as secure as necessary for the practical projects of life that determine their sense" (Husserl, 1970 [1937]: 125).

Science, Technique, and Bureaucratic Procedure. To the extent that bureaucracy expresses the same way of thinking about reality as does science, since both are very much parts of the modern world view, Husserl also speaks about bureaucracy. His argument requires following through a series of steps.

In modern scientific thinking we purposefully compare what we find in nature to models we already have constructed of it. For more exact comparing we measure. Measurement enables us to create *formulas* determining how elements of the *model* relate to each other and how reality relates to model: "If one has the formulae, one already possesses, in advance, the practically desired prediction of what is to be expected with empirical certainty in the intuitively given world of concretely actual life" (Husserl, 1970 [1937]: 43).

The totality of such a reducing of reality to measurement is the creation of a "formula world." Thinking of the real world in this way so far removes the scientist from real life as to create a concept that Husserl describes as "the formal-logical idea of a world-in-general." We are reminded of $E = mc^2$. But we hardly need remind ourselves how distant that formula is from our everyday experience of the world as particular to, and meaningful only from, our varying perspectives.

Against immersion in the formula world even scientists have revolted, especially Richard P. Feynman. The Nobel laureate in physics wrote in this connection: "We know so very much and then subsume it into so very few equations that we can say we know very little" (Feynman in Gleick, 1993: 325). But whereas the true scientist escapes into discovery, where instinct and knowledge both rule, there are enough equations for the bureaucrats of science—technicians—to immerse themselves in the details of calculation.

Eventually, Husserl (1970 [1937]: 48) shows, the original algebraic arithmetic of reducing reality to formulas is pushed to its "most extreme extension." This world of figures becomes referential only to itself. Its functionaries—technicians—focus on problems internal to the coherence and consistency of the formulas with themselves. (Today we are well acquainted with this phenomenon in the internal tests for validity used in social statistics regardless of their relevance to the world; similarly, bureaucrats use tests for the internal coherence and consistency of procedure without concern for its external adequacy.)

Scientists are reduced to technicians and become preoccupied with technique. Concern for the appropriateness of the models they use or their impact on the reality they study recedes into the background. (We can already anticipate the parallel to bureaucrats' preoccupation with procedure, selling short both the intent of policy and program outcomes in the reality administered.)

In the technization of science, increased attention is paid to the comparing of models and reality. Science is reduced to "a sort of *technique*" (46; Husserl's emphasis). But "technique is . . . a mere art of achieving . . . results the genuine sense of whose truth can be attained only by concretely intuitive* thinking actually directed at the subject matter itself" (46). In short, technique may declare an operation a success, but this claim ultimately can be tested only if we look to see whether or not the patient died. Similarly, a bureaucracy may have used perfect procedure but the baby in the welfare office in Chapter 1 nevertheless died. In neither case is there bad technique or bad procedure, nor even are there bad people: There are only good technicians and good bureaucrats who have lost any sense of the human purposes for which systems of science or bureaucracy are established.

As technique comes out of science, bureaucratic procedure comes out of policy. It is striking that technique in science functions just the same as does procedure in bureaucracy. The bureaucrat also has a model. It is the policy or the program. This defines ahead of time what can become real. The program or policy model is given; it is then the task of the bu-

---

*We will recall here, with Kant, that intuition (*Anschauung*) or "onlooking" means the primary organizing of direct experience of reality.

reaucrat to measure the distance or divergence that each relevant aspect of a client has from the model. Some potential clients too uncharacteristic of the model simply fall through the mesh. And like fish falling through the net, they lack the required surface characteristics—size, qualities such as roughness—that can snag a mesh of the net. Such outliers never become congruent with their picture contained in the model. They are, in terms of the model, unreal and must be ignored. Potential clients that do match the model are serviced: They are real.

Bureaucratic reasoning is fundamentally by analogy. The functionary compares the attributes of a "case" against the parameters of a program. We can also say that, in its concern with the measurement of reality against models, scientific reasoning is by analogy. Science is always a measuring of the divergence that actual objects have from the parameters of ideal models. Bureaucratic thinking and scientific thinking are very much of a piece. So are their limits.

Limits of Science. From the beginning, Husserl shows, modern science distances itself from how ordinary folk experience reality. This is so because science is not concerned with the particular behavior of anything in particular. In contrast, each ordinary human being is first of all concerned with things as they particularly affect that individual. Science—especially the queen of sciences, physics, on which modern sciences are modeled—is not concerned with any specific body. Instead it seeks to build the general formula governing the behavior of all bodies of that type. "One is not concerned," Husserl (1970 [1937]: 41) writes of physics, "with the free fall of *this* body; the individual fact is rather an *example.*"

One of the staunchest proponents of science, Bertrand Russell (1968: 19), agrees with this evaluation: "It is time to say something about scientific method. Science is concerned to discover general laws, and it is interested in particular facts chiefly as evidence for or against such laws." What a particular body is an example of is the formula or model constructed out of everything about any classified type of thing that can be captured in terms of its generality and measured in similar terms. This approach gives science immense power to penetrate (explain), predict, and control things or events *to the extent that their behavior is dependent on general rules or laws.*

But that same science does not give us knowledge of what to do when a particular one of such things or events has to be handled on the spot.

Science can design the general rules of jobs; it cannot advise how to apply such rules in the particular instance of work.

Such occasions science calls examples or accidents; but from the viewpoint of the ordinary client or the working individual, work is not an example and the world is full of such accidents. In fact, true managers are said to earn their money not through following routines but through using their brains to deal with the nonroutine. "We are not paid for doing what we are told to do, but for doing rightly that part of our job which is left to our discretion; and we rate our own and our fellows' jobs on our estimate of the weight of this discretionary element" (Jacques, 1983: 200). Elliot Jacques, to whom this observation is owed, found in one study that among all jobs, from the highest to the lowest, not one fails to involve some elements of discretion, some duty, essential to its performance that is not and cannot be specified in the instructions given to the holder.

Implications of Husserl for Bureaucracy. In summary, bureaucracy, like science, is distant from real life because its thinking tends toward distance from that of real life. This distance can be summarized in two ways:

1. Bureaucracy models reality. Its original modeling of reality becomes the standard for recognizing reality as something that is real *to* the model.
2. Bureaucracy, in time, becomes preoccupied with procedure. This dedication of its functionaries is entirely natural in view of human beings' tendency to immerse themselves in the infinite variety of technical problems that a technical approach opens up. But its focus on means rather than ends leads to a lack of concern with functionaries' own origin in real-life problems, for the solving of which the model was originally formed, and also the impact of the solutions.

As does technique in science, so does procedure in bureaucracy overshadow problem statement (policy intent) and solution (program outcome). Technique in science or logical procedure in modern organization truly is the art of achieving *precisely* what we want without due care for the human consequences. To the extent that people allow themselves to become functionaries of bureaucracy, they fail to ask the question that concerns us all: Why are we doing all this? In turning from everyday thinking, bureaucrats fail to be what Husserl (1970 [1937]: 17) called "functionaries of mankind."

Heidegger: Experience as Escape from
Bureaucratic Thinking

How can we think our way out of scientific, technological, and bureaucratic ways of thinking? This question concerns Martin Heidegger. (The
discussion here is based on Heidegger, 1984, and 1962: §54–60.) Thinking about it, he takes a different point of departure than does scientific
thinking. Scientific thinking defines what we are in terms of essences.
Ultimately the definition of any specific human being scientifically tends
to be reduced to discovering the constituent parts or the rules for how
the parts hang together: principles. These are supposed to be *essentials*
that make up the human being. Knowledge of these, science hopes, can
ultimately be reduced to a formula: for example, the genetic code. The
human being, however, does not experience life at the level of DNA.

In real life, even geneticists do not experience themselves in terms of
the genetic code. The attempt to reduce human life to essential building
blocks or formulas falls short of how we feel, sense, think our daily lives.
Science falls short of covering experience.

Say this is fundamentally so. Then to use science to understand what
human beings need, and to design methods of delivering it to them, can
suit human beings at best only accidentally. There is no automatic meshing between our experience of what we need and what science can know
about that experience.

But what if we then want to rethink scientifically designed delivery
systems? The first step would be to obtain a picture of *experience*. It may
then be possible to design delivery systems that fit human experience
rather than change it.

Heidegger shows that the experience of being human points not to
formulas but to just the opposite: openness, the undetermined nature of
the human being. Human experience, far from being reducible to a closed
formula, is wide open. Into this openness each of us throws him- or herself
every day. This hurling oneself ahead of oneself requires resoluteness
and courage; of this science knows nothing.

This is a point of departure from science. Heidegger's phenomenological approach—approaching things in their own terms—emphasizes
experience as the basis of the human being's own self-understanding.

We are reminded that we are able to rethink ourselves in terms of our
actual openness to future possibilities. For the human being, existence
itself does not turn around this or that constitution of being but turns

around the "freedom *for*" the ability to be. This has implications for organizations.

The Caring Organization. The lesson for organizations is clear. No organization can serve human beings if it proceeds from an already finished model of the human being; any organization in the service of human beings must allow these human beings to remain essentially open.

This does *not* mean a return to Social Darwinism and a noninterventionist state, government, or administration that lets an individual hang and twist in the wind as if he or she were alone in the world. Rather what is espoused is opening up a path on which each individual can recover his or her own freedom to be human *with* and *among* others (Heidegger, 1962: §25–27).

Nor does this mean a suffocating immersion in some kind of socialism. What Heidegger wants us to appreciate is our own experience: I feel myself to be most myself when I am suspended in the most caring relations with others, as in love or terror, guilt or courage (Gelven, 1989: 119).

Also, we are least ourselves when we treat others as objects. The task for the work of helping human beings be all they can be (for Americans there is here an echo of Abraham Maslow) therefore is not, as it would be if subject and object were separated by nature, to act as a kind of transportation medium that brings self and others together. The task is to help me develop for and by myself that form of self-awareness in which I recognize my original presence in the world as the being that is already in the company of others. Care opens up to that being with others.

Policy and Program Implications of Care. What is care? It is not possible to be myself unless I care for myself. What I care for when I care for myself is the maintaining and development of my innermost ability to be. That innermost ability to be is always oriented toward the future. The past has already made us what we are. We experience what we have become in the twinkling of an eye in the present. But what we are able to yet be is open only in the future. Therefore I care most for myself when I orient myself toward what I can yet become in the future. Without a future, the being that I am would have no possibilities, only actualities already enacted. My innermost definition of my being is therefore the exercise of the utmost openness of myself toward my future. By caring about my being in future terms, I open myself to all the possibilities of being that only the future can open up for me.

This has direct consequences for my responsibility in caring for others. Others also have their future. If I deprive them of it, by defining them in terms of what they were or have become, I limit not only their future but their innermost ability to be. There are, therefore, two ways of caring for others: caring as a standing in for others until they can get back on their feet and caring as taking the place of others, in effect displacing them (Heidegger, 1984: §39–44, 61–66).

This also has clear-cut implications for organizations. These perform the work through which a society cares for those in its midst who need help with their future. But this is all of us, whether this may involve concerns of national security (which ensures life itself) or the various forms of government regulation of the economy (which ensures the wherewithal for life) or the various forms of the so-called caring professions: psychiatry, health, welfare, education.

The guideline for programs of care is to be true to the human being's innermost truth. This is that each human being comes into its own only when it is free to look to a future to be and enact itself in the direction of that future. An enabling organization can be judged according to two standards: Is it engaged in the kind of caring in which the organization stands *in* for people in order to allow them to get back on their own feet and conduct their own lives? Or is it engaged in the kind of deficient caring in which the organization *takes over* people's lives and converts them into permanent clients, that is, examples of models of clients contained in policy programs?

To this latter kind of caring belongs all bureaucratic organization. By its nature, bureaucracy is a delivery instrument for programs predesigned from beginning to end for people in terms of their past. Only such programs can be applied in a way in which those carrying them out can judge whether the tools they assign themselves have actually been carried through, which is what we mean by control.

This does not mean that *all* predesigned programs condemn clients to live up to the past. Programs can be predesigned that leave the actual working out of that program open *for* the client. This opening *toward* the client helps orient him or her toward the future. But such programs cannot be bureaucratically administered. They cannot be subjected to the ultimate judgment to which every bureaucracy is subjected: Did you or did you not follow the rules—carry out the instrumental means of the program the way they were predesigned? The answer to such a question will determine the extent to which bureaucracy has exercised proper control over the program and is accountable to policy makers, but it says nothing about the *outcome* of a program.

All activities that determine the actual *outcome* of a program must be left to at least minimal participation by the enacting individual client helped by the worker.

Implications for Program Evaluation. In terms of prevailing statistical methodology of program evaluation, the evaluator of a program properly designed to help ensure the well-being of human beings is confronted, in the client's freedom to be, not with an *intervening* variable but with a variable unheard of in logic or statistics. Basing ourselves on phenomenology's fundamental insight into what makes us a human being—namely the freedom to be itself—we may call this an *originating* variable.

Beyond a certain point any supportive program cannot go. Beyond that point it is not possible to draw causal chains. Beyond that point no functionary of a program can be held accountable for what happens. What happens—that which comes into its own—is not up to the caring program but is up to what the client does with it. At that point all the caring program can do is get out of the client's way. This is well expressed in the epitaph for a program manager spoken in *The Soul of a New Machine:* "He set up the opportunity and he didn't stand in anybody's way" (Kidder, 1982: 274). Or, in the words often repeated by organization theorist David Carnevale: "Don't buy a fish for them, teach them how to fish. Don't try to control their lives, build capacity" (personal communication).

But at that moment, the client ceases to be a client and again becomes what the caring policy originally wanted: a human being capable of enacting his or her own future with an eye to preserving and enacting the freedom to be. At that moment, welfare programs take a turn and go beyond their own program standards: to produce either people faring well or faring ill. But so do defense programs. In a sense the quality of the original welfare program determines people's ability to pick up from where it leaves them off—to either fare well or fare ill, to be capable of defense or to be defenseless. But in a most profound sense that is *their* choice; no one can make the choice for them. I can procure for you the means to be happy, but I cannot—nor can anyone—make you be happy. I can help find the support to recover your authenticity, but I cannot force you into being yourself. I can outline, through reasoning and pointing to your own experience, what it means to be, but I cannot make you into a human being that confronts the choices and the terrors of what it means to face up to your being. Finally, I can teach you, but I cannot learn you.

This also applies to rethinking the design of organizations internally. Workers can be enabled to do good work, but they cannot be forced to do good work.

Post-Modern Critique: Derrida

The post-modernist Jacques Derrida, in exposing the border violations of reason, cuts to the heart of the great modern experiment. Moderns trust reason as the umbrella covering all thought. To expose when reason goes too far is to question a turn in the modern way of life. This original turn was the inversion of reason. After the turn, reason was driven by logic instead of remaining free. What calls for such questioning? Certainly, it is the evidence of dead-ends that our cultivation of this instrumental use of reason has got us into: "Specialist without spirit, sensualists without heart."

The performance of instrumentalists raises fatal questions for the Enlightenment project. Are they really claiming to cultivate us the way you cultivate agriculture or horticulture? Cast in doubt are the claims to special competence of experts and the special authority of modern organizations.

We can supply our own example from the days of missile defense set up during the Cold War. Imagine you are a defense manager. A blip appears on one of your radar screens. You are authorized to decide whether to consider a blip as a case of missile attack. You check whether what you see fits into the protocols. These are programmed into the system to achieve the system's purpose. If you are concerned with outcomes, the question is—or ought to be: Can the choice you are about to make logically lead to some measure of national defense?

What if *any* and *all* the decision paths laid out for you lead to the same outcome? What if any choice you make still leads to the total destruction of your own country's population? Then it might dawn on you that the frame you are working in is paradoxical.

Derrida makes it his business to expose paradoxical outcomes. His critique of rational policy making and program design focuses us on the fatal ascendance of instrumental reason (the preserve of experts) over imagination (an ability of all of us). Human reason can imagine human goals. Once these are set, logic can design means to reach them. But what if we design only goals that our logic can project? Then the means drive the ends. This is a different kind of reasoning from the imaginative reasoning that designs frameworks to begin with.

Derrida doggedly pursues precisely these questions. Is the invocation of reason itself rational when the decision framework nullifies not only reason but all human life? Immanuel Kant had already raised this specter. It is a misuse of reason to think it can *determine* what we come to know. One commentator suggests that Derrida sees such a system as "having far outrun its own self-regulating principles" (Norris, 1987: 162).

Derrida himself speaks of showing us the "outer limits of the authority and the power of the principle of reason." His way is to "*think the limits* of that principle of reason which has shaped the emergence of Western philosophy, science and technology at large." This way has its own label: deconstruction (Derrida, 1983: 14, cited in Norris, 1987: 162–63).

Deconstruction is not a method but moves. These moves question the reasonability of reason in our times. Reason may have been reasonably exercised by experts in the founding days of modern knowledge—the Enlightenment—but to exercise its procedures today puts us in a false position. Locked into a precast framework of decisions or choices, we are forced to come up with irrational results no matter how logically we proceed. This has serious implications for the claims of professionals and bureaucrats. Where the end of reason is reached, the rule of experts also falls by the wayside.

Gone is the expert's claim to a special competence, and hence authority. People will tell you: It's all very complex. They will tell you experts are needed in making so-called complex and sophisticated decisions for the rest of us. They are wrong. It's all very simple. The setup is: any choice and you are dead. One source of the impression of complexity is that the modern technological framework is the product of so many specialties that no single expert knows enough to imagine how to put all the pieces together. But critics of modernity see a further burden. Consider Derrida's thought, as worded by an interpreter, that experts' "very training in the logistics of calculated response may prevent them from seeing just how far the current situation has left such [classical "means-ends"] reasoning behind" (Norris, 1987: 164).

Heidegger already raised the suggestion that logic should depend on humankind's different states of being in different historical epochs. Derrida would alert us to the lack of fit between our logic and our new state of being in late modernity with these words: "The dividing line between *doxa* and *episteme* ["mere belief" and "knowledge"] starts to blur as soon as there is no longer any such thing as an absolutely legitimizable competence which is no longer strictly socio-scientific but techno-military-political-diplomatic through and through, and which brings into play the *doxa* or incompetence even in its calculations" (Derrida, 1984: 24, in Norris, 1987: 164–65; Norris's bracketed addition).

Now Derrida's point is not that reason collapses only in ultimate, extreme situations. Reason contains a paradox to begin with. It is the contradiction between the reasoning that allows us phantasy, the reason that imagines ends, and the reason that simply calculates means to these ends.

The more "rational" we get about implementing our imagination's products, the more we leave this to experts and logic-based organizations (like bureaucracies and computers). Result: the more the tension grows between reason as logic and reason as our power of the imagination. It follows that among the experts and the bureaucracies, imagination is devalued, and our very much human fate is left to mere calculations and operations of logic. A less global example: an administrator who has no sense for the work to be done may make great job allocations that are perfectly logical—but are unreasonable.

Emergent Rules

Imagine you are one of the managers deciding whether a space shuttle should fly. An engineer comes to you. He says that shuttle booster seals have failed in the past. Some did so at high, some at low, launch temperatures. There is no clear pattern. Do you figure the absence of a pattern means it is safe to launch? Or does the series of incidents without a pattern alarm you, and you scrub the launch? (Remember the *Challenger*?)

Modern thinking asks: What do the rules say?

Modern critique asks: Which rules apply?

Post-modern thinking asks: What is behind the rules?

Post-modern thinking challenges rule-bound thinking.

Modern self-critique already slices into the very idea that there are rules lying around just waiting to be applied. Post-modern critique now questions that there is a natural order. It lays existing rules open to see what is inside or behind them. It is not the rules that get work done; it is doing the work that discovers new rules as they emerge from working. Existing rules therefore need to be questioned especially when there is an emerging situation, one that does not quite fit previous patterns. This was the case in the pre-launch discussions that ended up sending *Challenger* and seven astronauts to a fiery demise.

What Jacques Derrida, along with other post-modernists, calls an attitude of "deconstruction" would get launch managers to worry. Their concern might focus not only on how an anomaly might fit into the launch pattern but whether the launch pattern is adequate to the anomaly.

Suspect patterns would become part of the normal thinking of the managing engineers themselves. They would constantly be aware that their normal management thinking and their normal engineering thinking involve different kinds of discourse. They would question any instances in which normal organizational dominance would impose itself on the other.

Dissociated Competencies

Despite being reticent to call deconstruction a method, Derrida himself gives an example of the results of deconstructionist critique.

In his critique of nuclear deterrence policy, Derrida questions two sacred cows of modern thought: *science and technology*, on the one hand, and the *organization of knowledge*, on the other. He tries to show what these sacred cows feed on: the accidents and incidents of a history of knowledge and power that might have developed otherwise.

In the event of a nuclear confrontation during the Cold War, there was no single source who both knew what was going on in a showdown and had the authority to act. Instead, Derrida writes, "there is a multiplicity of dissociated, heterogeneous competencies." Whatever knowledge various officials in these jurisdictions might gather, "such knowledge is neither coherent nor totalizable" (Derrida, 1984: 20–31, cited in Norris, 1987: 164). Translation: Knowledge didn't hang together and knowledge didn't add up. (This situation, even with the demise of the Soviet Union, is worse today because we are now faced with a growing number of new nuclear states, and possibly non-state actors who possess these weapons.)

The same issues prevail in the *Challenger* case as in the nuclear standoff. Belief and social interaction enter into what is normally presented as purely technical issues. Just so Derrida would consider the *Challenger* launch decision as colored by long-standing and unquestioned belief in how an organization should function. This includes: the relatively low status in the hierarchy of the one engineer with experience with O-ring failure, the social pressure on the one hold-out engineer to "put on your management hat" and join his management-engineer colleagues, the political pressure (real or imagined) for NASA to show what it could do to obtain future funding, and so on. None of these aspects that may have gone into the purportedly knowledge-based decision to launch was explicitly recognized at launch.

We could well argue that, with the help of a Derridaen approach to such decisions, the *Challenger* decision makers might have been aware of the dangers of the "techno-militaro-politico-diplomatic" mixture of belief (Norris's term, in Norris, 1987: 165) that Derrida pointed out in regard to nuclear deterrence policy. And they might have seen the rhetorical-social traps they were falling into. They might have weighed the human factor into the formulaic response to what appeared as a technical decision.

In short, this runs against what both engineers and managers today assume: that knowledge will hang together (science) and will add up (bureaucracy). They learn in school that to do engineering and to organize is possible because reality is so structured (science) or can be so structured (modern organization) that we can deal *normally* with just about any situation. This dogma ignores situations where knowledge just doesn't hang together and just doesn't add up. The modern tradition of thought insists that, to become knowledge, our experience must show some coherence (science). And our tradition of modern organization demands that such knowledge be centrally located and controlled (bureaucracy). Could it be that situations nevertheless arise that are real but cannot be captured by scientific concepts nor administered knowledgeably from a center?

In the absence of a pattern, the *Challenger* launchers fell back onto an unspoken and unquestioned series of *modern* assumptions: that there is an order, that it favors Man, and that it can be known by bringing our concepts in line with the way things are. Truth then becomes getting our thoughts in line with things. We say something is so, we empirically test our assertion, the natural order says, "Yes," and "Presto!" we have knowledge. Similarly, not only they but later critics and investigators simply took bureaucratic organization for granted. This disregarded the fact that you cannot centralize knowledge that is pre-conceptual and emergent. In short, the National Aeronautics and Space Administration was operating with ideologies of both science and organization that did not sufficiently allow for emergent knowledge. It tried to force tentative knowledge into finished patterns and these, in turn, onto a centralized decision platform.

Patterning and controlling may be part of a necessary faith for the advance of science and organization. But this faith ignores the consequences: the failure of entire social systems, mega-deaths, the unintended effects of globalization.

Hesitations

Deconstruction makes us hesitate in our thinking about reality. And yet it could have the function of having us hesitate over exactly the right things: expecting latent functions as normal in social policy, expecting externalities to perhaps outweigh benefits in economics, expecting anomalies to be the unavoidable result of the exclusions of science, engineering, technology.

Yet we may demand a closer payoff: What can we do with this?

A further problem is that the man who was perhaps the lead exponent of deconstruction, Jacques Derrida, considers it a philosophical approach best kept out of our hands and left to philosophers.

Deconstruction offers a warning that may be helpful to break open the rigid and unquestioned conceptual matrix of modern thinking. When we look at the origins of modern thinking, we find an increasing faith in the normalcy of order in which accidents are exceptions. We believe that there is a foundational order around us—which merely needs to be uncovered to put knowledge of it to use. Particular events that do not fit our system are treated as deviations, and specifically called anomalies (physics and engineering), latent functions (sociology), or externalities (economics).

It is, however, just as reasonable to assume that order is just the sum of a bunch of accidents. In that view, order was constructed out of such accidents. If so, order can be taken apart—deconstructed—down to its original foundations, if any. Deconstruction is post-modern philosophy's attempt to show us the plausibility of taking that position. In the words of the commentator Christopher Norris (1987: 162), deconstruction can be argued to be "a rigorous attempt *to think the limits* of that principle of reason which has shaped the emergence of Western philosophy, science and technology." But of what use is this?

This is a typically American question. It is derided by Derrida. Derrida does his best to isolate philosophy from demands for utility. His writing is turgid, full of technical words, and eschews good old Anglo-Saxon one-syllable substitutes, aside from being elusive and given to fits of "This is all very complex"—as against the more traditional efforts of philosophers that they not only think big but teach what is simple in what to the rest of us seems complex. Although he clearly hopes people will look into history before they leap into the future, Derrida damns those who do. He declares that "Deconstruction is not a method and cannot be transformed into one."

But, we may ask, is it not reasonable for people to draw the consequences of what you have thought?

Derrida, while allowing himself to undertake his application to nuclear policy, objects. "It is true," Derrida writes, "that in certain circles (university or cultural, especially in the United States) the technological and methodological 'metaphor' that seems necessarily attached to the very word 'deconstruction' has been able to seduce or lead astray." To this we may reply that Derrida here contradicts one of his own axioms. It is that the meaning of a grouping of thoughts expressed in words is undetermined. As an author of deconstruction—though the originator was Martin Heidegger—Derrida has lost his grip. He cannot command interpretation. He has loosed the sorcerer's apprentices.

"Deconstruction," the idea of tracing what and how we know today to its origins, does have its appeals and its fans. It happens to resonate with long-suppressed ideas that there is knowledge of particular things for which knowing the rule is inadequate. It opens up the possibility that the pre-scientific individual worker has know-how, and demands recognition for the holding that there is mostly tacit knowledge that—without being spelled out or written—fills the gaps between explicit rules and facts and connects them and the results into a system.

Aye, there's the rub. Derrida contends that writing comes in some sense prior to speaking. With that position, he is not likely to be sensitive to the priority of "talk" (*Rede*) between the worker and what he or she works on. Such talk is silent, pregnant in its taciturnity, and entirely decisive of whether the worker gets the work done. Derrida might like the anti-rule position, but he also might see the potential disaster to his own project of treating all human action as a "text" that can be read over and over again in ways that differ and vary. All knowing is a game we play, in language, with reality.

Applications

The problem for Derrida's ability to influence actual work—beyond his obvious ability to criticize texts—is that in some ways work is not a text.

In work, you can't take back your moves. Work is not social intercourse. There, when someone tells you he or she doesn't like what you said, you can take back your word and say, "I didn't mean it." In work, time and action run only in one direction. You may be able to fix or repair a move. But the move was made. Somewhere in the Brooklyn Bridge today, hidden under corrective cable, is the poorly spun cable of the crook who sold it years ago to the bridge builders.

There is a necessity in work that is not present in social interaction.

Deconstruction challenges all reified thought, including bureaucratic thought, which says there is always only one definition of a situation, with a finite number of interpretations (namely: one), and that this one interpretation is good. Real people in real life—as the example of the batboy shows at the beginning of this chapter—expect more from thinking.

This is also not the old perspectives approach. Deconstruction does not grant to every person his or her right to see a situation from his or her own point of view. And this is not an example of pluralism in which many experiences constitute the elephant.

Instead deconstruction asks what silently taken-for-granted assumptions we make in our thinking in anything from judging when to fire a batboy to when to launch a space shuttle. Deconstruction gets us to hesitate applying the same old rules to a situation when these seem to offer the only certainty. In defense of the philosophical turn at deconstruction, it can be argued that Derrida, despite his autistic writing that performs baroque do-loops in getting us to think at the very edge of thought, gives a defense and foundation to those of us who question the empire of rules.

Bureaucratic Thinking

Bureaucratic thinking, in sum, defines reality from the top down. In such thinking, we forget that life is lived from the bottom up. Bureaucratic thinking, because it does not reflect a natural order of things, can be effective only through force or the threat of force. It is the use of force that demonstrates the poverty of thought. Denying the self what he or she considers the luxury or corruption of imagination, and recognizing only the logic of reason, the bureaucrat must suppress all those little imaginations of ordinary people, who might imagine, when they face the program or policy, that things might be otherwise.

Such thinking insists on explicit definition of the names of things. It assumes that names relate to things. It tries to control the entire domain of thinking by setting the rules for acquiring knowledge. It spreads the notion that nothing that is not clearly thought and can be expressed in words is real, that what cannot be made explicit in words is not real. Yet a question haunts us: Can we know something without being able to say it?

We all have had the experience of being tongue-tied sometime in grade school and being told by some teacher, "Sit down, Johnny [substitute your own name]! If you can't say it you don't know it." The experience haunts you all your life. You don't forget it not because you are especially neurotic, but because that is what science also says. It is what technology says, what the calculations of economics, politics, administration, and the rest say.

There is, however, growing evidence that Johnny (or Jane) was right. People do know how to live and work in ways that are not made explicit in speech. And they know it *before* they can talk about it and sometimes without ever giving it labels or names.

This outcome has fatal implications for the knowledge/authority claims of modern organization. In the extreme, the idea that there is know-how outside of formal knowledge means that bureaucracy cannot simply order something to be done. Any such order must go through a translation. The efficacy of that translation is determined from the ground up not by mere adherence to rules, orders, or standards. In one of my favorite cartoons, a manager cries out in agony at a worker who has used no judgment: "Oh, my God! You did it exactly like I told you!" The efficacy of any such translation of an order or a rule depends on my applying what I already know from knowing my way around my situation.

In the office and in the factory, work is dependent not only on clear orders but on the vague: the know-how it takes to implement them. In the school or the university, learning is dependent on what students already know. In the family and daily life, the way you take what I say depends on what you—based on what life has already made you—make of it.

Evidence of all this becomes inescapable today, not because heavy thinkers have figured out something new, but because an old commitment of our civilization—the one we made to rationality—is now producing technologies that are logical in the extreme. They crash precisely because all that does not fit into reason has been extruded from them.

Aesthetics: The Rise of Know-How

Support is on the rise for know-how. It is resurrected as a distinct way of knowing what to do by being immersed in our work. The support comes not only from post-modernists. The path was laid by at least two of their founding fathers, Martin Heidegger and Ludwig Wittgenstein (see above). And it comes from some pragmatists (see below).

Both Heidegger and Wittgenstein focus on what makes it at all possible for us to understand each other and things. But this is not language, though that is there for us when we arrive as babies. Even language makes sense only in a context. Nor is it belief systems. What makes life and others intelligible for me and you is the fact that we share practices (Heidegger) or forms of life (Wittgenstein). In the words of the pragmatic philosopher Hubert L. Dreyfus, "This view is entirely antithetical to the philosophical ideal of *total* clarity and *ultimate* intelligibility." What makes sense does not depend on reason, but reason itself depends on what makes sense when we are in touch with things (Dreyfus, 1991: 155).

Reason reduced to mere logic saps the imagination. Instrumental (or purposeful) reason tends to immunize our sensibility to situations. Something may fit in theory, but not fit in practice. These are subversions of full reason to which post-modernists are especially sensitive (for example, Derrida, above). Yet they were well known already at the beginning of modernity. They were discovered by none other than the philosopher who laid bare the bones of science. (See Kant, above.)

In knowledge operations, Immanuel Kant distinguishes between two mental powers. There is our ability to have a sense for a situation—a state of affairs or people or things. This is sensibility. And there is our ability to elicit and clarify the pattern of such situations by the rules and categories of reason. This is logic. To obtain certain knowledge, we bring to bear on the matter at hand both the logic function of reason and our feel for things (in Greek, *aesthesis*).

The early Kant says the certain knowledge of science comes from reason putting sharp questions to nature. This left a residue of uncertain knowledge. Science soon demoted this leftover. It came to be derided as merely having a vague sense for what needs to be done or how to do it. It is devalued as hardly worth calling knowledge at all. Kant calls it "a mere stumbling around" in the dark (Kant 1781/1787: xiii; my retranslation; see Kant, 1965: 20).

Yet, the later Kant finds it necessary to correct this position. The measure of what we know is not just whether we can convert what we find around us into terms reason can handle; it is also the fit with the situation. The result is his *Critique of Judgment* (Kant 1790 [1987]).

There he develops a problem of interest not only to scientists but to any problem solver. We can also imagine applications to business or government administration. The problem is this: How we can judge that one way of knowing what confronts us is better than another?

Here Kant develops a new kind of judgment. Such a judgment he calls "aesthetic"—from the Greek *aesthesis* or being in touch. Aesthetic judgment does not itself produce cognitions. But it gives us a sense of their fit with their setting and with human reason.

Does this say anything useful to people who professionally make lots of judgments? Yes. What, for example, can an administrator gain if she frees her feel for the aesthetics of a situation in which she acts? She—or he—will find that, while a feel for the situation gets us to know nothing new, we will feel more in tune with one course of action than another. Aesthetics in this sense is a sense of fit. And imagining courses of action that fit with the situation will improve the quality of being in touch with people and their work. When we give free rein to our sense for beauty (or, Kant says, the sublime), our choice of courses of action or frames of analysis will also improve. What we will have done, in fact, is reawaken once again the part of reason that instrumental modernism has put to sleep: our ability to imagine frameworks for our own thought and ways of life.

Aesthetic judgment depends on a feeling. Often it is the feeling that the one way of acting is more "beautiful" than the other. This is a judgment. But it is not a rational judgment. It is not a product tailored by reason as logic, which cuts here, trims there, and makes things fit. It is not a judgment that compares what Kant calls an "intuition" to a concept to see if what we first look at and gather (intuition) fits under already existing categories of reason or an already existing concept. In fact, it is an experience *without* a concept.

Such judgments come to us because the way we think of something *as it is* harmonizes with our imagining of *how it might be otherwise*. The resultant feeling of harmony gives us pleasure. This feeling is the clue that we are making an aesthetic judgment, such as a judgment of beauty.

Here is justification for the claim of the worker who says he or she did a piece of work in a certain way, "because it felt right." Similarly, scientists speak of the more elegant solution. On occasion they even refer to the feeling of beauty or of the sublime as discriminants that make a solution to a problem "feel right" before ever being tested (see Gleick, 1993).

Martin Heidegger picks up on this role given to the imagination as a third force between reason and sensibility. To him, the entire society, not as for us mainly bureaucracy, greets the newcomer with a demand for conformism in which "every exception is short-lived and quietly suppressed" (Heidegger, 1992a: 246).

From this, I as an authentic individual can only free myself by paying attention to a feeling for the actual situation into which the tension between my projects and the prevailing understanding puts me. Heidegger calls this *Befindlichkeit*, literally a finding of where you are "at." Knowing where you are "at" takes care of a crucial problem: What do I need to look at that connects me to what I am going to do next? This is the problem of relevance. Without such a sense for where we are "at," we would be overwhelmed by a chaos of sense impressions. Without a concern for self and its projects, *Befindlichkeit* as an expression of concern, none of us can live or work for the sake of him- or herself.

7

Bureaucracy as Polity: Politics as Administration

In a modern state the actual ruler is necessarily and unavoidably the bureaucracy. . . . The place of "revolutions" is under this process taken by coups d'état.

—Max Weber

Do we need a theory of power? . . . The first thing to check is what I should call "conceptual needs." . . . We have to know the historical conditions that motivate our conceptualizations.

—Michel Foucault

Bureaucracy replaces politics. It is not enough to observe that bureaucracy converts politics into administration, or that it drains all political life out of administration, or that this was originally intended to strengthen the power of him or her who had legitimate authority over a particular agency. The knock of bureaucracy on the door of politics announces: Hi, I'm bureaucracy, I'm your replacement.

Where bureaucracy takes over, politics dies. Oh, it may seem at first that bureaucracy is a wonderful tool for the one who controls it, but the "tool" soon develops what seems like a mind of its own. And given its characteristic traits—all focused on rational and machine-like operation standards—that turn is inevitable: modern organization replaces human beings. Consider the following contrast:

Functions & Structures of Bureaucracy (See Weber in Chapter 3.)	Functions & Structures of Politics (By the present author.)
Hierarchy of offices: super- and subordinated offices. (See Weber in Chapter 3.)	*Hierarchy of humans*: super- and subordinated *citizens*.
Jurisdictions (areas of "competencies" staked out on the basis of legality); ultimately technical division of labor.	*Constituencies* as source of *authority* in functional or geographic areas. (*Politician's* right, having won political battles, to act on behalf of citizens.)
Selection based on training in skills of technical or administrative technique. Risk-free as long as rules of office are obeyed. No ownership of administrative means of production.	*Election of politicians* based on success in political battles at own risk. "Ownership" of electoral district won.
The files as tools for retrieving past official actions.	*Personal memory* as way of staying in touch with constituents.
Fulltime devotion to the job.	*Fulltime devotion to political life.*
Obeying *the rules*.	Making *the rules*.

The contrast is telling. Max Weber himself said that we politick at our own risk (*auf eigener Faust*, literally: by one's own fist). In contrast the bureaucrat has not stood the test of fire: political battle; he or she is the creature of the organization. To the politician, the bureaucrat is merely an afterthought. Lack of experience in fighting for one's own cause is also why bureaucrats usually do not make great leaders, and are usually prohibited from political leadership.

In considering the bureaucratization of politics, we look at two aspects:

1. Externally, public politics is increasingly bureaucratized and loses its human vitality.
2. Internally, bureaucrats—though forbidden to politick—develop in the division of labor their own source for a new kind of politics: the infamous office politics.

Finally, we consider what the experts have to say: both modern experts and post-modern.

How People Politick

The Bureaucratization of Politics

How do citizens experience the bureaucratization of politics? A clear path takes us from the earliest ways and byways of political organization to the takeover of politics by organization.

The Citizen-Politician

The traditional American political experience: perhaps nowhere is it so essentially reflected as in this tale. It comes from a political organizer in the heyday of the political machine:

> I had a cousin, a young man who didn't take any particular interest in politics. I went to him and said, "Tommy, I'm going to be a politician, and I want to get a folldown'; can I count on you?" He said: "Sure, George." That's how I got started in business. I got a marketable commodity—one vote. Then I went to the district leader and told him I could command two votes on election day, Tommy's and my own. He smiled on me and told me to go ahead. . . . Before long I had sixty men back of me, and formed the George Washington Plunkitt Association. (Riordan, 1963: 8–9)

Even today, machine politicians still act and speak alike. A hundred years ago, such initiative meant patronage for the newly arrived ethnics: Europe's huddled masses gathered under the light of the Statue of Liberty. Even today, I know a county where both the Democratic and the Republican leaders rose from their first jobs as janitors at City Hall. In the state where I work, business still picks mayoral candidates. Political leaders may also serve in the legislature and be affiliated with lobbying law firms. The business of politics is still in business.

The machine vision of politics may strike the idealist among us as wrong. Plunkitt describes politics as a business and votes as a marketable commodity. He organizes the business of politics. But we may recall that the Founders already called America "a commercial republic." And the entrepreneur must surely be rewarded.

Bosses and Reformers

We should not be surprised that beginnings like Plunkitt's led to the political machine of the late 1800s. But at least that machine was still in the service of human beings, even if only a few men took personal responsibility for the business. The man who exposed the fallen politics of the political machine, the muckraking journalist Lincoln Steffens, concluded that "politics is business." "That's what's the matter with everything," he wrote, "art, literature, religion, journalism, law, medicine—they're all business, and all as you see them" (Steffens, 1957 [1904]: 4).

America reformed after the exposé by Steffens and other muckrakers. But, as Steffens had predicted, reform did not take. In the cities and states, most reformers did not have what it took to do politics. Even where they saw what needed to be done, they lacked the unified will to do it. Unwilling to use force to back up its will, reform lost the contest to the bosses, who did not hesitate. Unable to understand that the system that saw politics as a business was not sick but, if not healthy, then normal, reformers denied themselves business methods: the contract, the deal, being on the take to share in the take—but most of all the utility of recognizing the bare fact that politics is economics.

Even today, scratch a reformer, and you will still hear the old verities. An interview with a wary advocate of reform bears out the difficulty in thinking our way free of its handicaps:

Interviewer:	Do you think reformers would ever resort to bribery?
Reform advocate:	Oh, probably.
Interviewer:	How would they get the means?
Reform advocate:	Do 'em a favor.
Interviewer:	So that's part of reform?
Reform advocate:	It's not consistent with the idea of reform.
Interviewer:	They prided themselves for not being crooks. . . . Would they ever use force?
Reform advocate:	I don't know what they did.
Interviewer:	It's inconsistent with reform to use force and bribery?
Reform advocate:	Yes, because they're rationalists: they think the world runs on reason.

The line of thinking that values reason is a legitimate one in American political thought. The lineage can be traced to the Enlightenment: subjects of kings, freed from the old order, would use their reason to create a new order. And there was the Protestant ethic to justify success in ultimate religious terms. (See Chapter 3.)

But new free citizens were not that free from the old order. They seemed to desire its return. It was to this desire—reminiscent of the old patriarchal and patrimonial order—that the machine bosses responded with tools tried and true: loyalty in return for protection, a share in the gains of the machine, upward mobility, and a boss who always showed up at funerals. Those of us today who have no understanding for such values are denying our own patrimony: what clouds our mind is that the members of the party machine rose up against the privileged or that our forebears *were* the privileged.

As for the outcome of machine/reform battles: Where reformers turned to experts on how things got done reform won . . . for a while. Teddy Roosevelt as a New York police commissioner hired police Captain Schmittberger, an honest crook known to be a straight arrow. He served his masters well. Just as reliably as he had collected the graft for the old crowd he now stopped prostitution and shut down the gambling halls for his new masters (Steffens, 1931: 266–84). A new kind of man started to take over the public service: not a good man taking over from bad men, but a neutral man.

In the long run, the political machines lost, in most places, their failure due to a mingling of private needs with the machinery of public production. Now almost by default, political functions in the cities—seeing to who gets what when how—fell to the increasingly bureaucratic agencies. Politics suffered: Voter participation, for example, in presidential elections plummeted from 80-plus percent, to our present low hovering around the 40s.

The government bureaucracies grew. Without fear or favor, bureaucrats subscribed to the values that everyone qualified should have equal access to government largesse. They replaced the political party and its machines. For more than half the American population the attraction of politics in the election of the chief executive was destroyed; participation dropped to the teens or lower when it came to local school boards or community governance. Politics ceased being—perhaps had never been—good business for the average citizen, though the corporations and moneyed interests still found paying for it worthwhile.

Presidents

The tide of bureaucratic rationalism was acutely felt in the late refuge of raw politics: the American Presidency. The public still expects presidents to lead, not just manage. When presidents do neither, their stock sinks, though their outlook may be restricted; their choices are preset not only by previous political commitments but their formulation and execution are limited by a bureaucracy.

George W. Bush. George W. Bush found it slow going in trying to bring together a coherent agency structure for defending the American territory. Policy responsibilities and interests were owned by some four dozen government departments, divisions, and bureaus. Even when these were put into the Department of Homeland Security, their allies, owning the committee structure and holding the purse strings in Congress, were loath to let go. (See Stivers, 2008.)

Fatal hierarchy and division of labor got in the way of security—as, for example, FBI bureaucrats ignored agents' early suspicions about an aerial attack by foreign nationals taking flying lessons while uttering anti-American opinions.

With notable foresight, a former State Department intelligence chief and friend of the Bush family argued organizational changes were not enough: "There has got to be a management solution, and that may require a lot of will, though I don't see any lack of will on the part of this administration" (J. Stapleton Roy, in Tyler, 2002).

There was nothing new in the structural aspect of this. Previous presidents also had felt surrounded, though perhaps few had surrounded themselves with so many acolytes who failed and stuck to them for so long. By 2007, the public administration of the United States had experienced what Max Weber meant when he said the only alternative to bureaucracy in the modern state was rule by dilettantes: in one case, a defense secretary able in Defense Department reform but playing amateur general and strategist in what was supposed to be an oil war or a preemptive strike at (nonexistent) weapons of mass destruction or a collision of civilizations or a religious war (you take your pick); a horse trainer holding down the top job in emergency management during a hurricane disaster; a spy service disintegrating under attacks by the vice president; loss of control over "outsourced" public services and business operations on foreign soil; collapse of major business corporations and at least one major accounting firm. The best and the brightest, a group of self-anointed elites, seemed intent on making a return engagement after losing the unsatisfactory experience in Vietnam.

In the center of it all, we find a president beset only by blame. To paraphrase President Kennedy, "sooner or later every problem mankind is faced with gets dumped into the lap of the president." A continuing handicap for the president is that, at best, the problems have been cleaned up into rational options—isolating the chief executive from what these mean in human terms. This has been and is the result of relying on even the best funded and highly competent civil service organized in bureaucracy form (as outlined by Weber in Chapter 3). But, the civil service by now had gone through a series of homefront attacks from people and politicians who lowered capacity indiscriminately, "reinvented" government administration by slashing manpower, ending up with what some critics welcomed as a "hollowed out" state. And yet no substitute organizational design had been found to carry the continuing administrative burdens. Perhaps John F. Kennedy had seen part of the problem most clearly.

John F. Kennedy.

> Sooner or later it seems that every problem mankind is faced with gets dumped into the lap of the president right here in the center of it all. But by the time it reaches here, the problem has been dissected, sanitized, and cast into a series of options—almost as though they were engraved in stone. What is missing is the heart behind them, what they mean in human terms. (John F. Kennedy, quoted in Harris, 1973: 15)

Even in public administration's heyday, a perceptive president identified the problem: If agencies and staff purportedly under the command of the chief executive are capable of pre–decision making because of their superior knowledge and information about issues, they are also entirely capable of independent decision making and of entering the political arena to get their own way.

Franklin D. Roosevelt.

> When I woke up this morning, the first thing I saw was a headline in *The New York Times* to the effect that our Navy was going to spend two billion dollars on a shipbuilding program. Here I am, the Commander in Chief of the Navy, having to read about that for the first time in the press. Do you know what I said to that?
> No, Mr. President.
> I said, "Jesus *Chr*-rist!" (Marriner S. Eccles, quoted in Woll, 1977: 207)

Roosevelt is reported to have continued:

> The Treasury . . . is so large and far-flung and ingrained in its practices that I find it is almost impossible to get the action and results I want—even with Henry [Morgenthau] there. But the Treasury is not to be compared with the State Department. You should go through the experience of trying to get any changes in the thinking, policy, and action of the career diplomats and then you'd know what a real problem was. But the Treasury and the State Department put together are nothing as compared with the Na-a-vy. (Ibid.)

Thus a president of sixty years ago experienced in a very practical sense the error of Woodrow Wilson's statement of 1887:

> Administration lies outside the proper sphere of politics. Administrative questions are not political questions. Although politics sets the task for administration, it should not be suffered to manipulate its offices. The field of administration is a field of business. It is removed from the hurry and strife of politics. (Wilson, 1887)

While recent presidents (Jimmy Carter and Ronald Reagan on to George W. Bush) have attacked bureaucracy, through reorganization and budget cuts, their control seems not to have improved much. Yet there are also examples of agencies not being bureaucratic enough.

During Ronald Reagan's presidency, a special White House unit, set up to go around existing bureaucracy, was claimed (by the president) to have escaped presidential control; a marine colonel and other aides had delivered arms to Nicaraguan insurgents against congressional policy and purportedly without the president knowing it.

The failure of the George W. Bush White House and the Department of Homeland Security in the Katrina disaster met Max Weber's dictum that "the choice is only that between bureaucracy and dilettantism in the field of administration" (Weber, 1968a: 223).

Clearly when there is an intellectually weak president, such as Ronald Reagan, but also under stronger minds, the country can expect muffled wars between departments competing in a policy area, such as the State Department and the Defense Department. Such wars can usually be understood as contests over turf and power—each department head following the imperative of maximizing survival for his agency through constantly expanding its imperium—and the public be damned.

The experience of chief politicians seems to be that, except for war, they feel surrounded by bureaucracy.

1. Presidents seem to sense that bureaucracy gets to problems before they do, *predeciding* decisions by *defining* the problem.

2. Presidents seem to feel that bureaucracy unduly *controls solutions*, manipulating them according to its own interests, which may not be the president's intent or the public interest.

Overall, modern organization has taken American public administration for a wild roller-coaster ride. Originally replacing quasi-feudal political machines and boss rule, bureaucratic structures reached a high point during the Roosevelt era of the 1930s and into the 1950s. By the year 2000, the federal civil service as a whole had reached a low in both public appreciation and employment. The federal civil service shrank from 2.2 million employees to 1.8 million between 1993 and 1999. This did not include contract workers, and, given the prevalence of bureaucratic structures in private business and industry to which government functions had been outsourced, we can say that the bureaucratization of America continues apace. From 1999 to 2006, the ratio of U.S. federal employees to private employees in government contractors shrank from 15 government employees for every 6 private contractor to 14 government employees for every 15 private employees (*Harper's*, 2007:17). In a sense, this confirms public management theorist Barry Bozeman's claim that, increasingly, all organizations are public, certainly in the sense that private business is increasingly publicly funded.

"Legislators"

How do private organizations like corporations, public organizations like government bureaucracies, and politics fit together?

Economist and political scientist Charles Lindblom: "The large private organization fits oddly into democratic theory and vision. Indeed, it does not fit" (Lindblom, 1977: 356). Yet somehow private organizations, public bureaucracies, and politics are made to fit. How?

Political scientist Theodore J. Lowi explains that lawmaking is achieved through what he calls a "triangular trade in politics" among private groups, public bureaucracies, and congressional committees. But to make political deals, each participant has to have a power base. It is easy to see where the power base of private groups, especially corporations, is: in money. But only Congress can make laws; it divides up this legitimate authority among its committees. The money groups can do nothing politically legitimate without the authoritative lawmakers; the lawmakers will not get reelected without support from the money groups. Each needs the other. Where does bureaucracy come in?

Political scientist Peter Woll suggests two reasons for bureaucratic power: First, Congress has delegated authority to government bureaucracies. It is hard to take this power back. Second, those who run congressional committees, where the deals are made, have a harder time lining up constituencies for each policy problem so that an iron triangle can be put together.

Bureaucrats as Transformers

The secret of bureaucrats' power lies in the fact that they are given time and space to develop their specialization and expertise. (No term limits!) Since this is true both for corporate bureaucrats and government bureaucrats, this puts lawmakers at a disadvantage. But the key to power may be bureaucracy's ability to function as a transformer of substantive human needs into satisfactions that act as surrogate answers to such needs but are actually far removed from the substance expected. Thus the demand for justice is answered by law, for peace by readiness for war, for help in doing well in society by welfare, for getting a job at a livable wage by workfare, for health by diagnostic related groups, for security by rigidity.

Bureaucrats themselves may not understand the destructive impact such solutions have on politics. Or such solutions, of which they are masters, may feed their natural antagonism toward their nominal masters.

Playing on modern human beings' search for stability and security, bureaucrats tend to attack politics.

A federal bureaucrat:

> We draw up good legislation in the national interest with all the parts fitting into the whole properly, and what happens to it when it hits the [Capitol] Hill is like a Christian among the heathen. . . . So we spend lots of time figuring out how we can do something we want to do and think we should do, without taking a new piece of legislation over to Congress. (From a rare survey of high-level federal bureaucrats, cited in Green, 1984: 185)

Apart from the use of engineering models in which all the parts neatly fit the whole, bureaucrats also tend to treat political issues as technical issues: matters for scientific research that will uncover the "facts" just waiting out there to be discovered.

Another federal bureaucrat:

> The bureaucrat has a program to carry out that he believes in. The question of whether or not Congress has authorized it is not so important to him. He figures that if Congress really had the facts and knew what was right, it would agree with him. (Ibid.)

Yet there is this third possibility: Bureaucrats are superior in being in touch with full modernity, while politicians live in the backwaters of modernity.

Lawmakers as Bureaucrats

Lawmakers themselves are seduced into accepting the bureaucratic approach, viewing politics as technical issues to be decided according to technical (problem-solving) rather than political (problem-shaping) standards. For example, a political scientist studying the increased use of staff and reliance on experts by members of Congress observed: "Overburdened and somewhat intimidated by the material the experts throw at them, they [Congressmen] are delighted when issues can be resolved in apparently noncontroversial, technocratic terms" (Malbin, 1980: 243–44).

In another example of creeping bureaucratization, two scholars (the author and Raymond Cox) arguing against setting bureaucratic standards for Congress at a national political science convention, found themselves on a panel with a consulting firm hired to train new members of Congress in bureaucratic organization. (See Cox and Hummel, 1988.)

In trying to compete with the organizational superiority of public and private bureaucracies, some state legislatures have tried to rationalize their politics by bringing in the foremost tool of bureaucratic rationality: the computer. However, early studies showed that an increase in legislative technology simply centralizes the power of decision making at the top and center. Legislative leaders or the governors gain. But there is no evidence of any improvement in the *political* process of shaping reality-based problems founded on a sensitivity to the experiences of citizens.

As an administrative theorist and former staff member of the Massachusetts legislature, observed: "A legislature can be entirely functional without being either efficient or productive" (Raymond W. Cox, personal communication).

Finally we get to citizens' experience of bureaucratized politics. Not surprisingly, their experience is as split as the two sets of values on which they operate: political values and bureaucratic ones.

Citizens as Functionaries

As early as 1973, citizens at large agreed by a majority of 65 percent with the statement offered by a congressional survey in 1973 that "the trouble with government is that elected officials have lost control over the bureaucrats, who really run the country." Agreement among elected officials registered at 57 percent (U.S. Congress, 1973: part II, 115; part III, 61).

When the question was put slightly differently, 73 percent of citizens and 80 percent of elected officials agreed with the statement that "Federal Government has become too bureaucratic" (Ibid.: part III, 60).

At the same time, citizens were carried along in a continuing decline of participation in official politics. In contrast to the era of the *political* "machine"—in which voter participation in presidential elections, for whatever reasons, reached about 80 percent (1880–96)—in the era of the *bureaucratic* machine such participation has hovered barely near the 50 percent mark (1952–84) (Hummel and Isaak, 1986: 83).

The correlation between the rise of perceptions of domination by bureaucratic power and the decrease in participation in official politics can hardly be overlooked. Learning how to work the bureaucracies pays; politics doesn't. People give up their citizenship and become client-functionaries of the bureaucracy.

In summary, just about everyone—presidents, aides, legislators, political scientists, and citizens—faces up to the growing experience that:

1. Bureaucracies, public and private, are increasingly *politically active.*
2. Bureaucracies are more than simple conduits for the flow of authority originating in the political sphere and serving to implement legal policies and programs; they *generate their own power.*

Something paradoxical, unintended, and dangerous happens when bureaucracies use this self-generated power politically: Politicians begin to see and resent that the tool of politics tends to become the master of politics in the polity at large. Internal politization ultimately would seem to threaten to undermine even bureaucracy's own power base if bureaucrats lose faith in their technical values and adopt political ones. We next turn to this second danger and what it means to the institution and society at large.

The Politization of Bureaucracy

One of the worst-kept secrets is that politics of a different sort is alive and well in agencies. Unlike constituency-based political power, the control power of bureaucracy is entirely self-generated. Control power does not arise from the consent of external constituencies allowing themselves to be led, but from internal structures of the organization. When Max Weber concluded from his comparative study of traditional and modern organizations that modern bureaucracy is a control instrument without compare, he pointed to specific sources of power within: hierarchy and division of labor.

Divided Labor as a Source of Power

Assume you go to work for a modern organization. You are given a job description and you are assigned to a desk or a production line position. Next to you are other employees with their own duty assignments. You don't do what the person next to you does, and he or she doesn't do what you do. This is division of labor or rule of jurisdiction.

The division of labor is the source of *control* power for hierarchy. While the division of labor runs contrary to human instincts (I naturally turn my head to see what the person working next to me is doing), it *is* the basis for modern organization of work. In fact, to the extent that I am not divided from what the co-worker next to me is doing, to that extent I am also not required, in a technical sense, to lift my head upward with the spoken or unspoken query: "Boss, what do I do now?"

But that turning of the head upward also makes me dependent not only on the superior knowledge of technical task division and coordination possessed by my superior—*it also makes me dependent on that superior in a personal, political way.* If that superior chooses to tell me to do things that express his or her personal self-interest rather than the requirements for scientific task design or technical task coordination, *I am no longer in a position to know or judge whether such demands are technical or political.*

The breaking apart of technical working together on a job also means the breaking apart of politically working together. Technically divided labor also surrenders political judgment. At the most basic level—two people working in a situation of divided labor—you and I are no longer able to judge whether what we are told to do by our superiors accords with the self-interest of the two of us—to say nothing of the public interest!

The potential for political misuse of technical control power is unlimited. This may explain why, next to bureaucratic structures and overlaying them (encapsulating their potential political power), we use civil service systems to control the narrowly political, self-serving misuse of technical power for personal political purposes of managers.

We are all acquainted with typical examples of the political misuse of technical control power by managers.* As bureaucrats we are subject not only to the bureaucratic experience but to the political experience within bureaucracy.

Political Managers

In personality, the politician is an individual who displaces his or her private motives upon public objects. So Harold Lasswell told us. Often childhood scripts of family passions are acted out again and again in adulthood as has been pointed out in regard to Martin Luther and Mohandas Gandhi by Erik H. Erikson (1958, 1969). On the more narrow stage of bureaucracy, balancing precariously on a platform provided by hierarchy and division of labor and hemmed in by civil service regulations, political managers act out their own psychological predispositions—their traumas, agonies, and pleasures—in more narrow ways. Their office politics gains in pettiness, intensity, and viciousness what it lacks in the broad, creative stroke. Nevertheless, with the bureaucratization of the world, the impact of the office politician can be worldwide and the sword just as cutting. We all recognize the type of political manager. Whether the politicized manager's impact is personal or national or worldwide in scope, the political attack is always experienced with considerable surprise by those who trust in the ideology that bureaucracy is nonpolitical. To the victim the political manager's actions are never trivial. History has shown us:

---

*Technical control aims to get work done; political power in the American mold aims to satisfy individuals' personal interests and passions.

1. The manager with a dislike for sweaty or moist palms—whose employees are driven to seek medical or psychiatric advice before facing an occasion on which they were expected to shake hands with him.
2. The manager who transfers an employee to Butte, Montana, on discovering the employee has uttered a critical comment.
3. The manager who forbids coffee drinking on the job, checks up on unmarried employees' sex life, and dismisses anyone knowing of illicit relations but failing to report them.
4. The manager who distrusts anyone who hasn't gone to the type of school he has gone to, especially those from higher-status schools, and gets others to ghostwrite academic articles for him.
5. The manager who, coming in on a cold winter's day that is blowing snow, will comment on the nice weather we're having—expecting and getting employees to agree with him.
6. The manager who projects a childhood need to protect the mother into an adulthood obsession to protect the country—and uses his office to engage in national witchhunts that reenact the childhood script against contamination from without.

All of the above were attributed to longtime FBI director J. Edgar Hoover (Ungar, 1976). More recent revelations support Lasswell's doctrine that political people project private motives onto public objects.

Manager–Employee Relationships

Why do bureaucratic employees put up with politicized managers?

A disturbing possibility is raised by the research of public administration theorist and planner Howell Baum about the institutionally created gap in knowledge between superior and subordinate in hierarchy. It is possible that this gap, so essential to generating the technical control power of the superior, also sets the superior up so that political manipulation is expected of him or her. When this manipulation, however, is actually applied to a subordinate, the subordinate goes into a syndrome of shame and doubt about his or her own autonomy. There is a shift from an emphasis on getting work done to pleasing the boss. The Baumian paradox is this: Apolitical bureaucracy itself creates superior/subordinate relationships that are technically necessary but which the human beings engaged in them translate into dominance/submission relationships. Bureaucracy creates both itself and its antithesis—politics. (See Baum, 1987.)

In summary, two dangers emanate when bureaucracy confronts politics:

1. Bureaucracy creates the illusion that all problems, including political ones, can be translated into administrative and technical ones.
2. Even when bureaucracy becomes unduly sensitive to the political authorities or generates its own politics, it produces a truncated politics that itself rests on bureaucratic assumptions, thereby obscuring the possibility of a full, human politics.

Against the first possibility, there are and have been recurrent "political" revolutions in America, including the cultural revolution of the 1960s and the cutback revolution of the 1980s. The second seems unavoidable. Can the world be rescued from the bureaucratization of politics? Can it be rescued from the narrowness of office politics? Can a fully human politics emerge out of and against bureaucracy, yet without a loss of the benefits of bureaucracy? The thinking of two modern experts orients our own thinking on these questions, followed by a challenge of a post-modernist.

What the Experts Say

Weberian Transformations

The foremost investigator of bureaucracy and politics at an early stage saw the threat of organizing politics. Max Weber expected a threat to individualism, a threat to democracy, and a threat to politics (Weber, 1968a: 1403). Today, where reason was to rule alone, we find its shadow twin—the re-enchantment of the world.

Bureaucracy transforms politics from the art of the possible to the calculation of the probable. What is calculated is the use of power in the struggle over who gets what, when, how. What is lost is the political imagination. Yet human beings, when they look at their reality, cannot help but wonder how things might be otherwise. Following the rule that the more you squeeze human potential out of reality, the more it will extrude elsewhere, a new politics appears.

Set up against, yet still within, the administrative background, a surface politics reappears. It forms as a paradox. People both reject politics as administration and rely on it as a safety net for the new politics. They

Figure 7.1   **Post-modern Politics-Administration Paradox**

Pyramid depicts administration as context; circles are political patches and their discontent

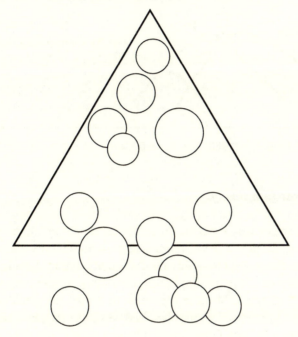

resurrect the art of the possible, but without claims to solutions that go beyond the situation and without claims to a system valid for all. Politics reappears as a way of finding ways for human beings to live together—but neither purely in the classical sense nor purely in the modern sense nor purely in the administrative sense. It becomes a series of temporary projects undertaken against a taken-for-granted background of stability secured by administration. If administration's hierarchy can be pictured as a pyramid, and each little political world as a circle, the picture might look like this: a patchwork of little political worlds flickering into existence and fading again against the backdrop of the pyramid (see Figure 7.1). The sequence of this development over time is depicted in Figure 7.2.

Bureaucracy achieves this transformation in two stages. The first stage is the direct consequence of bureaucracy: The transformation of politics into administration. In the second stage, people find the managed life not worth living, drop out in droves, and develop the paradoxical politics-administration.

Figure 7.2 **Stages of Political Development**

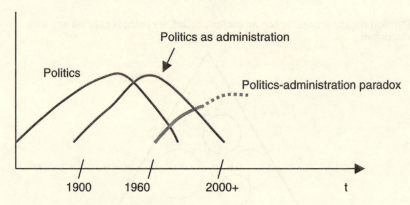

Toward Post-Citizenship

Freed by bureaucracy from the duty and rights of the politically responsible citizen, the post-citizen commits him- or herself only temporarily to
a political effort, often to political efforts that contradict each other. He
or she feels free of the personal responsibility of maintaining a position
in political struggle. Modern organization turns independent citizens
into clients with dependent psyches, and workers into quasi-beings with
truncated personalities. Government bureaucrat and client alike, corporate
bureaucrat and customer, become subscribers to an empty formalism of
values and thought.

What is left of the human being finds refuge in reservations of un-
thought speech and unspoken thought. Theirs cannot be a return to a
kind of pre-politics. Their solutions to the tensions between human
beings that require joint effort to resolve are created in the context of
modern, organized life—and yet, in a certain sense, they escape. Their
post-political islands are not separate from the modern organization, they
require it: post-politics are islands in the interstices, both permeated by
the post-modern condition and autonomous in it.

The essential parts of modern politics are, if not gone, then epiphe-
nomenal. Where is the acting subject of politics? Where the objects of
his or her desire? Where the conscious forming of alliances? Where the
individual creation and manipulation of power?

Across each great territory over which a state once exercised a monopoly of power, out of the gaps of management, arise patches of autono-

mous politics, often overlapping and incoherent. Each bears its own little truth, its pre-thematic issues. Its pre-objectifying subjects are diffused through neighborhood and interest group. Its diffusion of power courses through many overlapping non-systems. Consciousness, the power of the concept, theory no longer dominate. Each patch is just plain folks immersed uncritically and fully and directly in their daily lives. To echo a thought of the historian Eric Voegelin (1952): Each little patch is a little cosmos—a cosmion—illuminated with meaning from within.

How is this result produced by that instrument of the human will that was supposed to produce the exact opposite?

Bureaucracy transforms modern politics into administration. But administration is not the endpoint. Beyond transforming politics from the realm of imagining possibilities, bureaucracy forecloses possibilities, and, in so doing, creates a population both dependent on it and escaping from it.

This result echoes an anticipation of the post-modern theory of knowledge: The more you try to bring things under rules, the more they escape (Collingwood, 1939). Bureaucracy starts the process by imposing its rules on politics. It takes the spirit and the guts out of politics. It dulls the politician's appetite for battle. It dulls the political imagination. It blunts the politician's sense, not only for new ideas, but for new opportunities to test and enact them.

To senior bureaucrats who expect to lead their agencies, bureaucracy offers at best a surrogate for politics. In the maze of infinite management technique, they find refuge in a formalism that keeps content out of thinking. Their expertise is in the manipulation of subtleties in the rules and petty one-upsmanship of office politics. To street-level bureaucrats, it yields the pettifoggery of minimal discretion.

Dependent on bureaucracy's control over goods and services and submissive to enforced controls, citizens abandon politics for the bloodless and increasingly "rational" distribution of the goods. Citizens themselves are converted into clients. Politicians become administrators. From here it is only a short step to post-modern effects.

Post-Modern Challenges

By the time of post-modernity, the map of the political system itself has been cut up into functional zones of clients clustered around issue areas and headed by a politician-administrator. Where politics was structured as representative democracy, this development was built in from the begin-

Figure 7.3 **Stages of Overlap and the Present**

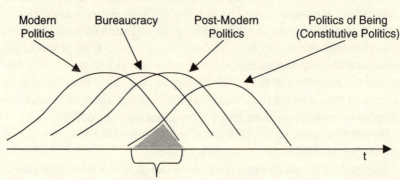

ning. Representative democracy filters out the passions of ordinary folk before issues are brought up to their representatives. It re-presents them as "rational men" all very much alike and therefore able to fit into one law that fits all—a familiar bureaucratic value. This is the same rationalism that is the foundation of bureaucratic thinking itself.

When bureaucracy's rationality begins to outweigh political irrationality, we get what post-modernists call "the ruin of representation." The thought that representative democracy could literally re-present the needs of actual people in the fullness of their lives is ended. Citizens drop out; the rest are transformed. The question arises, not how a relevant politics can be saved, but whether one can be built anew.

The sequence is political society [is transformed by] → bureaucratic rationalism → [into] representative democracy [which collapses from irrelevance to daily life of real people yielding] → the post-modern condition [yielding a search for a] → new politics.

The bureaucratic transformation of politics runs: modern politics → individual → representation → pluralism, distribution of overlapping interests, declaration of corporations as entities (Fourteenth Amendment) with political rights (Boston Bank case) → post-modern diffusion of individual, power seen as systemic → back to constitutive politics, for example, the Greeks.

The demise of politics was already expected by Max Weber early in the twentieth century, when he asked how freedom, democracy, and politics could at all survive the bureaucratization of the world.

First experience with this crisis is still seen as a collision between society and bureaucracy. We are still used to thinking of politics in terms of modern society in which bureaucracy was given a subordinate role. When the power of that role flares up, we see it as a temporary aberration. Such experience, and the tendency not to make too much of it, is reflected in early bureaucratic encounters of presidents, legislators, presidential aides, and citizens. Their experiences bespeak a more innocent time.

Modern politics begins with the individual joining another individual, each free in his will, to create a common public space to define what politics will be all about. By late modernity, the individual is absorbed into interest groups, individual interests become overlapping, and political freedom, once safeguarded by law, becomes so clearly defined by law that the citizen is transformed into a client. The constituent of politicians becomes the dependent of a bureaucracy. Representatives, in doing constituent service, increasingly need to know how the bureaucracy works and subscribe themselves to bureaucratic thought.

Representative government, the genius of modernity that allows only reason into the high precincts of decision making and forces passions to stay behind at the local level, shows itself to be subject to the same kind of rationality as is bureaucracy. Representation abstracts conceptually from everyday experience, whether in science, politics, or administration; the more we are represented, the more we become merely a concept for science, just another voter in a series of equally potent voters, or just a case.

Modern Critique

The future of politics, as a realm where leaders take *personal* responsibility for acting on behalf of citizens in making and applying policy, was already cast into doubt in the early twentieth century. Self-criticism of modern politics by modernists begins with Max Weber. The founder of interpretive sociology was as concerned as are today's behavioralists with describing politics how it actually "is," but he also stressed what politics actually means to people: a public place for imagining and disputing different ways of living a meaningful life together. The conditions permitting this, Weber noted, were already disappearing at the turn of the nineteenth to the twentieth century, and he points out the costs of denying political philosophy's hopes for freedom, democracy, and politics itself.

Ironically Weber's realism is picked up and directed against political philosophy itself—denouncing it as a vain hope—by a founder of modern political science, Harold Lasswell. Political science of the behavioral type abandons the traditional aim of political philosophy as it was to be used, in keeping with Enlightenment goals, to educate people for freedom, democracy, and a politics conducted by responsible leaders. Itself uninterested in the past and claiming not to be committed to any specific preference for the future, behavioralism looked only at "what is" in the present. Of course, the methodology has consequences. It leaves the arena wide open to late modern politics. The rationalism of that politics is now mirrored in the science designed to study it. Even the most irrational impulses are considered subject to exposition in rational categories. For even the craziest of leaders behavioral science hopes to be able to find what makes them tick and thus to predict and control their behavior. Endorsed by political science and with the use of campaign management, politics itself becomes the battleground not of opposing politicians but of the allocation of financial resources. Electoral politics becomes campaign administration. Public cynicism is the product. How did this become so?

We begin with Max Weber.

Weber

Prophetically, Max Weber foresaw the demise of politics under the impact of administration. His three rhetorical questions about this transformation deserve to be more fully reported:

> Given the fact of the irresistible advance of bureaucratization, the question about the future forms of political organization can only be asked in the following way:
>
> 1. How can one possibly save *any* remnants of "individualist" freedom in any sense? After all, it is a gross self-deception to believe that without the achievements of the age of the Rights of Man any one of us, including the most conservative, can go on living his life. But this question shall not concern us here, for there is another one.
>
> 2. In view of the growing indispensability of the state bureaucracy and its corresponding increase in power, how can there be any guarantee that any powers will remain which can check and effectively control the tremendous influence of this stratum? How will democracy even in this limited sense be *at all possible*? However, this too is not the only question with which we are concerned here.

3. A third question, and the most important of all, is raised by consideration of inherent limitations of bureaucracy proper. It can easily be seen that its effectiveness has definite limitations in the public and governmental realm as well as in the private economy. (Weber, 1968a: 1403-4)

This third question points to politics itself. How are politics and political leadership still possible in the essentially modern sense of "battle for personal power and what follows from that power: personal *responsibility for his own cause* [which] is the lifeblood of the politician as well as of the entrepreneur."

Political science by the mid-1950s crystallizes the modern answer in Harold Lasswell's behavioralism.

Lasswell

Harold Lasswell wrote a book on defining political science as a science. Its title was *Politics: Who Gets What, When, How.* It promised a method to report not how people were supposed to act but as they actually behaved. The family resemblance of this kind of politics to public administration is not accidental. The distribution of goods was at the center of both.

Politics had been treated as something entirely too immeasurable. Lasswell would remedy this problem. In the blunt words of his first paragraph, Lasswell redefines politics in such a way that science can take a measure of it: "The science of politics," he declared "states conditions; the philosophy of politics justifies preferences. This book, restricted to political analysis, declares no preferences. It states conditions." The study of politics would henceforth be the measurement of influence and the influential on who gets what, when, how: the distribution of the goods: "The influential are those who get the most of what there is to get. . . . Those who get the most are *elite*; the rest are *mass*" (1958: 13).

Gone is the concern over what goods—Lasswell calls them values— are to be valued to begin with. Gone also: the concern over preferences for what ought to be. Both concerns are replaced with a focus on *what is*. In short, there is now no concern for the origin of cultural categories within which we judge what is to be valued and through which we judge what are proper methods to achieve what we value. Behavioralism dictates opposition to a philosophy of politics or the study of preferences as expressed in constitutions. It drops the previous interest in constitutive politics. Lost is the definition of what a political community is all about: its hopes, its aspirations, its commitment to these. The inner light of the political community, which, as we have noted, the historian Eric Voegelin had once described as a little cosmos illuminated from within, flickers out in the clinical glare of science.

In summary, here are two modern social scientists describing a sea change in what we consider politics. The one regrets it, the other promotes it. But both demonstrate the ability of modern social science to detect the change. The question remains: What can post-modern critique add to what has already been said?

Post-Modern Critique

Foucault

The key question left for post-modern critics may be: How do we escape the bureaucratization of politics? Here we might expect the post-modern approach—given its claim of standing beyond modernity—to have something to say.

The outlook for politics as a way for people to design ways of living together now seems more dismal than modernists thought. Michel Foucault—the late French historian, sociologist, and philosopher—gives a particularly frightening answer. He finds an insidious connection of the forces that run our lives. Power as knowledge, knowledge as power, truth as the authorized knowledge of the established order—all are linked together in a giant system of oppression (Foucault, 1980).

Openings in Power

Are we to despair? The mind boggles at the connections exposed between knowledge, power, and establishment truth. But, while Foucault paints these in stark colors, he also points to power's discontinuities: chances for escape. By exposing what we do not ordinarily see—hidden practices, scientifically legitimated tortures, systemic delusions, contradictions, reversals, paradoxes—Foucault points to these as sources of their own independent and often conflicting power aims. These may or may not align themselves with neighboring power relations. Science may or may not support democratic politics. Bureaucracy may develop its own internal imperatives: techniques that devalue political power. Students may discover an interest in remaining students, rather than use their tickets, once punched, to enter the routine and thoughtless commercial world.

Foucault does not suggest all is lost. His hope rests on an expanded understanding of the diffusion of power. The so-called powerful in any historical era do not "have" power nor do they have a monopoly of power. Their power not only depends on the acquiescence of the relatively powerless, but on the coincidental and independent support of other power relations, fields of power beyond their own.

Such other power fields may have their own purpose and their own logic, what Max Weber called their *Eigengesetzlichkeit*—autonomous source of rules. They may or may not align themselves with two people's existing power relation—purely coincidentally, almost by accident. Thus, in an early version of the kind of thinking that is Foucault's, Max Weber already pointed to the "elective affinities" between the interests of modernity's rising industrial and merchant classes and the wholly independent power of a knowledge movement in religion: reinterpretation of Calvinist predestination doctrine supported the doings of the new classes. However, Weber's thinking, in contrast to Foucault's, is fatalistic: he tends to speak of inevitable movement toward a dictatorship of instrumental reason.

In contrast, Foucault emphasizes openings. These are provided by autonomous sources of knowledge and power. They occur in the fluctuations of the power/knowledge field induced by the accidental coincidence or affinity of interests, knowledges, truths. If power tended only toward a monopoly by central power holders, how could bureaucracy ever take over from political institutions of monarchy or democracy? Technical requirements of bureaucracy possess their own logic and their own aims. And these are asserted in daily struggles with the politicians.

Wherever a legislator is told by a bureaucratic expert she cannot pass a certain law because it would lead to impossible difficulties in implementation, the spread of power relationships beyond just a single one is apparent.

Wherever students discover that the professor's grading practices are not supported by future employers, the students may withdraw their submission to a school (power relation) that does not give numerical grades.

On the other hand, studies by the Educational Testing Service may show that the Graduate Record Exam is not a predictor of success in doctoral programs. Yet those in power may use the GRE to exclude the academically less well prepared—ignoring the effect of maintaining the status quo on racial and social-class opportunity.

Employers may continue to reduce the work force—until they discover their power to do so depends on the existence of consumers willing and able to buy their goods.

Foucault gets a hint of such openings from his early historical studies. Take for example, the impact of new ways of thinking and doing on state sovereignty. In Foucault's own words:

> In the seventeenth and eighteenth centuries, we have the production of an important phenomenon, the emergence, or rather the invention of a new mechanism of power possessed of highly specific procedural techniques, completely novel instruments, quite different apparatuses, and which is also, I believe, absolutely incompatible with the relations of sovereignty. (Foucault, 1980: 104)

All change depends on such countercurrents to the dominant powers in charge.

The Attack on Knowledge

Knowledge is from early on implicated in countercurrents to power. But we can find today's examples. Those who govern today no longer rely alone on claims to sovereignty, right, or law but also on housebroken professionals whose knowledges can safely be elevated to become established Truth. History, however, shows that such harmless Trojan horses hold warriors.

Post-modernists including Foucault argue there is no absolute capital "T" Truth. Knowledge is a function of power. Truth is the establishment of knowledge by those in power. The professionals involved in this shell-game are the members of the social sciences and their derivative helping professions. These range from policy analysts to mental health and social workers and probation officers, whose claims to scientific knowledge can be used to help legitimate the powers that be.

This will all sound very strange to us moderns, but especially to Americans. As moderns we are used to thinking that knowledge is power. If we acquire knowledge, we hope, we will be able to tell the powerful how it really is: to speak truth to power. Knowledge is considered something pristine and untainted by power. Should power interfere with knowledge acquisition, it would simply distort and invalidate what we learn. To now suggest, as Foucault does, that some knowledges are elevated to established truth by the powerful or by coincidence, to suggest that Truth is merely knowledge elevated by power, and to hold at the same time that such tamed knowledges might escape—all this seems outrageous.

Weber Recalled

The know-how of the disciplines both supports and undermines the legal order as each discipline claims its own origins in reason. The fact of the transition of power from politics to administration based on expertise had long ego been observed by Max Weber: "In the modern state the real ruler is necessarily and unavoidably the bureaucracy since power is exercised neither through parliamentary speeches nor monarchical enunciations but through the routines of administration" (1968a: 1393). And: "The power of all bureaucrats rests upon *knowledge* of two kinds: First technical know-how. . . . and official information" (1417–18).

The modernization of the state itself proceeds according to rational principles, Max Weber tells us. Also: "Within political parties bureaucratization progresses in the same fashion as in the economy and public administration" (Weber, 1968b: 1395). Legislatures become "a mere market place for compromises between purely economic interests, without any political orientation to overall interests" (1397). For bureaucracy he saw an opportunity to play off opposing economic interests and increase its staff (at the time through log-rolling with job and contract patronage) (1397). And, prophetically, regarding todays' campaign management: "In the course of the rationalization of campaign techniques during the last decades, all parties have moved toward bureaucratic organization" (1398).

Does post-modern critique have anything to add? Yes. For one thing, Weber suggests that knowledge will retain a tendency toward internal integrity and centralized unity. Foucault, by contrast, emphasizes diverging developments of sectors of knowledge.

In Michel Foucault's approach, this calls for an investigation into bureaucratic reason, what used to be called *raison d'état*. And this recognizes that all humans did not have our kind of reason at all times, that there in fact are many kinds of reason.

Today, in view of the capture of government and politics itself by agency interests and campaign managers, we may see rationalization—as the subjection of everything under bureaucratic reason—as proceeding apace. To escape it, we would need something resembling Foucault's challenge to theories of bureaucratic reason but also a new theory of power and politics and how these can be de-bureaucratized. Foucault is cryptic in his advice. But he does send us on our way.

Kinds of Political Reason

Foucault prides himself in going back to specific documents in history. Here he finds the specific historical entanglements of reason with power. Foucault specifically looks at the growth of state power in the sixteenth and seventeenth centuries (Foucault, 1980). It is there that he finds the origin of a politics that also is the origin of today's bureaucracy. This is a system based on "reason of state" (*raison d'état*). It prescribes a two-pronged system of rationality. This kind of reason is not only the forerunner of the modern state today; it contains within it the possibility that technical reason might split off from substantive political performance.

Reason of state succeeds the previous Machiavellian system. For Machiavelli, governing was all about a ruler holding on to a territory. The art of governing lay in the ability to mobilize anything that might enhance the power of the prince.

Against this idea, the so-called anti-Machiavellians recovered a yet older idea: the reasoning of the shepherd. Guarding and guiding, the shepherd would pay attention not only to the needs of the flock but to each individual member.

Raison d'état "marks the emergence of an extremely—albeit only partly —different type of rationality from Machiavelli" (Foucault, 2000a: 316). In this specific rationality rather than a general rationality lies the motivation of Weber's bureaucrat. It is the key to government's weak spot: the structure of its own reasoning. So Foucault would argue. The motivation for the bureaucrat lies in reinforcing the bureaucratic apparatus in all its work. Yet here, busy with internal technical matters, the bureaucrat is already tempted to forget that this aim had a further purpose: the general welfare.

The lost duality of motivation—publicly discursive and technically categorical—belongs to a peculiar kind of thinking. It has its own history. It has a presence still embedded in our concepts of the state, government, and bureaucracy today. The origins of what acts the bureaucrat considers rational lie in his or her subscribing to one rationality over another. The choice is between adopting the rationality of a government conducted for a prince and the rationality of a government conducted for its own sake but simultaneously for the purpose of assuring the general welfare. In the first, technique and purpose are one. In the second, there are two strands, each of which strengthens the other.

Both systems are rational. The first looks for logical means to prop up a prince's control over a territory. The second looks to gathering extensive knowledge. If government is to be a shepherd, it needs the kind of knowledge that, in being used to take care of the welfare of a population, also reinforces the power of the state to do more of the same: "The aim of such an art of governing is precisely not to reinforce the power a prince can wield over his domain: its aim is to reinforce the state itself" (316). Foucault focuses on a resulting paradox.

The state both coerces and frees. That is the paradox of reason that Kant encounters when he confronts Frederick the Great (see Chapter 3). In Foucault's words: "Rational government [of the shepherd type] is this, so to speak: given the nature of the state, it can hold down its enemies for an indeterminate length of time. It can do so only if it increases its own strength" (316).

To acquire that strength, the state must have knowledge. This is not an irrational thought. The state to survive must have knowledge of what each member of its population is doing and thinking at any given time. Only then can it use that knowledge to help the individual and the population at large build up the general welfare that is the wellspring of a strong state. Thus knowledge builds power and order.

Yet, protection of the individual goes hand-in-hand with intrusion into his or her most private lives or thoughts. This restricts freedom.

And, yet again, the security of order also supports freedom. A paradoxical truth is asserted for the political: Freedom and order are not opposites, but are the elements of reason. Knowledge is the source of what needs to be done to and for the individual, balanced by society's needs, to ensure the power of the state to do the same over and again. The relations of freedom and order are treated not as those of opposites but of complementarities.

Not only the origins of the entanglement of reason and order lie here. So does the entanglement of security of society at large as needing to be balanced by the welfare of the individual. While these may be seem opposites, modern state action treats them as mutually supportive: insecure individuals will not help the growth of general welfare, lack in general welfare will not support the state. In this sense, both the concepts of the state and of its apparatus (bureaucracy) partake from the beginning of the

Orwellian formula: order is freedom, knowledge is power, power is reason. We find here the origins of Foucault's interconnection of power, knowledge, and truth spelled out in his other writings on power/knowledge.

"Just to look at nascent state rationality," so Foucault concludes, "makes it clear that, right from the start, the state is both individualizing and totalitarian" (325). There is a lesson for revolutionaries in this: Think through what kind of rationality you are attacking. Dare to examine your own reason. Where do you stand on individualization versus totalizations? Foucault: "Liberation cannot come only from attacking just one of these two effects but political rationality's very roots" (325).

Do these exposures by a post-modernist say anything new?

A Way from Bureaucratized Politics

Does post-modernism show us an escape from the decline of politics into administration?

Modern self-critique exposed the heart of modern politics long ago in the work of journalists like Lincoln Steffens. The promise of modern politics rested on an ideal assumption. Each of us is able to imagine for him- or herself a set of goals and rules to live by that would be as binding on us as on all others. This was not the ideal assumption. The ideal assumption would already include the "I" in a context of "Others." Reason of this inclusive sort, however, collapsed into reasoning for oneself. While this promoted the satisfactions of self-interest, it could promote only *naked* self-interest. That which could not be pressed into the narrow confines of reason as self-interest—from intimate relationships to public matters or affairs of state (*res publica*)—was pushed into the background. At best, the public interest was defined as the heaping up of individual interests. At worst, these matters concerning what lives *between* us all—*inter-esse*: our being in the company of others—were defined in individual terms. But this meant they had no place on the political stage at all.

Modern Self-Critique

To steal an insight from the muckraking journalist Lincoln Steffens and apply it here: politics becomes a business: "That's what's the matter with everything—art, literature, religion, journalism, law, medicine—they're all business, and all—as you see them" (Steffens, 1957 [1904]: 4).

He might have added all other American institutions that involve more than one person: birth, raising children, learning, dating, getting a job, engagements, marriages, divorces, illnesses, and so on. All these are exchanges, potentially valuable, if not profitable. In these exchanges, the behavior and its goals and the human beings involved themselves become commodities. It was not a long step from this politics as commodities market to bureaucratic reason: politics as the distribution of scarce goods. The price was imaginative reason itself. This currency of imagination underwent a devaluation.

The Original Promise

The American political promise—like that of modernity elsewhere—rested on three pillars. In sequence: freedom, reason, and order.

Free human beings would meet. In public they would reason out their common purposes. And so they would design the order of their own polity (Kant, 1784). The American experience followed this script. Americans demanded *freedom* from the tutelary order of a far-away king. The announcement came in a declaration of independence. War ensued, and was won. From here on what actually happened is obscured by our tendency even today to read the script instead of the facts.

How free are men when defined in terms of property, as were all the delegates? Is their worth not already constantly measured by what they own not what they can imagine for self and others? Are they not set up to be bought and sold?

Delegates met in *public*. Or did they? How many journalists or ordinary citizens were present at the Constitutional Convention? Set that aside, for now.

In what way was *reason* the guide for the Founders? What kind of reason: self-reasoning in self-interest or reason on behalf of all? It certainly is referred to as a source of our order. But it is amputated from the human concerns that surround and give a context to Reason writ large: Reason for human being.

Instead of reason on behalf of self within a group of others, reason appeared in the context of the fear of others. It was a reason that trusted no one. Its appeal is recorded in the Federalist Papers and diaries like that of Samuel Adams; its early test rested on force of arms. The other source, intertwined with imaginative reason, was political experience itself.

Publicly displayed or not, the Founders' reason took into account what they had seen as the realities of the American citizenry. Established was not a perfect union, but a "more perfect" union. Citizens were not regarded as creatures of pure reason. Institutions were to be insulated from the mob.

The tree of government itself was to have branches that checked and balanced each other. Mused one of the Founders: "But what is government itself except the greatest of all reflections on human nature? If men were angels no government would be necessary" (Madison, Federalist 51).

The political imagination, firmly rooted in political experience, reflected an image of the citizen, of fitting institutions, of a suitable politics. These images were not determined by reason; they put reason in the service of what was possible.

Resurrecting the Promise

If the modern loss of participation in politics has taught us anything, it is this: The purpose of politics must be to unify once again reason with imagination and experience, but without creating a monster. The cure may, in bringing back imagination, end its separation from the mere unimaginative thought such as settled on bureaucracies. Put in traditional terms: Politics must find space and places to gather what can be said about the interest of *all* with what is the particular experience of every *one*. The alternative is internal emigration.

The Post-Modern Answer

For the challenger of modernism's thoughtless thought, the issue is what imagination will show us if we put being before thinking. Here there reemerges sensibility. Each one of us "finds" him- or herself in his or her situation. The measure of a successful politics is whether it opens up possibilities for being human for an entity for whom being is an issue.

For post-modernists, the task is to find a successor to the kind of order that uses force to fatten the sheep so it can feed its appetite to raise more sheep: *raison d'état*.

For those more modestly inclined, there is the search for *small* spaces for small groups to work out their humanity, spaces that modernism treats the way a bulldozer treats a landfill. The race is between human beings determined to find and exploit such openings even as the system, preoccupied with concern for strengthening its architecture, forecloses. This last thought is expressed when we reflect on what we may call Michel Foucault's political manifesto.

Commentary on Foucault's Manifesto

Foucault offers, consistent with his style of inquiry, a somewhat less than resounding call to political arms. Here are some fanfares with the current author's interpretation in brackets (from Foucault, 1983a: xiii–xiv).

- Free politics from all unitary and totalizing paranoia. [That is, reject the false sanity of a single source of authority that Weber already traced from the one God of ancient Judaism to the one-source systems of monarchy, sovereign, single-truth science, and totalizing bureaucracy.]
- Develop action, thought, and desires by proliferation, juxtaposition, and disjunction, and not by subdivision and pyramidal hierarchization. [Grow different versions of what you do, think, and want. Spread these abroad. Be open to encounters with the doings, thought, and desires of others. Find the pieces that do not fit with one another—keeping these intact instead of sacrificing to the consistency of little minds up the organization.]
- Withdraw allegiance from the old categories of the negative (law, limit, castration, lack, lacuna) that Western thought has so long held sacred as a form of power and an access to reality. Prefer what is positive and multiple, difference over uniformity, flows over unities, mobile arrangements over systems. Believe what is productive is not sedentary but nomadic. [This caution attacks the standard assumption of modern knowledge: that the categories of reason are universal and permanent, rather than changing products of our times.]
- Do not think that one has to be sad to be militant, even though the thing one is fighting is abominable. It is the connection of desire to reality (and not its retreat into forms of representation) that possesses revolutionary force. [Resurrect from Kant the pleasure and playfulness of an imagination driven beyond its "proper" limits.]
- Do not use thought to ground a political practice in Truth; nor political action to discredit, as mere speculation, a line of thought. Use political practice as an intensifier of thought, and analysis as a multiplier of the forms and domains for the intervention of political action. [Act so as to intensify thought beyond its balanced and appropriate limits. Find the gaps left by the established forms and domains of political action.]

- Do not demand of politics that it restore the "rights" of the individual, as philosophy has defined them. The individual is the product of power. What is needed is to "de-individualize" by means of multiplication and displacement, diverse combinations. The group must not be the organic bond uniting hieararchized individuals, but a constant generator of de-individualization. [Do not return to the individual as a source of rights. The individual him- or herself is the product of power. What is needed is to "de-individualize." This means to take the individual apart, rearrange the parts, draw unheard-of connections with other parts of the whole: diverse combinations. The group must not be seen as a refuge for the individuals caught up in a hierarchy. The group may serve as a renewable source for taking apart and "disappearing" the individual.]
- Do not become enamored of power. [Good advice. It exposes that power is just a name for the unspeakable acts we impose on each other. It, like all other concepts, must be reexamined for what they do to us. To be enamored is a temptation and a sign that we have failed to let go.]

How does the post-modern help? Most clearly in the realm of politics, amid all the critiques of modernity, post-modernism succeeds in ringing a single bell: the need to contemplate and rethink reason and trace it to its source in what makes us human beings.

Epilogue:
Bureaucracy, Modernity,
and Post-Modernity

What next? Can we predict the future that bureaucracy has prepared?

The preparations of today are the imperatives of tomorrow. Choices we have made in absence of knowing their consequences become a matrix: the mother of the future. Within that matrix, the future is conceived. *Imparare*—the root of imperative and emperor and empire—this word gives us a clue not to sit still for the preparations of the bureaucratic mind. The struggle is between the comfort of being prepared and the courage of exercising whatever is left of human freedom.

Consider the sum of bureaucratic achievement in transforming us. Do these "preparations" prepare us for democracy, aristocracy, monarchy, tyranny, dictatorship, totalitarianism? Think it through. Then, if you still can, judge for yourself.

Bureaucracy prepares:

- Beings without a sense of self-legislation
- Social identities without a sense of self
- Psychologies without soul
- Language without meaning
- Thought without purpose
- Politics without imagination

Let us review the results of such preparations. And let us credit and fault the relevant modern and post-modern criticism. In making your judgment, consider what you have to work with.

A Case Is Not a Cause

Under bureaucratization, free society and voluntary social life disappear. The *modern critics of modern times* already saw this. *Socially*, bureaucracy converts people into cases.

As cases we are made by others. As causes we used to make ourselves—though, as Marx said, not in circumstances of our own choosing. We used to think of ourselves as causes. Now, organizations tell us whom to work with and relate to. We are classified by that well-known department whose very name reveals what we really are. As human resources, each of us is just a part of the supplies needed for a particular job. Work, the way we accomplish ourselves in accomplishing a task, becomes the job set by others. Person, being in the world with some dignity, becomes the case. The human being becomes a commodity (Marx). The we-relations of social action (Weber) become they-relations (Schütz) and objectifications (Berger).

Post-modernism confirms this and points to the next step. This step affects society at large and sociality itself.

In his *Birth of the Clinic* and in *Discipline and Punish*, Michel Foucault questions the idea that each of us is him- or herself an independent centered subject. We are merely the effect of the powerful inscribing their own selves on us as bodies politic. Sociality is reduced to a mere function of power: not love or affection define our relations, but the deal. In the extreme, there is the loss of the social altogether: society falls apart into small circles each playing a different language game.

Jean Baudrillard speaks of us as mere atoms in random Brownian motion. "This 'atomization' of the social into flexible networks of language games," François Lyotard writes, "may seem far removed from the modern reality, which is depicted on the contrary, as afflicted with bureaucratic paralysis" (Lyotard, 1984: 17). Note the word "seem."

A Cult Is Not a Culture

Culturally, *modern social science* sees every culture as a set of values. Meaning is seen as derived by reference to such a core. It is this core that makes possible a shared social life.

In *late modernity*, the powerful try to manipulate this core. Culture is used as a tool. Perennial attempts try and fail and try again to throw away and overthrow values. The organizational culture movement tries to impose new values from above. Yet lists of values do not a culture make. The Neutron Jack of today is tomorrow's falsifier of his own résumé. Today's "courtesy, service, and consideration" are tomorrow's "speed, sell, and so long, suckers!" Manipulation of culture yields only one certainty: loss of trust.

Yet such manipulation is built into the very concept of culture. The very idea of culture is a historical anomaly. It is a product of the Enlightenment, with its belief that human beings can consciously cultivate themselves. Over time a culture's meanings and these purposes become second nature. People no longer are aware that this ultimate meaning is a product of their own making. In fact, at a further stage, when culture is used as a tool, the relativity of values dawns on people and ultimately the culture collapses.

The same in organizations. Repeated efforts to change an organization's culture from the top may, in fact, open the suspicion that not only is such "culture" artificial but that it is arbitrary and has no foundation apart from power. Then there is only one hope: to lower the consciousness of those affected, and turn the culture into a cult.

The cult of the organizational leader raining down values is today only a weak echo of its precursor in the society at large: that is, in the cult of a divinely sanctioned economics. When the divine endorsement of Western culture as economy is lost with the decline of the Protestant ethic (Weber 1958a [1904–05]), then the devolution into cults begins.

Post-modernism here is extremely helpful. It digs deeper and finds that culture manipulation induces the collapse of a sense of reality. We can bring to bear our own examples: stock market bubbles, CEO theft, the self-desecration of the priesthood of accountants, the narcolepsy of government watchdogs, and the complicity of the political powers.

Post-modern analysis sees in such events more than a mere straining of the cultural bonds, more than deceit, more than a perversion of the economic culture. Some post-modernists see a rupture in the structure of reality itself.

What cults of leadership and cults of organizational "cultures" prepare in organizations carries over to society at large. In both places, differences are obscured: those between subject and object, knower and known, valuer and values, the legal and the criminal, good and bad. This may be fatal. Our whole modern approach to things is based on assuming such polar structures. To see these is to us a natural way of looking. We consider the result to be the structure of what we call reality. Yet in late modern times, we witness the disappearance of such poles as self over here and world over there. The distance shrinks between where my fist ends and your nose begins. With this disappearance of distinction, other poles also disappear: those of the valued and the nonvalued, the worthwhile and the non-worthwhile, good and evil, morality and immorality, and so on. Since all oppositions and distinctions disappear, no society can look into the mirror and see what it has lost. "No society knows how to mourn the real, power, the *social itself*"—so writes the post-modernist Jean Baudrillard (1994: 26; his emphasis).

This, however, says Baudrillard, is exactly the situation in which we now find ourselves (or more correctly, lose ourselves): "and it is through an artificial revitalization of all this that we try to escape this fact" (26). He calls this process of artificial resuscitation "simulation."

Previous troubles with reality dealt with distortions—that there was *something* to be distorted was taken for granted. For example, false consciousness assumed there was a reality to be falsely conscious about: the exploitation of labor by capital. In simulation, however, there is no reality, only the simulation of one. There is a new phenomenon here, and it needs a name. Baudrillard does not hesitate to give it: *simulacrum*.

Simulacra are symbols. Symbols are markings that stand for something. But the simulacrum is a symbol of a new kind. The ordinary symbol's function is to refer us to a reality even where there is misrepresentation. When W.C. Fields wiggled the fingers of one hand, pleasantly insinuating "Never do my fingers leave my hands," we could be sure his other hand was palming all four aces. By contrast, the *simulacrum* has no other hand. It has no reality to refer to, but functions otherwise. It engages our attention to cover up the fact that there is nothing behind it. Examples: television news, stock market numbers, television commercials, any ad with a scantily dressed woman in it. . . . Result: we live in a virtual reality or what Baudrillard calls a "hyper-reality." We shop in the "hyper-markets." We buy the sideshow spiel, when there is no sideshow.

All this is happening with reinvestment capitalism still in place, except it now fulfills a human need greater than all the human material needs it once claimed to fulfill: the need for reality itself. Observing that we have become a society wide open to markets, Baudrillard asks what such markets produce. He finds that our main production effort is directed at the reproduction of reality. The *simulacrum* is what is sold to reconstitute the individual by the same producers that first took him or her apart. (See the section "Identity Is Not a Personality" below.) *Simulacra* give the illusion there is no fragmentation of the self and that the culture still holds together. Bureaucracy's shaping of the citizens' minds into the dependent mind of the client and the mindless "needs" of customers, of course, played a major role in that fragmentation.

Baudrillard signals the defeat of the Enlightenment project. In fact, we may consider the Enlightenment project to be at fault in its own decline. With it, "Man" became his own object to be manipulated like any other object. With the cultivation of everything, he soon encountered nothing that he had not himself made. Here is the source of the collapse of the distance and relationship between Man and reality, the knower and truth, the realizer and the real. Now what you see is what you get: Appearances are "immortal, invulnerable" (164). This is not what the designers of the Enlightenment had in mind. Whether it refers to economic or other values, late modern culture murders reason. The institutions intended to nurture it are accomplices. Awareness of this begins with a run on the culture bank.

An Identity Is Not a Personality

Psychologically, modern analysis easily shows the personal experience of fragmentation. All we need to do is to compare modernity's early vision of the masterful psyche, active and self-determining in society at large, with the remnants of a psyche that we find in modern organization. Masterful workers are not exactly what personnel managers have in mind when they transform people into personnel that will fit in.

The modern organization actively destroys the psyche. The organization grants organizational identity; personality is what we brought with us before we were pigeonholed into our jobs. At best only truncated personalities are tolerated. Everything not needed for the job is pruned away, and the trainee is bent to the job the way a rose is trained to the trellis. (Hence the idea that organizations can "cultivate" personnel in organizational cultures.)

A new entity emerges. The worker's self now is diffused. In this diffusion it is also fused with the manager. Some modern observers speak of narcissism (Schwartz, 1990), a dual psyche (Baum, 1987), or organizational identity (Diamond, 1993). And there is the concept of a psyche with its mastery and conscience functions extracted; what is left is bound up with managerial control in a "work bond" (Hummel, 1977). Again, a new entity presents itself: the transpersonal psyche as a new unit of analysis. Only in this structure do functions of mastery and conscience (claimed by the manager) meet up with the energy of the worker. It is difficult to see how traditional psychology can still take either the worker or the manager as unit of analysis. Individual psychology just doesn't fit the reality. One solution has been to try to heal the interaction of employees and managers in groups—as in object-relations psychoanalysis (see Diamond, 1993).

Here is where *post-modern psychoanalysis* performs a crucial, though devastating, service. The psychoanalyst and philosopher Jacques Lacan suggests that a decentered psyche is perfectly natural. The problem is not that of an alienated psyche that can be restored to some original authenticity. The problem now is seen as getting each of us who thinks of himself/herself as an isolated and autonomous entity to face up to this fact: We are not.

Instead of making the individual the unit of analysis, Lacan focuses on insatiable "desire," the psychological dynamic *between* biological entities called human. The dynamic of desire ties us to one another in an unsatisfactory relationship. Desire, in this sense, is the inability of the child to express what it needs in terms the parent can fully understand and reciprocate. As the child grows into an adult, language becomes the focus of analysis.

The previous psychotherapeutic hope—that a breach in ego, superego, and id can be healed—is now contradicted. Nothing can heal the gap left by desire. It separates us, but it also originates us. The work bond—that bond introduced by bureaucratic structure that destroys any hope for autonomous individuality—appears as perfectly natural. The Enlightenment project has failed because it must fail. Freedom and reason do not—cannot—produce an order that is an escape from dependence. The problem of subjection to others is not one that freedom and reason can solve; they can only paper it over.

Silence Speaks

Linguistically, bureaucracy leaves us speechless. The loss of speech is the clearest indicator of what has gone wrong with bureaucracy's mission as carrier of the modern project of Enlightenment.

Taking our hints about the future of humankind from our experience with bureaucracy, we find always in the forefront the quest for total control. In regard to language, too, bureaucracy seeks total control. If it can control this matrix, it can control what can be said and what not said, the speakable and the unspeakable. Bureaucracy's power lies in its command over silence.

The model for the future human being is not George Orwell's boot stomping on a human face—forever—but the capacity of the modern organization to keep silent when ordinary folk address it, to enforce silence when workers attempt back talk, to speak in a meaningless combination of empty phrases, to deny that silence speaks. Lost is Martin Heidegger's point that, by working things out, we silently articulate things as they surround us (*Rede*) before we ever speak (*Reden*). Thus, being forced to speak at work also is to be forced into the intelligibility of the average expression and the mediocre that leaves the full experience behind. "Language makes manifest . . . it does not produce anything like discoveredness" (Heidegger, 1992a: 262).

The modern institution, however, tries to control both speech and silence within the matrix of "language" it designs. This much can be observed by drawing on modern critics of modernity (Wittgenstein, Searle). How much of what needed to be said is lost when silence is enforced? And how fare things, matters, states of affairs that needed silence to be kept?

What does *post-modern critique* add? This question can be put in terms of usefulness. But usefulness is always for a purpose. I will here confess my purpose: it is to find hope that my mother tongue and my freedom to say what I want to say in my own terms will not be lost.

Useful in this sense is Jacques Derrida's attack on bureaucracy's infuriating attempts to exercise authority through controlling language. Here we find hope in Derrida's demonstration that the attempt fails, which has implications for computer advocates in the artificial intelligence field. The bigger the system designed to fully control language and the more fully perfect it is, the more the opportunities for freedom of interpretation—for which see his *The Post Card* (1987) (see Chapter 5).

Useful also is Jean-François Lyotard's suggestion that what we say does not derive its meaning from a heaping up of phrase after phrase in a line that runs from the past to the present. Instead, he says, this meaning derives always from our anticipating what the other is going to say to our saying—even unto, and from, the last phrase. (Martin Heidegger's last "phrase" was "Danke!") Lyotard: "Must it be imagined that there exists a 'phrase-power,' analogous to labor power, and which cannot find a way to express itself in the idiom of this science and this politics?" (1988: 12)

The most difficult contention made by a post-modernist (Jacques Derrida) is that life is a text. The modernist's life may be an open book, but to live life is not the same as reading that book. Life is not a text.

Thinking Isn't Knowing

Cognitively, in a world of modern thinking, we become aware of ourselves as individual subjects, capable of knowing the world and changing it. Each one of us is a thinking and knowing subject. In the bureaucratic modification of reason not only is thinking reduced to thinking by analogy, but we treat ourselves as objects: as mere cases, mere examples of general laws and rules constructed by others.

The case model is definitive of bureaucratic thinking. It states what we must be in order to come to the attention of the bureaucracy. As long as people can be induced to accept the organization's case definitions of themselves, the bureaucrat's moving concepts of cases around in his or her mind has the same effect as moving people around. In traditional bureaucracy, when this happens, power is never far from the scene. But there may also be technical circumstances: We must, to become computer-literate, totally adapt to the computer. Otherwise, it simply will not work for us. However, Kant already warned against the consequences. Bits of information without context, rationalism without content: it is no virtue to let these rule our thought if we want to know and understand what is going on in the world.

Moving concepts around is thinking, but it is not knowing. Reason thinks up laws and rules. But laws and rules, when applied to the empirical world, at best capture only how we are all similar. They do not capture our differences, even though each of us is who and what he/she is because of our differences. Generalizations alone cannot tell us about the individuality of actual people—even those who volunteer to act like cases: that is, as mere examples of the law or rule. The result is the creation of a false reality in case managers' minds. The case model captures enough of people and things to create the illusion of total control within the standards of the program. But this illusion is vitiated by the constant production and intrusion of "anomalies," "latent functions," "unintended consequences." Some of these can be hidden, some excused, some rationalized.

But, among *post-modernists*, Jean Baudrillard shows such problems are not easily fixed. He points to the ultimate rupture of modern reality: "Illusion is no longer possible, because the real is no longer possible" (1994: 177). The real and the unreal are both simulated.

To this we might reply with a blow to the chin and the invitation: Simulate this! In doing so we would be giving the game away. We would be admitting that what is called real has no other basis than what can be imposed and policed by the powers that be. But that would mean to give up on Truth, knowledge, and the scientific and helping professions—which is exactly the post-modernist's point. (See also Foucault's map below.)

Kant might say that the real is the whatness of an entity that makes an initial comprehension by us possible. But today, if we could get him to lose his need to assume an ordered nature, we might get him to admit that how we pull indications of a real entity together is arbitrary—and our knowledge of the entity therefore less than real. It is precisely statements like Kant's that we must *assume* an orderly nature for our model of knowing to work that open up our system to suspicions of being "made" real or an unreal. If the great philosopher himself needed to paper over such a yawning gap, then in our less certain age, we may have to do more of the same. (Kant, of course, has thought about these problems, and answers our belated criticism in his *Critique of Judgment* and the function of aesthetics.)

Post-modernism serves a disruptive function, and possibly an ideological one, when it points out that increasingly we live in a world that must paper over rips and rends in reality. As noted above on language, this is done by means of symbols that stand for nothing: *simulacra* (Baudrillard, 1994). Thinking in this state of hyper-reality means a regression to pure reason: we become experts in moving concepts around. This does not get us in touch with the world, though. What we are doing is constantly reconstructing an outer hull around the world. Material production of Karl Marx's time is replaced by the need to reproduce the real even if only symbolically. But if everything is eventually covered by simulacra, who is to know if there is a world? In the meanwhile, an immense need for producing the reproductions of the real opens up.

Thinking isn't knowing. Logic is not full reason. Logic alone descends into technique that obscures its source. These were principles of knowing in modernity. But what was obscure then, now is let out of the bag. Reason in our day has lost its source in the imagination, which constitutes how we look at things.

Administration Is Not Politics

In constitutional times, when it came to defining who we are as a nation, Americans drew on the Enlightenment faith. On this continent, too, free men would use reason to form an order more fitting to human beings than ever before—a more perfect union. So goes the national Legend. To tell any other national story is to insult History. To suggest any innovation that cuts to the root of the Constitution is tantamount to treason. This may explain why students of American politics have not come up with a new idea in two hundred years.

It is an embarrassment to see that the public administration—the designated carrier of this New World of New Men—was given no formal place in the Constitution. But it is an even greater scandal that it takes a Frenchman—actually a clique of them—to tell us the system does not really work the way we suppose it does.

For we Americans are wise to politics. Just as wise as we are to economics. We ferret out the powerful. We can tell that a founder of Microsoft has clout. And we can psych out the enemies of the common man and woman. And we can spot corruption among the elite. To know what is going on is to be armed with the truth. But do we understand the link between the elite, truth, knowledge, and power?

An immigrant named Henry Kissinger gets spotted by an elite talent scout. Next thing he knows he is running a city for the post–World War II occupation authority in Germany. Back in America he is recruited into the academic elite, say Harvard. He establishes a respectable academic record, say with a Ph.D. thesis on a member of another elite, say Metternich. He writes a brilliant book that rethinks foreign policy under the nuclear umbrella. At the next stage, he is seconded into government service: National Security Adviser to the President, then Secretary of State. Next thing we know his books, having become policy, are required reading in colleges and universities. Entire schools of thought spring up propagating the thinking of this knowledge-in-power. Changes in the established truth (and in funding) give a new angle to, or even create, fields of study or disciplines. These in turn develop new knowledge to be inculcated into the best and the brightest in elite education and hence into government on the next go-round. Apparently all this is in good fun, for as our hero himself proclaimed: Power is the best aphrodisiac.

Among such personal illusions and delusions, politics becomes the matrix of the administration of goods and services. These are defined in

Figure 8.1   **Production of Pseudo-Knowledge**

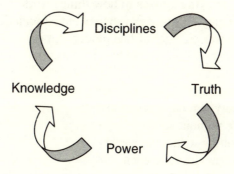

terms of the absolute values and knowledge of official truth. This truth, once accepted, defines and maintains the boundaries of knowledge for a self-serving elite.

Do we really need a French philosopher and sociologist named Michel Foucault to draw us a verbal map of this? Something like in Figure 8.1?

The drawing stands as an icon of what we already know. Knowledge is submitted to the judgment of the powerful. Their positive assessment makes it part of the established Truth. Under Truth's umbrella funding supports new disciplines. These in turn produce new knowledge—within the framework of accepted Truth. Do we need *any* philosophy or social science to draw the curtain from the obvious?

Look again at the map. It is one thing to read this map as the icon of the circulation of elites, and another to pay attention to what this map actually says.

- There is no Truth as such.
- Truth is the product of power.
- Power is the product of knowledge.
- Knowledge is a product of disciplines set up by those in power.

So, okay, the more cynical among us will say: Sure, that's how it's done at the top. But the people—the people—down here doing their daily work, living their daily lives, they believe there is Truth, they believe knowledge will speak to power, they believe power can only distort knowledge, and, besides: What is all this talk about disciplines?

Not until we begin to ask how the local judge works—in criminal court, but also in family court, drug court, DUI court—do we discover that Foucault's drawing applies to how things work in *all* of American society, and not only all American society but all societies blooming one last time by the waning light of late modern times.

Inconclusions

- A society without individuals
- Culture without values
- Psychology without a psyche
- Language without speech
- Thinking without thought
- Politics without politicking

Are these absences likely to prepare us for a democracy, for a politics of freedom, for government by the people for the people? Or are they preparations for something else?

Bibliography

Adams, Guy B., and Danny L. Balfour. 1998. *Unmasking Administrative Evil.* Thousand Oaks, CA: Sage.

Andrews, Edmund L. September 28, 2002. "Financial Leaders Back New World Debt Framework." *New York Times*, National edition: A6.

Arendt, Hannah. 1973. *The Origins of Totalitarianism*. New York: Harcourt Brace.

———. 1982. *Lectures on Kant's Political Philosophy.* Ed. Ronald Beiner. Chicago: University of Chicago Press.

Baker, Al. August 7, 2002. "New York City Faces Exodus of Firefighters." *New York Times,* New England edition: A1 and A18.

Basler, Barbara. December 20, 1985. "A Blind and Deaf Infant's Short Life on the Rolls of New York's Homeless." *New York Times*: B1 and B5.

Bass, Alan. 1987. "Translator's Introduction" to Derrida, 1987: ix–xxx.

Baudrillard, Jean. 1994. *Simulacra and Simulation.* Tr. Sheila Faria Glaser. Ann Arbor: University of Michigan Press.

Baum, Howell S. 1982. "Psychodynamics of Powerlessness among Planners." In R.P. Hummel, *The Bureaucratic Experience.* 2nd ed., New York: St. Martin's Press.

———. 1983. *Planners and Public Expectations.* Cambridge, MA: Schenkman.

———. 1987. *The Invisible Bureaucracy: The Unconscious in Organizational Problem-Solving.* New York: Oxford University Press.

Berger, Peter L., and Thomas Luckmann. 1967. *The Social Construction of Reality.* Garden City, New York: Doubleday-Anchor.

Berger, Peter L., Brigitte Berger, and Hansfried Kellner. 1974. *The Homeless Mind: Modernization and Consciousness.* New York: Vintage Books.

Bird, Harry. November, 2002. From CNN Report.

Borowski, Tadeusz. 1976. *This Way for the Gas, Ladies and Gentlemen.* Tr. Barbara Vedder. New York: Penguin Books.

Bourdieu, Pierre. 1990. *The Logic of Practice.* Tr. Richard Nice. Stanford, CA: Stanford University Press.

Bozeman, Barry. 1987. All Organizations Are Public. San Francisco: Jossey-Bass.

Carnevale, David C. 2003. *Trustworthy Government: Leadership and Management Strategies for Building Trust and High Performance.* Boulder, CO.: Westview-Press.

Collingwood, R.G. 1939. *An Autobiography.* Oxford: Oxford University Press.

Cox, Raymond, and Ralph Hummel. 1988. "A Congressional Declaration of Independence: Why Legislative Politics Cannot and Should Not Be Managed," paper delivered at the annual meeting of the American Political Science Association. Washington, D.C., September.

de Certeau, Michel. 1988. *The Practice of Everyday Life.* Tr. Steven Rendall. Berkeley: University of California Press.

Deleuze, Gilles, and Felix Guattari. 1983. *Anti-Oedipus: Capitalism and Schizophrenia.* Trs. Robert Hurley, Mark Stern, and Helen R. Lang. Minneapolis: University of Minnesota Press.

Denhardt, Robert B. 1981. *In the Shadow of Organizations.* Lawrence, KS: University of Kansas Press.

Derrida, Jacques. 1978. *Writing and Difference.* Tr. Alan Bass. Chicago: University of Chicago Press.

———. 1983. "The Principle of Reason: The University in the Eyes of Pupils," *Diacritics,* vol. 13: 3–20.

———. 1984. "No Apocalypse, Not Now (full speed ahead, seven missiles, seven missives)," *Diacritics,* vol. 20: 20–31; cited in Norris, 1987.

———. 1987. *The Post Card: From Socrates to Freud and Beyond.* Tr. Alan Bass. Chicago: University of Chicago Press.

Diamond, Michael A. 1993. *The Unconscious Life of Organizations: Interpreting Organizational Identity.* Westport, CT: Quorum Books.

Dilman, Ilham. 1974. "Wittgenstein on the Soul." In Royal Institute of Philosophy, *Understanding Wittgenstein.* New York: St. Martin's Press.

Dreyfus, Hubert L. 1991. *Being-in-the-World: A Commentary on Heidegger's* Being and Time, *Division I.* Cambridge, MA: MIT Press.

Dreyfus, Hubert L., and Stuart E. Dreyfus. 1988. *Mind Over Machine.* New York: Free Press.

Dreyfus, Hubert L., and Paul Rabinow. 1983. *Michel Foucault: Beyond Structuralism and Hermeneutics.* 2nd ed. Chicago: University of Chicago Press.

Erikson, Erik H. 1958. *Young Man Luther: A Study in Psychoanalysis and History.* New York: Norton.

———. 1969. *Gandhi's Truth: On the Origins of Militant Nonviolence.* New York: Norton.

Federal News Service, Inc. June 7, 2002. "Excerpts from Senate Judicial Committee's Counterterrorism Hearing." *New York Times,* New England edition: A20.

Feynman, Richard P. 1989. *What Do You Care What Other People Think?* New York: Bantam.

Fire Department of the City of New York. Nd. *McKinsey Report: Increasing FDNY's Preparedness.* New York: McKinsey Consultants. Retrieved on Aug. 19, 2002 from www.nyc.gov/html/fdny/html/mck_report/index.html.

Fischer, Frank. 1980, *Politics Values and Public Policy.* Denver, CO: Westview Press.

Forester, John. 1989. *Planning in the Face of Power.* Berkeley: University of California Press.

———. 1999. *The Deliberative Practitioner: Encouraging Participative Planning Processes.* Cambridge, MA: The MIT Press.

Foucault, Michel. 1973. *The Birth of the Clinic.* Tr. A.M. Sheridan Smith. New York: Pantheon.

———. 1979. *Discipline and Punish: The Birth of the Prison.* Tr. Alan Sheridan. New York: Vintage Books.

————. 1980. "Two Lectures." Tr. Colin Gordon et al. In Colin Gordon, ed., *Power/Knowledge: Selected Interviews and Other Writings, 1972–1977*, pp. 78–108. New York: Pantheon.

————. 1983a. "Preface" to Deleuze and Guattari, 1983: xi–xiv.

————. 1983b. Interview with Gerard Raulet, *Telos,* 16–55: 195–211; reproduced as "Structuralism and Post-Structuralism," in James D. Faubion, ed., *Foucault: Aesthetics, Method and Epistemology.* Tr. Robert Hurley et al., pp. 433–38. New York: New Press, 1998.

————. 1984. "What Is Enlightenment?" Tr. Catherine Porter. In Paul Rabinow, ed., *The Foucault Reader,* pp. 32–50. New York: Pantheon Books.

————. 2000a. "Omnes et Singulatim." In J. D. Faubion, ed., *Foucault Power.* Tr. Robert Hurley et al., pp. 298–325. New York: Free Press.

————. 2000b. "Questions on Method." In J.D. Faubion ed., *Foucault, Power.* Tr. Robert Hurley et al., pp. 223–38. New York: Free Press.

————. 2000c. "The Subject and Power." In J. D. Faubion, ed., *Foucault, Power.* Tr. Robert Hurley et al., pp. 326–48. New York: Free Press.

Freud, Sigmund. [1922?]. *Group Psychology and the Analysis of the Ego.* New York: Boni & Liveright.

————. 1955. *The Standard Edition of the Complete Works.* Ed. James Strachey. London: Hogarth.

Friedrich, Carl Joachim. 1937. *Constitutional Government and Politics: Nature and Development.* New York: Harper.

Fuery, Patrick. 1995. *Theories of Desire.* Melbourne: Melbourne University Press.

Gelven, Michael. 1989. *A Commentary on Heidegger's Being and Time.* Rev. ed. Dekalb, IL: Northwestern University Press.

Glater, J.D., and K. Eichenwald. June 28, 2002. "Audit Lapse at WorldCom Puzzles Some Professionals." *New York Times,* New England edition: A1 and C4.

Gleick, James. 1993. *Genius: The Life and Science of Richard Feynman.* New York: Vintage Books.

Goodsell, Charles. 2003. *The Case for Bureaucracy: A Public Administration Polemic.* Chatham, NJ: Chatham House.

Green, Mark, with Michael Waldman. 1984. *Who Runs Congress?* 4th ed. New York: Dell.

Habermas, Jürgen. 1971. *Toward a Rational Society: Student Protests, Science and Politics.* Tr. Jeremy J. Shapiro. Boston: Beacon Press.

Hamilton, Alexander, John Jay, James Madison. *The Federalist: A Commentary on the Constitution of the United States.* Ed. Robert Scigliano. New York: Random House.

Harmon, Michael. M. 1981. *Action Theory for Public Administration.* Burke, VA: Chatelaine Press.

Harper's Index. 2007. *Harper's Magazine,* April, p. 17.

Harris, Louis. 1973. *The Anguish of Change.* New York: Norton.

Heidegger, Martin. 1962. *Being and Time.* Trs. John Macquarrie and Edward Robinson. New York: Harper & Row.

————. 1973. *Kant und das Problem der Metaphysik.* Frankfurt: Vittorio Klostermann.

————. 1984. *Sein und Zeit.* 15th ed. Tübingen: Max Niemeyer.

————. 1992a. *History of the Concept of Time: Prolegomena.* Tr. Theodore Kisiel. Bloomington: Indiana University Press/Midland Book.

———. 1992b. *Parmenides*. Trs. R. Rojcewicz and A. Schuwer. Bloomington: Indiana University Press.

Hummel, Ralph P. 1977. *The Bureaucratic Experience*. 1st ed. New York: St. Martin's Press. (Previous editions 1977, 1982, and 1994.)

———. 2002. "Back to the Future: The Twenty-First Century and the Loss of Sensibility." In Jong S. Jun, ed., *Rethinking Administrative Theory*, pp. 187–97. Westport, CT.: Praeger.

———. 2004. "A Once and Future Politics: Heidegger's Recovery of the Political in *Parmenides*." *Administrative Theory & Praxis*. 26(3)l: 279–309.

Hummel, Ralph P., and Robert A. Isaak. 1980. *Politics for Human Beings*. 2nd ed. Monterey, CA: Brooks/Cole-Duxbury Press.

———. 1986. *The Real American Politics*. Englewood Cliffs, NJ: Prentice-Hall.

Hummel, Ralph P., and Camilla Stivers. 1998. "Government Isn't Us: The Possibility of Democratic Knowledge in Representative Government." In Cheryl Simrell King, Camilla Stivers, and collaborators, *Government Is Us: Public Administration in an Anti-Government Era*. Thousand Oaks, CA: Sage.

Husserl, Edmund. 1970 [1937]. *The Crisis of the European Sciences and Transcendental Phenomenology: An Introduction to Phenomenological Philosophy*. Tr. David Carr. Evanston, IL: Northwest University Press.

Jacques, Elliot. 1983. *Measurement of Responsibility* (Tavistock Publications), paraphrased by Geoffrey Vickers, "The Art of Judgement," in D.S. Pugh, ed., *Organization Theory: Selected Readings*, 2nd ed., pp. 1–36. New York: Viking Penguin–Penguin Books.

Jameson, Fredic. 1991. *Post Modernism, or the Cultural Logic of Late Capitalism*. Durham, NC: Duke University Press.

Jennings, Kate. July 14, 2002. "The Hypocrisy of Wall Street Culture." *New York Times*, Week in Review section: 15.

Johnson, George. July 14, 2002. "To Err is Human." *New York Times*, Week in Review section: 1–7.

Kant, Immanuel. 1781/1787. *Kritik der reinen Vernunft*. 1st ed. (A) and 2nd ed. (B). Riga: Johann Friedrich Hartknoch.

———. 1784 [1964]. "Beantwortung der Frage: Was ist Aufklaerung?" (Answer to the Question: What Is Enlightenment?) *Berlinische Monatsschrift*, December 5, 1784. In Kant, *Werke*, vol. 6, Wilhelm Weischedel, ed., pp. 53–61. Frankfurt am Main: Insel Verlag.

———. 1790/1793. *Critik der Urtheilskraft*. Berlin and Libau: Lagarde und Friedrich. In Wilhelm Weischedel, ed., *Immanuel Kant: Werke*. vol. 5, u.d.: Insel-Verlag. (Referred to as 1790 edition = A; 1793 edition = B).

———. 1790 [1987]. *Critique of Judgment*. Tr. Werner Pluhar. Indianapolis: Hackett.

———. 1800. *Logik. Ein Handbuch zu Vorlesungen*. Ed. Gottlob Benjamin Jäsche. Königsberg: Friedrich Nicolovius.

———. 1965. *Critique of Pure Reason*. Tr. Norman Kemp Smith. New York: St. Martin's Press.

Kidder, Tracy. 1982. *The Soul of a New Machine*. New York: Avon Books.

Kipling, Rudyard. 1941 [1897]. "Recessional." In T.S. Eliot, ed., *A Choice of Kipling's Verse*. London: Faber & Faber.

Kramer, Robert. 1996. "Insight and Blindness: Visions of Rank" in Robert Kramer, ed. *Otto Rank—A Psychology of Difference: The American Lectures*, pp. 3–47. Princeton: Princeton University Press.

Lacan, Jacques. 1977. *Ecrits*. Tr. Alan Sheridan. New York: W.W. Norton.

———. 1978. *The Four Fundamental Concepts of Psychoanalysis*. Ed. Jacques-Alain Miller, tr. Alan Sheridan. New York: W.W. Norton.

———. 1997 Lecture #7, In *The Ethics of Psychoanalysis 1959–60*. Jacques-Alain Miller, ed., trans. Dennis Porter. New York: W. W. Norton.

Lasswell, Harold. 1958. *Politics: Who Gets What, When, How.* Cleveland and New York: World Publishing Company/Meridian Books.

Lee, Jonathan Scott. 1991. *Jacques Lacan.* Amherst: University of Massachusetts Press.

Lindblom, Charles E. 1977. *Politics and Markets.* New York: Basic Books.

Loewith, Karl. 1970. "Weber's Interpretation of the Bourgeois-Capitalistic World in Terms of the Guiding Principle of 'Rationalization.'" In Dennis Wrong, ed., *Max Weber,* pp. 1–122. Englewood Cliffs, NJ: Prentice-Hall.

Lukacs, Georg. 1923 [1967]. *Geschichte und Klassenbewusstsein* (History and Class Consciousness). Berlin: Malik.

———. 1971. *History and Class Consciousness.* Tr. Rodney Livingstone. Cambridge, MA: MIT Press.

Lyotard, Jean-François. 1984. *The Post-Modern Condition: A Report on Knowledge.* Trs. Geoff Bennington and Brian Massumi. Minneapolis: University of Minnesota Press.

———. 1988. *The Differend: Phrases in Dispute.* Tr. Georges Van Den Abbeele. Minneapolis: University of Minnesota Press.

Madison, G.B. 1988. *The Hermeneutics of Postmodernity.* Bloomington: Indiana University Press.

Malbin, Michael. 1980. *Unelected Representatives: Congressional Staff and the Future of Representative Government.* New York: Basic Books.

Mayer, Carolyn E. June 3–9, 2002. "Read it—or Weep." *Washington Post,* National Weekly edition: 19.

Mitchell, Alison. November 4, 2001. "Dispute Erupts on Ridge's Need for His Job." *New York Times,* National edition: B7.

Norris, Christopher. 1987. *Derrida.* Cambridge, MA: Harvard University Press.

Oakeshott, Michael. 1991. "Rational Conduct." In *Rationalism in Politics and Other Essays.* Indianapolis: Liberty Fund.

O'Neill, Thomas P., Jr. 1984. "Congress: The First 200 Years." *National Forum,* vol. 54, no. 4 (Fall).

Parsons, Talcott. 1951. *The Social System.* Glencoe, IL: Free Press.

———. 1937. *The Structure of Social Action.* New York: McGraw Hill.

Peters, Thomas, and Robert H. Waterman, Jr. 1982. *In Search of Excellence.* New York: Harper & Row.

Polt, Richard. 1999. *Heidegger: An Introduction.* Ithaca, NY: Cornell University Press.

Rabinow, Paul, ed. 1984. *The Foucault Reader.* Tr. Catherine Porter et al. New York: Pantheon.

Riordan, Paul. 1963. *Plunkitt of Tammany Hall.* New York: Dutton.

Roazen, Paul. 1968. *Freud: Political and Social Thought.* New York: Knopf.

Roelofs, H. Mark. 1976. *Ideology and Myth in American Politics: A Critique of a National Political Mind.* Boston: Little, Brown.

Rohr, John. 1985. *To Run a Constitution: The Legitimacy of the Administrative State.* Lawrence: University of Kansas Press.

Rossiter, Clinton. 1963 [1948]. *Constitutional Dictatorship: Crisis Government in the Modern Democracies.* New York: Harcourt, Brace & World/Harbinger Books.

Roth, Güenther. 1968. "Introduction." In Max Weber *Economy and Society: An Outline of Interpretive Sociology.* Güenther Roth and Claus Wittich, eds., Trs. Ephraim Fischoff et al. New York: Bedminster Press.

Russell, Bertrand. 1968. "The Art of Rational Conjecture." In *The Art of Philosophy and Other Essays*, pp. 1–36. New York: Philosophy Library.

Schütz, Alfred. 1967. *The Phenomenology of the Social World.* Evanston, IL: Northwestern University.

Schwartz, Howard. 1990. *Narcissistic Processes and Organizational Decay.* New York: New York University Press.

Searle, John. R. 1969. *Speech Acts: An Essay in the Philosophy of Language.* London: Cambridge University Press.

Seely, K.Q. May 3, 2002. "E.P.A. Surprises Its Leader and Interior Chief on Snowmobiles." *New York Times,* National edition: A1.

Sennett, Richard. 1972. (with Jonathan Cobb) *The Hidden Injuries of Class.* New York: Knopf.

Shelby, Richard C. 2002. "Senator Richard C. Shelby; A Reaction to September 11—'This Is a Massive Failure of Intelligence.' The *New York Times*, Sept. 10, National edition, p. A14.

Simon, Herbert. 1971. "Decision-Making and Organizational Design: Man-Machine Systems for Decision-Making." In D.S. Pugh, ed., *Organizational Theory: Selected Readings,* pp. 189–212. Baltimore: Penguin.

Snow, C.P. 1964. *Corridors of Power.* New York: Scribner.

Steffens, Lincoln. 1957 [1904]. *The Shame of the Cities.* New York: Hill & Wang.

———. 1931. *The Autobiography of Lincoln Steffens.* New York: Harcourt, Brace.

Stiglitz, Joseph E. 2002. *Globalization and Its Discontents.* New York: W.W. Norton.

Stivers, Camilla. 2008. *Governance in Dark Times: Practical Philosophy for Public Service.* Washington, D.C.: Georgetown University Press.

Teichman, Jenny. 1974. "Wittgenstein on Persons and Human Beings." In Royal Institute of Philosophy, *Understanding Wittgenstein.* New York: St. Martin's Press.

Tyler, Patrick E. May 19, 2002. "An Eye on the Ballot Box." *New York Times,* National edition: A1–A20.

Ungar, Sanford J. 1976. *FBI: An Uncensored Look behind the Walls.* Boston: Little, Brown.

U.S. Congress. Committee on Government Operations, Subcommittee on Intergovernmental Relations. 1973. *Confidence and Concern: Citizens View American Government.* Washington D.C.: U.S. Government Printing Office.

Van Natta, Don, Jr. March 31, 2002. "Full Disclosure." *New York Times*, Week in Review: 10.

Vesey, Godfrey. 1974. "Foreword." In Royal Institute of Philosophy, *Understanding Wittgenstein.* New York: St. Martin's Press.

Voegelin, Eric. 1952. *The New Science of Politics: An Introduction.* Chicago: University of Chicago Press.

von Humboldt, Wilhelm. 1993 [1854]. *The Limits of State Action.* Ed. J. W. Burrow. Indianapolis: Liberty Fund.

Weber, Max. 1913. "Ueber einige Kategorien der verstehenden Soziologie." Reprinted in Johannes Winckelmann, ed. *Gesammelte Aufsäetze zur Wissenschaftslehre,* pp. 427–73. Tübingen: J. C. B. Mohr.

———. 1920. "Zwischenbetrachtung: Theorie der Stufen und Richtungen religioeser Weltablehnung" [Interim observation: theory of stages and directions of religious rejection of the world]. *Gesammelte Aufsätze zur Religionsoziologie.* Volume 1. Tübingen: Verlag von J. C. B. Mohr.

———. 1958a [1904–05]. *The Protestant Ethic and the Spirit of Capitalism.* Tr. Talcott Parsons. New York: Charles Scribner's Sons.

———. 1958b [1919]. "Politik als Beruf" [Politics as Vocation]. In Weber, *Gesammelte politische Schriften* [Collected Political Essays], ed. Johannes Winckelmann, pp. 493–548. Tübingen: J. C. B. Mohr.

———. 1958c [1919]. "Parlament und Regierung im neugeordneten Deutschland. Zur politischen Kritik des Beamtentums und Parteiwesens" [Parliament and Government in a Reconstructed Germany: Contributions to the Political Critique of Officialdom and Party Politics.] In Weber, *Gesammelte politische Schriften* [Collected Political Essays], ed. Johannes Winckelmann, pp. 306–443, Tübingen: J. C. B. Mohr.

———. 1968a. *Economy and Society: An Outline of Interpretive Sociology.* Güenther Roth and Claus Wittich, eds., trs. Ephraim Fischoff et al. New York: Bedminster Press.

———. 1968b. "Bureaucracy." In Max Weber *Economy and Society: An Outline of Interpretive Sociology.* Güenther Roth and Claus Wittich, eds., trs. Ephraim Fischoff et al., pp. 1381–1469. New York: Bedminster Press.

———. 1968c [1918]. "Parliament and Government in a Reconstructed Germany." In Max Weber *Economy and Society: An Outline of Interpretive Sociology.* Güenther Roth and Claus Wittich, eds., trs. Ephraim Fischoff et al., pp. 1381–1469. New York: Bedminster Press.

———. 1968d. Der Sinn der 'Wertfreiheit' der Socialwissenschaften" [The Meaning of "Value Freedom" in the Social Sciences]. In Johannes Winckelmann, ed., *Max Weber: Soziologie, Weltgeschichtliche Analysen, Politik*, pp. 263–310. Stuttgart: Alfred Kröner.

White, Jay D. 1999. *Taking Language Seriously: The Narrative Foundations of Public Administration Research.* Washington D.C.: Georgetown University Press.

Wilson, Woodrow. 1887. "The Study of Administration." *Political Science Quarterly* 2 (June: 209–10). Reprinted in Jay M. Shafritz and Albert Hyde, eds., *Classics of Public Administration.* Oak Park, IL: Moore Publishing Company, 1978.

Wittgenstein, Ludwig. 1953. *Philosophical Investigations.* 3rd ed. New York: Macmillan.

———. 1956. *Remarks on the Foundations of Mathematics.* Oxford: Basil Blackwell.

Woll, Peter. 1977. *American Bureaucracy.* 2nd ed. New York: Norton.

Index

About the Author

Ralph P. Hummel (Ph.D., New York University) is a professor of public administration at the University of Akron and a co-director of the non-profit Institute for Applied Phenomenology. His original edition of *The Bureaucratic Experience* was the first book explicitly critical of the study and practice of American public administration. It has been widely used in courses of political science, sociology, organizational psychology, culture studies, language studies, and organizational philosophy, and has become in five editions one of the longest-published books in public administration. Dr. Hummel's other works include, with Robert A. Isaak, *Politics for Human Beings,* which criticized an increasingly managerial political science, and *The Real American Politics,* which cut below the veneer of America government courses to the foundations. Dr. Hummel is at work on a critique of business and public organizations under the title *Pyramids of Knowledge/Pyramids of Power.*